THE MEIJI CONSTITUTION

The LTCB International Library Trust

The LTCB (Long-Term Credit Bank of Japan) International Library Trust, established in July 2000, is the successor to the LTCB International Library Foundation. It carries on the mission that the foundation's founders articulated as follows:

> The world is moving steadily toward a borderless economy and deepening international interdependence. Amid economic globalization, Japan is developing ever-closer ties with nations worldwide through trade, through investment, and through manufacturing and other localized business operations.
>
> Japan's global activity is drawing attention to its political, economic, and social systems and to the concepts and values that underlie those systems. But the supply of translations of Japanese books about those and other Japan-related subjects has not kept pace with demand.
>
> The shortage of foreign-language translations of Japanese books about Japanese subjects is attributable largely to the high cost of translating and publishing. To address that issue, the LTCB International Library Foundation funds the translation and the distribution of selected Japanese works about Japan's politics, economy, society, and culture.

International House of Japan, Inc., manages the publishing activities of the LTCB International Library Trust, and Chuo Mitsui Trust and Banking Company, Ltd., manages the trust's financial assets.

THE MEIJI CONSTITUTION

THE JAPANESE EXPERIENCE OF THE WEST
AND THE SHAPING OF THE MODERN STATE

TAKII KAZUHIRO

TRANSLATED BY DAVID NOBLE

Transliteration of Foreign Words

The Hepburn system of romanization is used for Japanese terms, including the names of persons and places. Except for familiar place names, long vowels are indicated by macrons. The older Hepburn practice of using m instead of n before p, b, or m is followed. An apostrophe is used to distinguish syllable-final n from n at the beginning of a syllable. The spelling of non-Japanese words that have been incorporated into Japanese reflects the way these words are pronounced by Japanese speakers.

With regard to Japanese personal names, we have followed the local custom of placing the family name first.

Photo credit
Jacket and Cover: Photo of Ambassador Iwakura and the four vice-ambassadors courtesy of Ōkubo Toshihiro and Kume Museum of Art. Meiji Constitution photo courtesy of National Archives of Japan.
Page 7: Memorial Picture Gallery, Meiji Shrine.
Page 15: Ōkubo Toshihiro and Kume museum of Arts
Page 86: Rudolf von Gneist Papers in the Family Archives and Papers section of the Secret Central Archives, Prussian Cultural Heritage Foundation.
page 99: Memorial Picture Gallery, Meiji Shrine.
Page 102: Kensei Kinenkan (Constitution Memorial Hall).
Page 122: Archives Department, Ministry of the Interior, Czech Republic.
Page 137: National Archives of Japan.
Other photos appear in this book curtesy of Kosansha Ltd.

This book was originally appeared in Japanese, as *Bummei shi no naka no Meiji kempō* (Tokyo: Kōdansha Ltd., 2003). International House of Japan retains the English-language translation rights under contract with Takii Kazuhiro and through the courtesy of Kōdansha Ltd.

First English edition published March 2007 by International House of Japan
11-16, Roppongi 5-chome, Minato-ku, Tokyo 106-0032, Japan
Tel: +81-3-3470-9059   Fax: +81-3-3470-3170
E-mail: ihj@i-house.or.jp

Printed in Japan
ISBN978-4-924971-20-2

CONTENTS

Preface to the English Edition   vii

Introduction   ix

CHAPTER ONE

The Iwakura Embassy
From the Law of Nations toward a Constitution   1

1. The Journey Begins   1

2. Strange Voyage   6

3. Scenes from the Tour   12

4. The Iwakura Embassy's Perspective on National Institutions   27

CHAPTER TWO

Itō Hirobumi's European Research
From Constitution as Law to Constitution as National Structure   49

1. The Political Crisis of 1881 and Itō's Return to Europe   49

2. Melancholy in Berlin:
Heavy Weather for the Parliamentary System   60

3. Resurrection in Vienna: Awakening to "National Structure"   69

4. Later Research   84

CHAPTER THREE

Yamagata Aritomo's European Tour
A Different Kind of Constitutional Research   91

1. The Promulgation of the Meiji Constitution   91

2. Yamagata Aritomo's European Study Tour   107

3. The Other Constitutional Investigation   124

CONCLUSION

The Meiji Constitution Seen from Abroad   131

Afterword   145

Appendix: The Constitution of the Empire of Japan (Meiji Constitution)   149

Notes   163

Primary Sources   185

Index   187

PREFACE TO THE ENGLISH EDITION

Gakumon is one Japanese word that can be used to translate the English word "science." *Gaku* means to study, while *mon* means to question. Studying and questioning—is this not a wonderfully apt expression of the scientific method? A Spanish priest who lived for many years loved this sense of the word *gakumon*, and used to say he would like to see it spread to Europe and America.

On the other hand, there is an English word I cannot help wishing could be transplanted into Japanese, and that is the word *constitution*, the theme of this book. Of course there is already a Japanese translation of this word. But the word *kempō* in Japanese does not adequately convey the rich connotations of the English term. *Kempō* signifies only the legal document prescribing the fundamental structure of the state; the English *constitution* contains a double sense of both the structure and its formation or establishment. In other words, *constitution* seems to point to a process by which something is created and then becomes subject to ongoing analysis and verification. Like the Japanese word *gakumon*, it is a very dynamic concept.

What I hoped to depict in this book was this constitutional dynamism. I wanted to demonstrate that the Meiji Constitution was not merely a written document, but the "shape of the nation" of Meiji Japan as it was formed and transformed by the thought and hopes that people invested in it. Beyond that, I hoped to write a history of the Meiji Constitution that would make possible a dialogue with the research in constitutional history being done in other countries. For understanding that desire, and for making this English translation of the book possible, I would like to express my heartfelt thanks to the individuals at the International House of Japan who were involved in this project, and especially to Mr. Saji Yasuo, to whom I am indebted for his editorial work, and to the translator, Mr. David Noble.

Takii Kazuhiro
February 2007

INTRODUCTION

THE MEIJI CONSTITUTION

THE JAPANESE EXPERIENCE OF THE WEST
AND THE SHAPING OF THE MODERN STATE

"Imitation should have its limits"

On February 11, 1889 (Meiji 22), the Constitution of the Empire of Japan, commonly known as the Meiji Constitution, was promulgated. Nitobe Inazō[1] happened to be in Berlin to greet the news of East Asia's first modern constitution.

Not long before, Nitobe had been invited to a dinner party at the home of a German acquaintance and was drawn into the following dialogue with one of the German guests concerning the anticipated Japanese constitution:

"I hear that your country will soon have a constitution."
"Yes, that's what I hear."
"But it's odd that the Japanese constitution should be exactly the same as the German one."
"No, I don't think it will be exactly the same; I am sure there are some differences."
"No, it's the same."

And back and forth they went, straight through the meal. Then the German pressed his point even further:

"Japan is a different land, a different people, with a different history, so it is strange that its constitution should be the same as Germany's. Imitation should have its limits."
"No, no, I think what you are saying is really not the case."
"No, I am sure it is correct."

Here, Nitobe seized the initiative and countered by saying:

"Well, I suppose you might say that in the main it is not that different. If countries with their different histories and peoples and geography each came up with something completely different, then we probably could not call it a constitution. Since what we call a constitution is basically something enumerating the rights and duties of the rulers and the ruled, it's only natural that for the most part the constitution of any single country is going to resemble that of the others and not be some strange and completely different beast."

But the stubborn German was not about to give up any ground.

"No, there's a limit to resemblance. I am shocked by the fact that Japan's constitution is copied almost word for word from the German constitution."

At this point, Nitobe abandoned rational discourse and began to respond emotionally.

"Is that so? If that's the case, then it would seem the German constitution is just an imitation of the American one. The German constitution simply changes the words *president* to *Kaiser* and *republic* to *Reich* and translates *congress* as *Reichstag* and otherwise is just a copy of the American constitution. If the Japanese constitution resembles Germany's it is because both countries learned from the American model, so there's nothing strange about the fact that they resemble each other is there?"
    "No, that's not true. Germany is an empire, America is a republic, and there is an enormous difference between the two.
    "As I have just said, that's merely a difference in terminology. Insofar as constitutions define rights and duties, there is not a great deal of difference between them. Have you read the American constitution?"
"No, I have never looked at it."[2]

And so on they went, without resolution.
    Nitobe himself did not have that clear an idea of the similarities or differences between the U.S. and German constitutions. He was simply

responding in kind to the German's stubborness. The whole episode might be dismissed as the sort of wrangle to be avoided at a fashionable dinner party, except that it raises some interesting points about the Meiji Constitution.

The image of a secondhand constitution

The first point is the image of the Meiji Constitution as nothing more than a secondhand version of the German constitution. Even today, the assessment of the Meiji Constitution as an authoritarian document following the German model, with strong and extensive imperial powers supported by a superficial constitutionalism, holds common currency and is entrenched in academic circles. Ienaga Saburō, one of the standard-bearers of postwar Japanese historiography, summed up the establishment of the Meiji Constitution as "an attempt to control popular thought with a blend of Confucian and German conservatism," paying no heed to the various constitutional concepts put forward from among the people and "drafted in utmost secrecy by a handful of bureaucrats and their German advisers." Ienaga flatly characterized the document as "the product of a reaction against the prevailing trend toward the reception and assimilation of modern constitutional thought beginning in the initial years of the Meiji era."[3]

Certainly, as Ienaga states, the domestic opposition the Meiji government was facing from the Freedom and Popular Rights Movement (Jiyū Minken Undō) provided an impetus for the Meiji government to seek its model for constitutional government in Germany and, more specifically, in Prussia. Contemporary public opinion believed this to be the case, and in fact, it was a firm and carefully considered government policy.

After the Political Crisis of 1881 (Meiji 14) that resulted in the expulsion from the government of Ōkuma Shigenobu and other proponents of British-style party politics, Inoue Kowashi, the *éminence grise* behind the drafting of the Meiji Constitution, proposed that "we should encourage only Prussian [constitutional] theory . . . and silence the headlong rush toward the British model."[4] It is also well known that after the establishment of the Meiji Constitution Japanese legal scholars devoted themselves almost exclusively to the importation of German constitutional law. So it is an undeniable reality that the Meiji Constitution bore the heavy stamp of German influence, and the appraisal of it by Nitobe's anonymous

German debating partner is testimony to the fact that this image of the Meiji Constitution was prevalent internationally even before the constitution was promulgated.

The era of national legal codes

Another point raised by the exchange between Nitobe and the German is how to interpret Nitobe's counter to the rumor that the Meiji Constitution was simply an imitation of Germany's. Was Nitobe's retort nothing more than a wild remark tossed off in the heat of the moment by a young intellectual from a developing nation, straining to assert himself on unequal ground? If we dismiss Nitobe's argument as such, we risk overlooking a significant aspect of constitutional history.

Nitobe's assertion was that because any document called a constitution is "something enumerating the rights and duties of the rulers and the ruled" there should, in essence, be little difference among them. In this, Nitobe expresses an orthodox interpretation of constitutionalism. The sixteenth article of the French Declaration of the Rights of Man, which in 1789 raised the curtain on the history of modern constitutionalism, reads, "A society in which the observance of law is not assured, nor the separation of powers defined, has no constitution at all."

In this sentence, a touchstone of modern constitutionalism is succinctly expressed. It is a political declaration that no state structure can be considered constitutional if it does not provide for the rights of the people and a separation among the powers of the state.

Grounded in this ideal, the nations of the West began to enact constitutions beginning in the late eighteenth century. They might differ in whether they adopted a republican or a monarchical form of government, but insofar as they embraced constitutionalism there was not a great deal of difference in the basic principle of governance. Rejection of despotism and acceptance of the overarching principle of guarantees for the rights of the people was something that all constitutional governments held in common. Nitobe's argument was right on the mark.

So, was Nitobe's German opponent simply and stubbornly holding to a position based on ignorance and prejudice? We must also be careful in coming to this conclusion.

By the time of their conversation, a century had passed since the American and French revolutions that inaugurated the era of modern constitutionalism. The universal principle of constitutionalism was not the only element that had shaped European politics during that time. The nineteenth century was, above all, an age of nationalism. Amid the repercussions of the Napoleonic Wars, national consciousness was awakened throughout the countries of Western Europe. In the public sphere of politics and economics, the evolution of the nation-state was the hallmark of the era.

Law was no exception to this trend. One of the leading legal historians of postwar Germany, Helmut Coing, calls the nineteenth century "the era of the compilation of national legal codes." According to Coing, this should be seen as a quite unusual period in the history of European law, one in which the formulation of legal systems was carried out on the basis of the individual nation-state, drawing a distinct line of demarcation between itself and earlier periods, in which the legacy of ancient Roman law had shaped Europe into a single legal entity. The result was a variety of legal codes compiled and enacted by individual nations, such as the Code Civil of France and the Bürgerliches Gesetzbuch of Germany, so that even today we speak of the French and German civil codes, differentiating these laws by naming the country of their origin.[5]

The same is true of constitutions. In the course of the nineteenth century, all the European nations enacted constitutions, and it might be noted that this became a symbol of the political liberation of their citizens. This was not simply because these constitutions abolished despotism and absolutism and guaranteed the enhanced political status of the citizenry. Amid the rising nationalism of the era, a constitution was a political proclamation of the independence of the people domestically and internationally.

Taking this into consideration, if we revisit the dialogue between Nitobe and the German a further interesting point arises. Underlying the German's aggressive mocking of the Japanese constitution as a copy of Germany's was no doubt a sense of superiority rooted in Japan's selection of the German constitution as a model, and it is not difficult to see Nitobe's remarks as an attempt to defend the originality of the Japanese constitution. Their exchange may have been no more than trivial political banter, given that they were discussing a document neither of them had seen, but in it we get a glimpse of the high value placed on national constitutions by the educated classes of that era and of the nationalistic fervor with which these documents were interpreted.

The subtle nuance of the word *constitution*

So what is a constitution? When we hear the word, we immediately think of Japan's prewar and postwar constitutions or the constitution of the United States; in other words, a document codifying the fundamental laws of a nation. The debate between Nitobe and his adversary concerned the nature of this type of legal document. But this understanding is quite limited if we consider it in terms of the original meaning of the word *constitution*.

Look up *constitution* in an English dictionary, and you will find that the word also means the composition or structure of something. So in addition to the way in which we normally think of the word, we should be aware that it also implies the structure and composition of a country's overall system of governance.

Satō Kōji is a constitutional scholar who, as a member of the Administrative Reform Council (1996–98) and Judicial Reform Council (1999–2001), has played a leading role in the significant governmental reforms under way in Japan today. He maintains that at the beginning of the Meiji period (1868–1912), *constitution* was translated into Japanese as *kempō*, a compound derived from two Chinese characters meaning laws, rules, or regulations. As a result, Satō says, "when we hear the word *kempō* the first thing that comes to mind is a legal document, and the subtle nuances originally possessed by the word *constitution* are lost." He goes on to say,

> This reinforces our tendency to think of constitutional issues in terms of law and legal language and has hindered our efforts to speak of the shape and form of our nation in ordinary, everyday terms and to reform it. In other words, what is important is for us to try to understand the present state of our nation, sketch out a vision for what we would like it to be, and if there is a gap between the two, figure out why that is and how to fill it. Whether or not we change the legal document and its wording is, if you will, the exit, but somehow it has been confused with the entrance.

Satō then quotes with approval Kōsaka Masaaki, a specialist in international politics, who says that as a Japanese term for "the ineptly translated word *constitution*.... I think Shiba Ryōtarō's 'shape of the nation' (*kuni no katachi*) is more appropriate."[6]

As Satō has observed, if we interpret the concept of a constitution in the narrower sense implied by the word *kempō* and conceive of it as a single codified political text, we lose sight of the "subtle nuances" of the original word. We should see a constitution as connoting both the systemic aspect of the nature and mechanisms of national governance and the practical political aspect of conceiving, deciding upon, and managing that system of government.

This book takes as its theme the process by which the Meiji Constitution was formulated. In doing so, it is concerned with more than the constitution in the narrow sense and places particular emphasis on the "shape of the nation" that was constructed around this central constitutional axis and that will be referred to here as the Meiji state.

Ancient Rome and Meiji Japan

As I have just indicated, the concern of this book is the formation of the Meiji state, focusing on the Meiji Constitution. I will approach this topic from the perspective of cross-cultural contact: the experience of the West by the leaders of Meiji Japan.

For the countries of East Asia, the nineteenth century was the era of Western impact. Spurred to action by its collision with Western civilization, Japan opened itself to the West and under the new Meiji government launched itself on a program of "civilization and enlightenment." The establishment of the constitution may be interpreted in this context. But was this quintessentially Western concept of constitutional government something the leaders of Meiji Japan embraced without hesitation? Was it not instead a grand plan for governing the nation in the midst of a clash of civilizations, arrived at after much deliberation and implemented with great caution?

If we think of it in the latter way, we might see the development of the Meiji state into a constitutional system as a process of encounter and negotiation with the principles of Western civilization resulting in their eventual acceptance and assimilation. The experience of the West has been chosen as the vantage point of this book to emphasize this process.

In fact, the first half of the Meiji period was one in which the Japanese study and incorporation of Western thought proceeded at a rapid pace. Lorenz von Stein (1815–90), the professor of political economy (*Staatswissenchaft*) at the University of Vienna who was Itō Hirobumi's mentor in constitutional matters and who became the object of the "Stein pilgrimage" so popular among Japanese scholars of the mid-Meiji period, wrote the following:

> At present, from their island nation in the Far East, not just young students but full-fledged adults set out for Europe, intent on studying these lands, their institutions, and their laws. What is it we embody that inspires them so? There is probably only one other example in human history that could be compared with this state of affairs.[7]

The example to which Stein alludes are semihistorical accounts of Rome in the middle of the fifth century B.C. Having just made the transition from a monarchy to a republic, the Romans supposedly sent a mission to Greece to study national institutions. The rising power of Rome learned the essence of its civilization from the more advanced Greeks and on that basis formulated the Law of the Twelve Tables (*Lex Duodecim Tabularum*). According to the third volume of Livy's *History of Rome*, three Roman ambassadors—Spurius Postumius Albus, Aulus Manlius, and Publius Sulpicius Camerinus—were dispatched to Athens with orders to study the celebrated laws of Solon and the institutions, customs, and laws of the other Greek states as well.[8]

Whether or not this Roman mission to the Greeks was truly historical has been debated. Stein mentions this himself. However, that this historical tale continues to be told is due primarily to its appeal in terms of world history.[9] The three Roman ambassadors took up the torch of classical civilization from the Greeks on behalf of the Romans, and with it the leading role in world history for what would culminate in the grandeur of the Roman Empire. It is a story that has fired the imagination of historians, and it is regrettable that Livy does not provide more detail.

In any case, Stein saw a comparable instance of this transmission of civilization from Greece to Rome taking place in his own time, between two peoples situated at opposite ends of the earth. The nation he introduces as the new Rome, dispatching its study missions to assimilate the principles underlying the civilized institutions of Europe, his present-day Greece, was none other than Meiji Japan. Just as Rome had crafted the Law of the Twelve Tables on the basis of Greek institutions, Japan was expected to produce a constitution as a result of its study of European institutions.

With these words of Stein's as its point of departure, this book attempts to depict the history of the creation of the Meiji Constitution in terms of Japan's assimilation of Western civilization. Or, to put it another way, as a record of Japan's voyage in search of civilization in the form of constitutional government.

The Romans sent three ambassadors to Greece. Here, we will investigate three study missions sent by the Meiji state to the Western nations: the Iwakura Embassy of 1871 (Meiji 4); Itō Hirobumi's 1882 (Meiji 15) mission to Europe to study its constitutions; and Yamagata Aritomo's tour of Europe in 1888 (Meiji 21).

The Meiji state in world historical perspective

This book is an attempt to reinterpret the formation of a constitutional system in Japan not only from the perspective of Japan's domestic history, but also from that of cross-cultural contact and the comparative history of civilizations, grounded in the circumstances of the advance of Western civilization into East Asia.

Traditionally, the history of the Meiji Constitution has been written with a focus on the power struggle between the popular rights movement and an oligarchic government dominated by a clique composed of a handful of men from the domains that forced the collapse of the Tokugawa shogunate. This interpretation, evident in the assessment by Ienaga Saburō referred to earlier, has solidified the image of the Meiji Constitution as having been imposed from above by a reactionary, authoritarian regime for the purpose of suppressing the spread of progressive, democratic thought. This methodological approach, however, fails to grasp Japanese history from a world historical perspective.

As noted earlier, the nineteenth century was the era of the Western impact and of nationalism. It was an era in which other cultural spheres were integrated into a world system centered on Europe and North America, and one in which the institutions and spirit of the nation-state, a product of Western Europe, began to permeate international society.

Watching intently as Qing-dynasty China was devoured piecemeal by the Western powers, Japan made the decision to engage in a program of nation building modeled on Europe and the United States. The goal that took shape in the eyes of the Japanese amid this reform of their national institutions was a Japanese constitution, for the nineteenth century in Europe was also the age of constitutions. With the two great revolutions in America and France as impetus, the Western nations came to embrace constitutionalism and to place constitutions at the heart of their political systems. A constitution functioned as a symbol of what it meant to be a civilized nation.

Thus, the adoption of constitutionalism became a crucial national goal for Meiji Japan. By establishing a constitutional government, Japan could assert its independence as a civilized nation, secure the reform of the unequal treaties it had signed with the Western nations, and become a full-fledged member of international society. There was little in the national aspiration for a constitution that separated the government oligarchs from the popular rights activists. In fact, it is safe to say that the government leaders, absorbed as they were in the actual administration of the state and in negotiations with the Western nations, were even more acutely aware of the task at hand and the stakes involved than were their opponents outside the government. The leading political figures of the Meiji period, from Kido Takayoshi and Ōkubo Toshimichi in the early years to Itō Hirobumi and Yamagata Aritomo somewhat later, were dispatched to Europe and America, where they were immersed in the civilization of the West. What vision did they shape for the introduction of constitutional government to Japan as a result of this experience? This is the question that will be pursued in the discussion that follows.

Today, in response to a call from many quarters to reconsider "the shape of the nation," Japan is again in the midst of major reforms of its administrative and legal systems. The situation has been likened to "a third opening of the country," after the first, in the mid-nineteenth century, and the second, in the wake of Japan's defeat in World War II.[10] An effort, therefore, to reconsider from an international perspective the thought and behavior of our predecessors at the dawn of Japan's constitutional order should have value in defining the historical and cultural position of contemporary Japan as it plunges into this major transformation of its national institutions. Keeping this in mind, we will take a detailed, individual look at the direct experience of the West by the leaders of the Meiji government. By doing so, we will be able to grasp their views on

Western civilization and the constitution and their concept of constitutional government and thereby gain a foothold in our efforts to situate the Meiji state in world historical perspective.

CHAPTER ONE

The Iwakura Embassy
From the Law of Nations toward a Constitution

1. The Journey Begins

A unique perspective on civilization

On the morning of December 23, 1871 (Meiji 4), the skies over Yokohama were clear. Iwakura Tomomi, the emperor's ambassador extraordinary and plenipotentiary, and a party including vice-ambassadors Kido Takayoshi, Ōkubo Toshimichi, Itō Hirobumi, and Yamaguchi Masuka boarded the steamship *America*, which rode at anchor in Yokohama harbor. The Iwakura Embassy was preparing for departure. There were forty-six members in the official delegation. If students and other members of the entourage are included, the embassy numbered more than one hundred individuals, from the highest to the most humble.[1]

For the next year and a half, until its return to Japan in September 1873, the embassy would make a circuit of the United States and Europe, meeting with the heads of state and the leaders of the great powers, and studying the cultures and institutions of the Western nations. Iwakura, Kido, and Ōkubo were Japan's most important leaders at the time, and the fact that they would together leave their country for such an extended period was extraordinary.

For what purpose was this embassy dispatched? The reasons usually given are (1) to make diplomatic courtesy calls on the great powers, (2) to request a postponement of the negotiations for treaty revision scheduled for the following year, and (3) to make firsthand observations of Western civilization. Yet something more fundamental underlay these reasons: the unique way in which the concept of civilization was understood by the

Meiji government. The following analysis of the motives for the dispatch of the Iwakura Embassy is indebted to Takahashi Hidenao, whose research has raised this important point.[2]

The document defining the objectives of the Iwakura Embassy was the "Jiyūsho" (Statement of Purpose). It charged the mission with "carrying out courtesy calls to further enhance our relations of amity in the context of the recent renovation of our form of government" and "to convey to and discuss with the governments of the various nations the aims and intentions of our government with regard to the subject of treaty revision." Treaty revision was accorded the top priority. The "Jiyūsho" defines the issues and policy on treaty revision as follows:

> If we are to revise the existing treaties, this must be based upon the law of nations. Where the national, civil, commercial, criminal, or customs laws of our nation differ from the law of nations, they must be altered or revised. To carry out such alterations or revisions, we must investigate the procedures and methods involved.[3]

In search of Japan's constitution
What were the methods employed to accomplish this goal? As previously quoted from the "Jiyūsho," the embassy was to "to convey to and discuss with the governments of the various nations the aims and intentions of the government." Its approach was to give the Western nations an unvarnished report of Japan's current situation and issues in an effort to elicit from them guidance and techniques for national reform. The "Jiyūsho" continues:

> In these reports and discussions, if we anticipate the points that they will raise, and inquire of them what they desire of us, then it is likely that the talks will proceed smoothly, our message will be conveyed, and they will be moved to give us considerable guidance and advice. If we accept this guidance and advice and give it due consideration and deliberation, then it should not be difficult to persuade them to give us more time (ideally about three years) to actually implement it.[4]

The idea was to seize the initiative, anticipating what the Western powers sought from Japan and demonstrating the intent to proceed with reforms along the lines they indicated. The scenario envisioned was optimistic. It was hoped that this approach would be followed by constructive discussions, the transmission of the know-how the Japanese desired to implement reforms, and a postponement of the impending negotiations on treaty revision for which Japan was clearly unprepared. This position is also explicit in the official letter of credence from Emperor Meiji to President Grant that the ambassadors carried with them:

> With this object, we desire to fully disclose to the United States Government the condition of affairs in our Empire, and to consult upon the means of giving greater efficiency to our institutions, at present and in the future; and as soon as the Embassy returns home we will consider about the revision of the treaties and accomplish what we have expected and intended.[5]

Pointing to this passage, Takahashi describes the government's intent as "postponement of the following year's negotiations on treaty revision and determination of a plan for domestic reform based on consultation with the Western powers; implementation of these reforms upon the embassy's return to Japan; and opening of talks on treaty revision."[6]

In short, the embassy was charged with frankly and openly appealing to the advanced nations of the West for instruction and with utilizing the results to formulate a program for the reform of Japan's national institutions, thus laying the foundation for treaty renegotiation. In this sense, there can be no doubt that the Iwakura Embassy was dispatched as a fact-finding mission with regard to Japan's constitution; that is, its national structure.

Trusting in the law of nations

What is odd is the almost childlike dependence upon the Western nations displayed by Japan's leaders.

Traditionally, diplomacy involves a mutual probing of intent in a coldly calculated game of maneuver and rivalry among nations motivated by the pursuit of power and dominance. There is, however, no sign of this from either the Iwakura Embassy or the Meiji government. As Takahashi puts it, "There was an expectation with regard to the goodwill of the Western nations much like that a student has toward his teachers." This is clear from the expressions of faith in what is referred to as "the law of nations" in previously quoted passages.

The law of nations was the contemporary term for international law. But it expressed a concept that went beyond what we think of today as the rules of international society based on legal agreements between sovereign states. At the time, the law of nations was embraced almost as a slogan for the new era. It embodied Western civilization and was a national goal for Meiji Japan to pursue. This naive trust in the law of nations is evident in the "Jiyūsho":

> The law of nations enables the nations of the earth to maintain their powers of independence and sovereignty and stand amid the ranks of the other nations without disturbing the balance of power. It preserves their pledges of mutual intercourse, and allows them to share equally in the profits of commerce. It alone makes it possible to contain the power of both strong and weak, and control that of the many and the few, so that the just laws of nature and of man are served. Thus it may be said that it is specifically because the existence of the law of nations that an equality of rights among nations exits.[7]

There is clearly a sense that for Japan, thrust precipitously into an international political arena dominated by the Western powers, the law of nations offers the sole refuge.

Under the Tokugawa shogunate's policy of national seclusion, Japan had long conducted its foreign relations according to its own unique standards. Elsewhere in the surrounding East Asian region, an international system now known to scholars as the Chinese world order was generally accepted. China was regarded as the center of civilization, and in return for delivering tribute to the Chinese emperor, a benevolent despot, the surrounding nations were granted the right to govern their territories. In short, China was seen as ruling the world. This arrangement, also known as the tribute system, was the fundamental concept of world order in East Asia.[8]

Incursions from the West ended China's hegemony, and ultimately even Japan had little choice but to bow to Perry's gunboat diplomacy and open itself to participation in the new paradigm of a Western-dominated international system. Even this, however, seems to have resulted in the reemergence in the minds of contemporary Japanese of an older concept of order in which a host of lesser nations grouped themselves under the virtuous rule of a great power. At the time of the Iwakura Embassy, the Japanese implicitly believed in the existence of a new benevolence—the conduct of politics and foreign policy in accordance with the law of nations—that would protect them and provide them with "a path for avoiding the assaults and depredations" of other countries.

Thus, the law of nations emerged as the embodiment of virtue for the new age, replacing the earlier notion of a central source of civilization. The issue for Japan now became how it was to assimilate the "virtue" demanded by the law of nations. The "Jiyūsho" does not hesitate to address this point:

> If one looks back over the recent past and pursues the reason why we were unable to obtain equality [with regard to the treaties], the inequality stems from the fact that because of the different nature of our national institutions and political customs it has been impossible for us to deal with other countries on the basis of the law of nations, or to accord their nationals the just treatment and civil rights that are commonly expected. If, in the light of reason, we recognize this situation as unacceptable, then we should study policies for restoring equality, which will require alterations and reforms to our national institutions and political customs.[9]

The document clearly and unequivocally states that Japan is not being treated as an equal by the Western nations because Japan is still ill prepared to deal with other countries on the basis of international law and that to put itself in the position to do so Japan must carry out fundamental governmental and political reform. Once more, we can see in this passage the unconditional trust being placed in the law of nations.

The standards of European civilization
What was the virtue embodied in the law of nations? In a word, *civilization*. International law and a nation's eligibility for participation in it were predicated on what was termed "the standards of the civilized nations." Of course, the civilization being spoken of here was European civilization, so to enjoy the benefits of the law of nations a nation had to be recognized as civilized by European standards.[10]

An influential textbook of international law from the period, James Lorimer's *The Institutes of the Law of Nations*, states that, "as a political phenomenon, humanity in its present condition divides itself into three concentric zones or spheres—that of civilized humanity, that of barbarous humanity, and that of savage humanity." Lorimer argues that "it is with the first of these spheres alone that the international jurist has directly to deal. . . . He is not bound to apply the positive law of nations to savages, or even to barbarians, as such."[11] According to Lorimer the sphere of civilized humanity extended to "all the existing States of Europe, with their colonial dependencies, in so far as they are peopled by persons of European birth or descent; and to the States of North and South America . . ."; the sphere of barbarous humanity "to Turkey in Europe and in Asia, and to the old historical States of Asia which have not become European dependencies—viz., to Persia and other separate States of Central Asia, to China, Siam, and Japan"; the sphere of the savage "to the residue of mankind."

In this Eurocentric model, the only nations subject to international law are those inheriting the mantle of European civilization. Another contemporary treatise on international law makes plain that for other countries to be eligible for the application of international law and for equal treatment alongside the European nations, "they must do something,"[12] i.e., remake themselves in line with European standards.

The significance of the Iwakura Embassy must be understood within this historical context. The embassy is frequently described as a voyage in search of "the shape of the nation."[13] It is important to note, however, that powerful forces demanded that this "shape" be acceptable to European civilization.

2. Strange Voyage

Under Western eyes

With the voyage of the Iwakura Embassy, the Meiji state set course for the shores of Western civilization. At 10:00 a.m. on December 23, 1871, Iwakura Tomomi, ambassador extraordinary and plenipotentiary, boarded a steam launch that would convey him to the ship to the accompaniment of a nineteen-gun salute. The rest of the mission members would soon follow. A painting by Yamaguchi Hōshun vividly conveys the scene (see illustration on opposite page). Iwakura is flanked by vice-ambassadors

Kido Takayoshi and Ōkubo Toshimichi. In contrast to Iwakura, who is in traditional court dress, Kido and Ōkubo are attired in Western-style suits. That the head of the delegation chose traditional attire might be read as a minor display of spirit vis-à-vis the Western nations on the part of Japan's new government, which was formed under the banner *ōsei fukko* (the restoration of imperial rule and a return to antiquity). And, in fact, before the official departure ceremonies a religious ceremony was held at the Ministry of Rites (Jingishō) to pray for the safe travels and success of the mission. Politics in

"Ambassador Iwakura Dispatched to Europe and America" by Yamaguchi Hōshun

Japan still had a sacred dimension quite apart from European standards of civilization, in which government was *matsurigoto*, a sacred sphere involving the observance of proper rites and ritual. The contrast between Iwakura and Kido and Ōkubo displays the janus-faced quality of the new Meiji government, which looked simultaneously toward civilization and antiquity.

Even so, throughout their journey the members of the embassy sought to conceal Japanese traditions in favor of observing the etiquette of civilization. Not long after departing Yokohama, Iwakura assembled them and issued the following instructions:

Civilized manners are displayed in our ordinary behavior and gestures, and if even a minor point is missed, major embarrassment often results. In your contacts with foreigners you must not forget this. The ranking members of this mission have been selected by each of the ministries of our government, and many of the students are of noble families. You will all be models of our nation; the foreigners on board will be watching you and will see in you the reflection of our nation's honor. All of you should be aware from the outset that this means the words and actions of even a single individual are of no small consequence.[14]

Iwakura here hints at his anxiety as the leader of such a large entourage. One of his solutions to this problem was to divide the embassy's members into smaller groups whose members were ordered to keep an eye on each other.

This may seem excessive on Iwakura's part, but he had in fact been ordered to take exactly these precautions. Before his departure, Iwakura was handed a set of official instructions from the government informing him that his duties were to communicate Japan's position and policies, to work to benefit its interests, and to spread its prestige throughout the world. It also told him what he later would tell his charges, that since any misstep could damage Japan's position, and invite disaster or bring shame upon the nation, he was to pay careful attention to smallest details of his speech, behavior, and deportment. "The ambassador's behavior—whether walking, standing, sitting, or lying down—is being watched intently by the people of every nation" who, he was told, are trying to gauge Japan's "national character."[15]

Iwakura's subsequent instructions to the other members of the embassy thus were merely an extension of the discipline that he was required to impose on himself. The members of the embassy as a whole had to know that while theirs was an inspection tour of the West they—and the Japanese nation—would likewise be continually under the scrutiny of Western civilization.

Slack discipline amid the rank and file

Whereas the ocean voyage of the Iwakura Embassy began amid an air of tension for Iwakura and its other leaders, the atmosphere among its lesser members was, if anything, unconstrained. This contrast was apparent during the boarding of the vessel. Iwakura boarded with dignity to the pomp of an artillery salute. The rank and file that followed, however, put on an embarrassing display, vying with each other to see who could clamber aboard first.

Sasaki Takayuki, accompanying the embassy as the commissioner from the Ministry of Justice, wrote that while the ambassador and vice-ambassadors had looked splendid, the other members of the embassy, including the commissioners (*rijikan*) dispatched as representatives of the various ministries of the new government, "competed with each other to see who would be first aboard, creating a confusion that was amusing, yet also pathetic, and quite an embarrassing spectacle to have foreigners behold." Sasaki adds, "I could not help grumbling a bit myself."[16] For the embassy's leaders, ordered to be acutely aware that the eyes of civilization would be upon them throughout their journey, this must have been an inauspicious beginning. All members of the embassy were thereafter required to learn Western etiquette—table manners, personal grooming, and so on—as the voyage progressed.

Yet many of the embassy's members were seasoned veterans of the upheavals attending the fall of the Tokugawa shogunate, some of whom fancied themselves modern versions of the folk hero Momotarō, setting forth for the Isle of Demons.[17] So it would have been surprising if everyone had submitted without complaint to Western customs. The struggle, in fact, between discipline and license produced a number of unusual episodes on board ship, a few of which I will relate here.

The impaled beefsteak

Among the personnel accompanying the embassy was Hiraga Yoshitada. He was a former samurai from the domain of Fukuoka in Chikuzen who had been sent by his domain to study in America in 1867, on the eve of the Meiji Restoration. He joined the Iwakura Embassy in the entourage of Sasaki Takayuki, and seems to have been generally disliked for the Western airs he put on. But Hiraga won favor with Iwakura, and an episode ensued in which he distributed a leaflet on Western table manners to the embassy's members and attempted to instruct them in the etiquette of Western dining. Written out of a concern that the embassy's "deportment and manners were crude and might invite the contempt of Westerners," the leaflet dispensed such advice as "speak quietly when giving orders to the waiters" and "do not slurp your soup or make noises with your spoon."

The embassy had been dispatched from a society in which the voices of unrest remained unstilled, despite the restoration of imperial rule. Among its members were many who had devoted themselves to antiforeign agitation during the last years of the shogunate, and who had yet to rid themselves of such prejudices. Given the character of the embassy, it is not difficult to imagine why some instruction with regard to behavior seemed necessary.

Embassy members with some knowledge of the West, from the secretaries (*shokikan*) on down, "passed it off with a smile as old news." But the majority of the party greeted it with "derision or anger." At breakfast on the morning following the pamphlet's dissemination, an amazing scene unfolded that Kume Kunitake recalled in later years:

> That morning, Okauchi [Shigetoshi], seated across from me, made a show of eating his soup—rattling his spoon, noisily grabbing the bowl with both hands, slurping down its contents, and smacking his lips—and then bellowed instructions to the waiter. Murata Shimpachi, who was sitting beside him, looked on with a smirk, and when a large beefsteak in the American style was brought to the table, he grabbed his fork in his right hand, speared the steak as if it were a roast yam, brought it to his mouth and tore into it.[18]

Following this, in Kume's words, "a variety of other rudenesses were performed," clearly as a "demonstration" for the benefit of Hiraga.

But was this merely a childish rebellion against someone with greater experience of the West? Japan's new government may have adopted "civilization and enlightenment" as its watchwords, but for the members of the embassy known as the incorrigibles (*gankōron*), who remained attached to the antiforeign heroics of the recent past, this display of rudeness in the mess hall was not merely a personal dig at Hiraga. It was also a spirited reaction against "civilization" that was a legacy of their political activism.

The button incident

After table manners came personal grooming. Here, too, Kume has left us a very interesting reminiscence of what came to be known as Itō's Shitty Speech. A crude title, perhaps, but for the new Japan, launched on its voyage to the civilized world, apparently an "urgent message."

> From the morning after we departed Yokohama, a gradually increasing number of black buttons began to appear on the floor of the ship's lavatory, like so many scabs, and eventually someone relieved himself outside the urinal. From the Japanese paper that had been placed over the result, it was deduced that the culprit was Japanese. Urged by the ship's captain to issue a warning,

Vice-Ambassador Itō assembled the members of the embassy on deck and delivered an address imploring them not to stain the honor of Japan in such a fashion—which everyone mocked as "Itō's Shitty Speech."[19]

Behind this rather comic incident, however, were serious issues that had their origins in the radical changes in customs and manners taking place in Japan. Kume explains this as follows:

> Where Westerners use buttons, Asians use cords. Some members of the embassy were not well acquainted with the use of fly buttons. At that time, Western clothing was just becoming fashionable, and as Japanese are quite handy by nature, they were able to turn out high-quality Western-style clothing; but at first they fumbled with the buttons, especially the undoing and doing up of trouser buttons. It is said that about this time an important government minister attended the imperial audience on New Year's Day in formal Western attire with the buttons on his trousers undone, which to his mortification and shame he did not discover until he returned home and began to undress. Particularly when time was of the essence, buttons were difficult to manage, and unable to hold back any longer, some ripped off the buttons in their haste, or relieved themselves before they managed to make it all they way into the lavatory. If one imagines their distress and urgency, one really should not laugh.[20]

The image of torn-off buttons scattered across the toilet floor certainly does invite laughter today. For the men of the time, though, who already had squeezed uncomfortably into this unaccustomed garb, the buttons were extremely vexing. The leaders of the embassy must have been acutely embarrassed to be cautioned by the ship's captain on so delicate an issue shortly after leaving port. Aware that the eyes of civilization would constantly be upon them, this was for them certainly no laughing matter.

The mock trial

Nagano Keijirō, who accompanied the embassy as a second secretary, had been a member of the Tokugawa shogunate's first embassy to the United States in 1860. He was well-liked in America, where he was nicknamed Tommy and where he even had a polka written about and named after him.[21] Nagano had been especially popular with the ladies during his U.S.

visit, and as the voyage got underway flirted with one of the female Japanese students accompanying the embassy, attempting to give her dance lessons under the pretext of teaching her Western social skills. The young woman became quite upset at his advances, went straight to Ōkubo to complain, and quite a tempest ensued.

Ōkubo delegated Itō Hirobumi to handle the matter. Itō decided to hold a shipboard mock trial, with himself as the judge, to deal with Nagano. Nagano probably thought he was doing little more than killing time on the long sea voyage by making a pass at the young woman, but there were plenty of other bored voyagers, and soon the ship was abuzz with news of his actions.

Itō seized the opportunity to set up his kangaroo court as an effort to "learn from Western forms by imitating them."[22] And so a minor flirtation was turned into a major shipboard event, with Nagano and the female student dragged embarrassingly before everyone on board to be judged.

Sasaki Takayuki, who detested Itō, wrote in his diary that putting this nonsense on public view was humiliating not only for Nagano and the young woman but for the entire embassy. Sasaki voiced his objections but was talked down with assertions that this was common practice among Europeans and Americans. He nonetheless felt that precisely because Japan was a country "that had just set its steps on the path of civilization" it should refrain from such monkey-see, monkey-do antics as this mock trial.[23] He felt especially strongly about not doing so at sea, far from Japan, with Westerners present and watching intently as the proceedings unfolded. No matter how bored they all might be, his conviction was that such nonsense was unbefitting an embassy warned that the eyes of civilization were upon it. This quasi-lynching was certain to sully the reputation of Japan's ambassadors.

Sasaki's anger was not without grounds. Yet at the same time, it is amusing that despite its intimidating power, the concept of civilization was still being apprehended in terms of such naïve imitation.

3. Scenes from the Tour

Buying Western clothing

The embassy arrived in San Francisco on January 15, 1872. This was the beginning of a tour of inspection of the United States and Europe that would continue for a year and a half until the embassy's return to Japan in the autumn of 1873. The embassy would spend half a year in the United States, four months in Britain, two in France, one in Germany, and two weeks in Russia. It also would briefly visit Belgium, Holland, Denmark, Sweden, Italy, and Austria—an official Grand Tour of almost incredible proportions.

The members of the embassy had already put on quite a show aboard ship on the way to America, and the rest of their journey was eventful as well. Let's glance briefly at the embassy's leading figures: Iwakura, Itō, Ōkubo, and Kido.

Given the awe with which the Western nations were regarded, it is easy to imagine how much more awed the embassy's members were when they finally set foot on American soil. Free of their shipboard confinement, they beheld the vastness of America, that stronghold of the West, spread out before them as far as they could see.

On board ship, the ever-present notion of civilization had generated a tense dynamic. The embassy's leaders expended considerable anxious energy on such trappings of civilization as clothing and table manners and other aspects of Western etiquette and deportment. Meanwhile, there was among the rank-and-file members a wild and uncouth element resisting the Western civilization of Japan. Once, however, the embassy had landed on actual "civilized" soil, and its members found themselves alone amid the Western camp, exposed on all sides to the gaze of civilization, even the roughest among them seemed to lose resistance to Western ways.

Upon their arrival in San Francisco, they were welcomed from every quarter and invited to a succession of banquets, plays, and other entertainments. According to Kido Takayoshi, "We were more than a little surprised at the lavish welcome given us by the people, for it appears that at this port alone nearly $100,000 was spent on the reception given to the Japanese embassy."[24]

Given a welcome far warmer and more enthusiastic than they had anticipated, the members of the embassy hurried off to buy "semiformal attire" soon after landing. It had been decided before the embassy left Japan that traditional Japanese court dress would be worn for formal state functions. For privately sponsored social events and appearances at other, more-intimate public venues, though, this must have seemed a bit excessive. Even as their ship neared America, Kido remarked that "it is likely that wearing formal Japanese dress every time we appear in public is going to become unbearable," and it was decided, as per his suggestion, to wear "the formal dress that is customary in foreign countries."[25]

"Cramped and uncomfortable"
So it was that the members of the embassy decided to buy Western outfits to supplement their Japanese ceremonial dress. As Sasaki Takayuki wrote in his diary:

> At the time we left Japan, it was understood that we would use Japanese dress on formal occasions, and all of the members of the embassy brought theirs, but do not have Western dress suits. Embarrassing, but what can be done?[26]

Sasaki describes the Western tailcoat as "ungainly clothing like a *haori* with the sides cut away," but writes that "since no one had brought one, we had to rush to buy them." Sasaki's irritation at being forced to abandon his traditional attire for such an "ungainly" Western garment is obvious. His diary continues:

> Since the shoes are also big and quite ugly to Japanese eyes, everyone bought small ones. They are cramped, hurt the feet, and are quite uncomfortable.[27]

Buttons, leather shoes, suit coats—Western attire certainly has an overall constraining effect on the body quite different from the looseness of traditional Japanese dress. But annoyed as they might be by the discomforts of "civilization," the members of the mission had to adopt its ways. Soon, Western suits would become the mission's uniform, even for Ambassador Iwakura.

Iwakura gives up Japanese dress
There is a photograph that is almost always displayed whenever the Iwakura Embassy is mentioned. It shows the ambassador extraordinary and plenipotentiary Iwakura Tomomi surrounded by his four vice-ambassadors (see page 15). It is said to have been taken not long after they arrived in San Francisco, and it is interesting to note the way Iwakura is dressed.[28] As in the Yamaguchi Hōshun painting mentioned earlier, Iwakura's vice-ambassadors are in formal Western attire, whereas Iwakura

is in Japanese dress and traditional hairstyle and has relaxed deeply into his chair, the very embodiment of the Meiji ideal of "Japanese spirit, Western learning" (*wakon yōsai*).

After about a month in America, however, Iwakura, too, abandoned Japanese for Western clothing. Sasaki's diary gives this account:

> At some point, Ambassador Iwa-kura also cut his hair short and changed from what he had been wearing into Western clothes. I don't know whether this repre-sents "enlightenment" or if he's just caught the American mania. Someone said that some of the aides had ingratiated themselves with Ambassador Iwakura's son, who had spent some time study-ing abroad, and convinced him to speak directly with the ambas-

Ambassador Iwakura and the four vice-ambas-sadors (from left: Kido Takayoshi, Yamaguchi Masuka, Iwakura Tomomi, Itō Hirobumi, Ōkubo Toshimichi).

> sador, telling him that if he did not adopt the Western style he would be looked down upon by the foreigners, and thus it came about that he cut his hair and changed his clothing. From my habitually conservative point of view, this seems like a miscalculation. In light of current trends it may be all well and good to cut one's hair and wear a suit. But it is one thing for the vice-ambassadors, who made the decision to do this before they left Japan, and quite another for the ambassador, who alone among them continued to dress in the Japanese style during the voyage across the Pacific and even after we had landed. Changing in mid-course like this seems quite imprudent. If he had cut his hair and changed his attire after completing the tour abroad and returning home, it would not present such an issue in terms of his dignity.[29]

Sasaki's writing grows increasingly bitter. He adds that in a foreign land it is vital to behave circumspectly; that influential people in foreign coun-tries, noting Iwakura's lack of gravitas, probably felt they had Japan's measure and were laughing up their sleeves. Sasaki concludes tartly that the term "civilization and enlightenment" does not simply mean imi-tating anything and everything other people do.

In truth, practically everyone in the embassy, including Sasaki, was probably equally guilty of rushing off the boat in a mad scramble to buy foreign clothes. Clearly, though, Sasaki had hoped that at least Iwakura, as ambassador plenipotentiary and head of the mission, would show a little more national pride by continuing to wear his country's traditional dress.[30]

Iwakura attired and groomed in the Western manner, as depicted in the October 12, 1872, edition of the Illustrated London News.

As for the "aides" that Sasaki denounces, it is probably safe to assume from other remarks in the Sasaki diary that this refers to Itō Hirobumi and his associates. Sasaki was convinced that Itō and others, infatuated with Westernization, had conned Iwakura into so precipitously abandoning his traditional clothing and replacing it with Western attire.

If this is the case, then the photograph mentioned earlier is significant. It is almost as if the four vice-ambassadors have surrounded the traditionally attired Iwakura to coax him into Western dress. Indeed, the photograph reveals that Iwakura is already wearing Western shoes. Soon this Westernization will extend to the rest of his body. We can only wonder what he thought at personally experiencing the discomfort of civilization and enlightenment for the first time.

The constitution as clothing

The Western-style suit, tailored to emphasize the contours of the body, can be applied conceptually to the shape of the nation, the central theme of this book. Western constitutionalism and the rule of law clothe and constrain the body of the state in legal statutes. In this regard, Kume Kunitake's reflections on Western dress are worthy of attention:

> Westerners like things to be neatly defined, while Orientals prefer them to be looser. For example, Westerners delight in the smallest detail, and their clothing is carefully fitted from head to toe, while Oriental clothing is flowing and roomy. This difference in character might be thought of as an aesthetic preference in terms of what to put in and what to leave out; Westerners take

pleasure in detailed and realistic depiction of the human form, while Orientals depict an unnatural nature in the name of elegance and refinement, savoring paintings in which the number of brush strokes has been reduced to the necessary minimum. Perhaps we can understand this as arising from some mysterious effect of the differing environments in which the artists live.[31]

Kume sought an explanation for the differences between Oriental and Western civilizations in a divergence of aesthetic practice; that is to say, in the contrasting methods and spirit each brought to the act of creation. Against the Western emphasis on detailed pictorial realism, he seems to view the mystery of the East as residing in elegant ambiguity.

If we apply this way of thinking to national institutions, then just as Western clothing is carefully tailored to the form of the human body so, too, is the nation shaped by the clothing of its laws. The nation, once an ephemeral ideal, gains definition through the workings of legislation to emerge as an entity with form and function. Annoyed by his new and uncomfortable Western suit, could Iwakura have possibly imagined the constitution that would eventually clothe his nation in this way?

Itō in his glory

Itō Hirobumi was by far the liveliest of the embassy's leaders. Unlike Iwakura, Kido, and Ōkubo, he had experience abroad. He was valuable because he was considered an equal by the former shogunal retainers and Western experts he had accompanied on the first Japanese embassy to the United States and thus was able to exert influence over them. We have seen something of this in his being asked by Ōkubo to sort out the uproar over Nagano Keijirō's dalliance with the female student.

It is clear from the rather childish episode of the mock court, however, that Itō's speech and behavior could just as equally antagonize. The self-styled conservative Sasaki constantly records his irritation with Itō:

> During the voyage across the Pacific the behavior of the secretaries and others was remarkably ill-mannered, but I was also shocked by Itō, whose talents apparently exempt him from having to comport himself in a fashion appropriate to a vice-ambassador. But this is the way of the world at present, where such manners are practiced, and gaining the upper hand.[32]

We can only imagine the show Itō must have put on. The embassy was a kind of national pageant, and it is likely that Itō saw it as his once-in-a-life-time chance to perform on a grand stage—especially since the embassy's other leaders knew little about the world beyond Japan. The dispatch of the embassy, moreover, had been due in part due to a proposal from Itō.

From November 1870 to May 1871, Itō had been in the United States to gather information on its economic system. In a position paper sent back to Japan he proposed that a mission be sent to the United States and Europe to prepare for the upcoming treaty revision negotiations in 1872.[33] This idea eventually developed into the Iwakura Embassy. So Itō, return-ing to America in a group that was the very embodiment of contemporary Japan and its aspirations, must also have secretly felt that he was the embassy's true leader.

Itō's ebullience is conveyed in his famous "Rising Sun" speech.[34] At a welcoming reception on December 14, a week after the embassy had arrived in San Francisco, Itō rose and addressed his American hosts. He began by emphasizing the rapid progress made since the opening of Japan, and continued as follows:

> Japan cannot claim originality as yet, but it will aim to exercise practical wisdom by adopting the advantages, and avoiding the errors, taught her by the history of those enlightened nations whose experience is her teacher.

He then characterized the embassy's aspirations:

> As ambassadors and as men, our greatest hope is to return from this mission laden with results valuable to our beloved country and calculated to advance permanently her material and intellectual condition. While in duty bound to protect the rights and privileges of our people, we shall aim to increase our commerce, and, by a corresponding increase of our productions, hope to cre-ate a healthy basis for this greater activity.
>
> As distinguished citizens of a great commercial nation, prepared for busi-ness, desirous of participating in the new commercial era now dawning auspi-ciously upon the Pacific, Japan offers you her hearty co-operation.

Itō concluded the speech with the rhetorical flourish by which it came to be known:

The red disk in the center of our national flag shall no longer appear like a wafer over a sealed empire, but henceforth be in fact what it is designed to be, the noble emblem of the rising sun, moving onward and upward amid the enlightened nations of the world.

It is not difficult to imagine Itō, proudly displaying his command of English, basking in glory. Sasaki noted that since the other ambassadors "were not conversant in the language," they had lost the authority they possessed at home, and it was Itō who wielded power as a result of his fluent translation and reading abilities. Sasaki, given his dislike for Itō, was apprehensive: "This is a most dangerous state of affairs; my heart is filled with concern." A month later, Sasaki was reviling Itō, whose embrace of radical Westernization had extended to advocating freedom of religion, as a "rude upstart who forgets the hard work of the government ministers back home and wields in its place a shallow Japanese cunning."[35]

Many instances of Itō's speech and actions, as we've seen, provoked Sasaki's indignation. But what seems really to have bothered Sasaki was the extent to which Itō made himself the central figure in the embassy and behaved more or less as he pleased.

Itō, we are told, was "spending absurd amounts of money and living it up."[36] Numerous anecdotes have survived regarding his extravagances: smoking an entire box of expensive cigars by himself in five days; wearing a hat that cost more than 15 ryō (a gold coin of considerable value at the time); and so on.[37] There is even a story that he set a match to the dress of a nightclub dancer, saying that he wanted to see whether the chiffon she was wearing would burn.[38] Itō was running riot, and his reckless behavior on "civilized" soil belied his affectation of Western manners and gives us a glimpse of his true colors.

"This is a calamity!"

Before long, reality would put a damper on Itō's revelry. The embassy arrived in Washington on January 21, 1872, and commenced discussions of treaty revision on February 3. Its goal was modest—merely a postponement of the scheduled renegotiation of the treaty. Heartened, however, by the warmth of their reception, the ambassadors overestimated the Americans' goodwill and began to think they might achieve an immediate and favorable revision of the unequal treaty with the United

States. When Secretary of State Hamilton Fish pointed out that they lacked the credentials certifying their plenipotentiary powers to enter into such negotiations, they were undeterred. Ōkubo and Itō, who was already claiming that "the prospects are splendid for bringing off a revision of the treaties," returned to Japan to obtain the necessary documents.[39] What the excited Japanese did not realize was that the Americans' display of goodwill hid ulterior motives, as shown in the research of Shimomura Fujio and Ishii Takashi.[40]

Japan interpreted the American willingness to sit down at the negotiating table as a major step toward ending extraterritoriality and restoring Japan's tariff autonomy. But what the U.S. had in mind was "the immediate conclusion of a new treaty with Japan aimed at expanding its own interests."[41] Specifically, in return for making certain concessions regarding Japan's legal rights vis à vis foreign countries and the tariff issue, America would seek freedom of travel for Americans within Japan's interior; guarantees on the rights of Americans to conduct business with Japanese; permission for U.S. vessels to call at ports not yet opened to foreign shipping, ostensibly for coaling; and authorization for Americans to acquire real estate in Japan.

An even bigger issue was the nonreciprocal most favored nation clause contained in every treaty Japan had negotiated with Western nations. This clause automatically extended any advantageous agreement Japan had concluded with one country to all of the other countries it had signed treaties with. "If," as British chargé d'affaires Francis Adams noted, "the United States won a number of concessions from Japan as a condition for lowering import and raising export duties, we [the British] would, thanks to the most favored nation clause, not only be able to demand the same concessions but also be able to refuse renegotiation of the treaty."[42]

The mechanics of this clause were explained to Iwakura and Kido by German ambassador to Japan Max von Brandt, who was in Washington at the time, and by Ozaki Saburō, a Japanese student in London who had rushed to Washington. Iwakura was puzzled by the unfamiliar term "nonreciprocal most favored nation clause." When its meaning was made clear to him, he is said to have shouted, "This is a calamity!"[43] As Ishii remarks, Iwakura was learning a harsh lesson in the realities of diplomacy. In the end, on June 17, 1872, the very day that Ōkubo and Itō returned from

Tokyo with diplomatic credentials, the embassy decided to suspend treaty negotiations.

Failure
The foregoing displays the diplomatic ineptitude of the Iwakura Embassy. Much of the blame lay with Itō. As we have seen, during his earlier visit to the United States, Itō proposed an effort to regain tariff autonomy and promote Japanese domestic industry and urged that a mission be dispatched to America and Europe to secure the necessary treaty revisions. Itō's ultimate goal, as clear from his "Rising Sun" speech, was to position Japan as a modern commercial nation and an important constituent of a Pacific trade zone centered on the United States.

Blinded by the American goodwill offensive, the Japanese had overlooked the nonreciprocal most favored nation clauses at the core of the unequal treaties. Far from achieving Japan's autonomy as a trading nation, they would have courted disaster had they persisted in negotiating with the Americans. Opening the interior of their country to foreign residence and trade and permitting foreign use of unopened ports would have invited a surge of foreign capital into Japan, rendering Japan attractive prey for imperialism.

Worse, American hints at a willingness to restore Japan's tariff autonomy in line with Itō's thinking were, in fact, duplicitous. The Americans would disguise the preservation of existing tariff agreements through the ruse of minor rate adjustments; they had no intention of restoring Japan's tariff autonomy. For Itō, this was a humiliating failure.

An irritated Kido
Itō's and Ōkubo's absence to secure plenipotentiary credentials brought the embassy to a halt in America for four months, from February to June 1872. The pause led to reflection and, ultimately, to recrimination, directed at Itō. It was Kido Takayoshi who led the charge. Given that the result of the embassy's time in America was a failure akin to the mountain laboring and bringing forth a mouse, criticism of Itō's rashness is understandable.

From virtually the moment that Itō and Ōkubo had been dispatched to secure negotiating credentials for the embassy, Kido had been apprehensive about treaty revision. Itō had managed to cajole the ambassadors into immediately entering negotiations. But in his absence, the time to think led them to foresee the possible benefits as pathetically small. Kido felt what was being proposed were "all things which the foreigners will delight in having": the opening of several new ports, the right of foreigners to travel the interior of the country within certain specified conditions, and the expansion of the areas open to foreign residence in Japan. "When I examine our course," Kido wrote, "I regret that we relied on Itō and Chargé d'Affaires Mori [Arinori] who know a bit about foreign lands, without holding thorough discussion of the Imperial instructions two or three times. We are indeed remiss in this."[44]

It goes without saying that things turned out pretty much as Kido had feared. Already sensing the coming crisis, it was no doubt extremely irritating for Kido to have to wait so long for Itō's return while the embassy bogged down in such a clumsy departure from its original agenda.

"It is," Kido writes, "a mere twenty years, after all, since our country began to have diplomatic relations with foreign countries. In no way do our diplomatic techniques and tactics measure up to those of the nations of America and Europe—which is, of course, inevitable, considering the time which the respective parties have spent at this." Nevertheless, he adds, "if we make promises, then trample them underfoot, no matter how trivial they be, and if we do not stick firmly to our position on matters concerning our country, I fear the world will lose faith in our country."[45] Kido's thoughts reveal a concern that the embassy—which had precipitously dispatched two of its leaders to secure credentials from the emperor and was now cooling its heels to no purpose in a foreign land—was becoming an international laughingstock.

And so Kido came to harbor great ill feeling for Itō's recent activities. In Kido's eyes, Itō's radical advocacy of modernization, including his haste with regard to treaty revision, was shallow and without sufficient consideration for Japan's national interests—being based primarily on Itō's desire for fame and his fancy of himself as an expert on the West. This impression was bolstered by the behavior of Mori Arinori. Another advocate of radical modernization, Mori teamed with Itō to push for immediate treaty renegotiation and in Itō's absence antagonized the other members of the mission with his arrogance. When his opinions were not accepted in a meeting with other members of the embassy, Mori stormed out and even traveled independently from the embassy for a time. Mori's opinion of himself as an American expert was the basis for a number of instances of rude behavior toward Kido and other members of the embassy.[46] Because of this, Kido began to distance himself from the radical modernizers, such as Itō and Mori.

Kido Takayoshi

The Kido who awaited Itō's return to Washington, therefore, was not the sympathizer and protector of old. In later years, Itō spoke of this in vague terms and tried to shift the blame for the change in Kido onto Ōkuma Shigenobu and Inoue Kaoru. "When I got back to America and saw Kido again," Itō maintained, "and the conversation turned to Ōkuma and Inoue, Kido's attitude toward me changed."[47] The truth was that Kido's gut-level distrust of Itō's frivolousness and superficiality had simply solidified. For the rest of the embassy's journey, Kido treated Itō with a coldness palpable even to outside observers.[48]

For Kido, the situation was painful. Only two months after arriving in America he expressed in a letter his misgivings about participating in the embassy: "Accepting the order to go with the embassy was the biggest mistake in my life. I regret it terribly, but at this point there is nothing to be done."[49]

A major cause of Kido's flagging spirits was that linguistic difficulties impeded his ability to gather information. Added to this, though, was his distrust of Itō and others in the modernizing faction. Kido openly displayed his distaste for how they showed off their knowledge of the West and for their high-handed efforts to dominate the embassy. Mori Arinori in particular rubbed Kido the wrong way, and Kido referred to Mori as "that bastard" (*kiyatsu*).[50] To Kido, the modernizers were soulless advocates of "half-baked enlightenment" (*nama kaika*).[51]

> They make a big fuss about "enlightenment, enlightenment" but it is simply for honor and gain. They forget their old friends and acquaintances, lose sight of what is fundamental, and make a habit of superficiality.[52]

Kido viewed the advocates of rapid modernization as a shallow lot, unable to see beyond the trappings of Westernization and motivated solely by self-interest. He felt keenly that the grand design of the Japanese nation could not be left to such people.

Yet the criticisms Kido voiced must have been directed in part at himself. He, too, saw himself as a progressive and was now being forced to reevaluate his advocacy of "enlightenment." For Kido, the embassy thus became his search for a new guiding principle for Japan to replace the "enlightenment" he had previously espoused. Was he able to find that guiding principle, and overcome his distress about the embassy? This question will be dealt with in some detail later. For the moment, let us look at another of the embassy's key figures: Ōkubo Toshimichi.

A melancholy Ōkubo

Travel across the great expanses of North America and in Europe was, of course, by rail. I write "of course" to emphasize that the first Japanese railway did not open until September 1872, in the midst of the embassy's journey. When the embassy left Japan, this railway was still under construction, with track laid only from Yokohama to the harbor fortifications at Shinagawa.

Anticipating the train travel they would face, however, it was felt that "were [the party] to never have ridden on a train until they reached the United States it would be an embarrassment." So according to one participant, Makino Nobuaki, "we all went to the seaside at Shinagawa, boarded the train directly from the beach, as there was no station or platform, and rode as far as Yokohama."[53] All in all, a rather pitiful exercise in national pride.

This dress rehearsal behind them, embassy members then experienced rail travel in the United States. One is curious to know what they thought, rocked by the motion of the train as it raced across infinitely greater distances then they had traveled before. Kume Kunitake gives us a glimpse of what it was like aboard the train with the ambassadors:

> In those days their railway cars were built to carry six people to a car. The one I rode in contained Ambassador Iwakura, Ōkubo and Kido, and also Yamaguchi Naoyoshi, another of the vice-ambassadors; Hatakeyama Yoshinari, [at the time known as Sugiura Kōzō] and I rounded out the number to six. Throughout our journey we six were always together.[54]

Where was Itō? Kume tells us that "Itō always traveled separately. Among the vice-ambassadors he
was odd man out." Kume adds, dryly, that Itō was
known as "quite a rake" and "was probably off chas-
ing women or something."[55]

But it is Ōkubo who concerns us here, and Kume
appears to almost always have been with him:

Ōkubo Toshimichi

> Thus we had a fairly deep connection with Ōkubo, but
> Ōkubo was in any case a man of few words, and riding
> the train he always just sat there smoking a cigar.
> When we went by horse and carriage to tour someplace, and everyone else was
> chatting away, excited by all the novelty, Ōkubo simply puffed away on his cigar,
> and kept quiet.[56]

According to Kume, Ōkubo was an interesting contrast to Kido. "On the
train, it seemed that Iwakura and Kido were always talking about something, and if Hatakeyama and I were talking Kido would soon join in the
discussion, but Ōkubo just sat there with a smile on his face, saying not a
word."[57] Even the smile was austere, scarcely more than a flicker around
the mouth. Most of the party seems to have been in awe of Ōkubo and to
have given him wide berth. Kume recounts that "during the entire course
of the trip you could have counted the number of times Ōkubo opened his
mouth. He was that taciturn."[58]

But the stern and intimidating demeanor that kept others at a distance
concealed Ōkubo's profound melancholy. From among the handful of
words Ōkubo spoke during the voyage, Kume records the following:

> We overthrew the shogunate in order to restore rule to the emperor, and with
> that task nearly accomplished, we have done about all we can do. Yet somehow
> I see trouble ahead. After getting a first-hand look at the West in this way, I
> don't think we are fit for such a world of progress.[59]

The work of Takahashi Hidenao indicates that the Restoration government just prior to the dispatch of the Iwakura Embassy was brimming
with confidence and optimism. It had just executed a series of crucial
reforms abolishing the feudal domains and introducing a centralized

system of national and local government. "This euphoric state, intoxicated with success," according to Takahashi, "was reflected in their views of the United States and Europe and led to an overly optimistic assessment of the situation in terms favorable to Japan."[60] That optimism also reveals itself in the guileless explanation of Japan's situation and request for assistance in implementing reforms contained in the official letter borne by the embassy abroad.

Actual contact with the West forced the ambassadors to reassess their views. The affluence of Western civilization forced them to acknowledge the magnitude of the gap between Japan and the West they were looking to as a model and validated Ōkubo's lament.

For Ōkubo, the shock was great. Added to a sense of having been too sanguine in his assessment of the West, he must also have felt chagrin at returning to Japan to secure certification of the mission's plenipotentiary powers—at having been duped by Itō into becoming an accomplice in a senseless enterprise that disregarded the nation's interests. Ōkubo, moreover, was as irritated as Kido at his lack of competence with Western languages. In Paris, he expressed his frustration, contemptuously describing himself as being "like a wooden dummy." [61]

According to Kume Kunitake, Ōkubo was in extremely low spirits in England, the embassy's destination after leaving the United States. Kume recalls Ōkubo muttering, "An old man like me is going to be totally useless from now on. I can't keep up with the times, so all I can do is get out of the way."[62] This sort of self-criticism can only have fueled Ōkubo's gloom.

For Kido and Ōkubo, therefore, the embassy was no pleasure cruise. Quite the contrary. It caused them to look upon their country's future with foreboding. A true leader, though, responds to adversity by opening new frontiers, and as the journey continued, Ōkubo's spirits began to revive. Both he and Kido sought to break out of their malaise by applying themselves to the study of the Western civilization that so overwhelmed them.

What political vision did Kido and Ōkubo derive from their experience of the West? Before dealing with this question, it may be useful to touch on Kume Kunitake's assessment of Western civilization in his careful record of the embassy's progress.

4. The Iwakura Embassy's Perspective on National Institutions

A brilliant comparative analysis of civilizations

The closest thing we have to what Tanaka Akira describes as "a detailed official report" of the Iwakura Embassy is Kume Kunitake's *Ō-Bei kairan jikki* (A true account of a journey of observation through the United States and Europe; hereafter referred to as *Jikki*).[63] Kume went on to become a professor at Tokyo Imperial University and one of the leading historians of the Meiji period. Known for employing a rigorously empirical approach to the study of history, Kume is also famous for his dismissal from the university in 1892 after publishing the controversial article "Shintō wa saiten no kozoku" (Shintō as an ancient custom to consecrate heaven).

Kume accompanied the Iwakura Embassy as its recording secretary and was at the side of its two major figures, Ōkubo and Kido, for most of the journey across America and Europe. In a sense, he served as their eyes and ears in observing Western civilization. So it is fair to say that the image of Western civilization in *Jikki* encompasses the impressions of Ōkubo and Kido.

Jikki provides more than a detailed account of the embassy's movements and observations. It also offers a brilliant comparative analysis of civilizations. There are numerous studies of this landmark in the travel literature of modern Japan, notably the outstanding achievements of Tanaka Akira, Nishikawa Nagao, Haga Tōru, and Izumi Saburō, that should be consulted for an overview of the embassy and for a detailed discussion of its observations of the West. Here, however, I offer my own approach to *Jikki* and to extracting the essence of its discourse on Western civilization.

The uniqueness of Western political thought

Chapter 89 of *Jikki*, "Europa-shū seizoku sōron" (A general survey of political practices and customs in Europe), yields Kume's deeply interesting discourse on comparative political culture. It ranks as a highlight of his voluminous work.

> According to European racial theory, the race which inhabits East Asia (that is, China and Japan) . . . are remarkably civilized, and it is the custom of their rulers to practice benevolent and compassionate government. Because the principles of law and principles of morality became intermingled, however, the

rules which govern relations within the family came to be the model for relations between between ruler and subject. These peoples lack a sense of shame, so the [idea of a] right to autonomy has never arisen among them.[64]

Kume accurately captures two major aspects of Western political thought. First is the distinction between the "principles of law"(or social norms) and "principles of morality." Second is the stress on the autonomy of the individual. The first also signifies a divorce between politics and morality, the implications of which will be discussed later. For the moment, let us consider the second point.

Fukuzawa Yukichi, the influential writer and educator, had already praised the autonomy and self-reliance of the individual as the essence of Western civilization in his famous formula: "When the individual is independent, the nation is independent." According to Fukuzawa, "When the people of a nation come together of their own free will to defend the nation and secure their own rights and honor, this is what we call the independence or the civilization of a nation." In other words, he believed that a civilized, free, and independent nation was possible only when the people actively preserved their rights and honor and guarantees of these were maintained. Fukuzawa further asserts that "The independence of our nation is the goal, and the civilization of its people the means to achieving that goal." What he is saying is that a civilized people—a collective of autonomous individuals—is a prerequisite for national independence.[65]

Kume shares this thinking. Perceiving the autonomy of the individual as a salient characteristic of Western civilization, Kume saw the development of national strength by an "autonomous people" (jishu no tami) as among the major tasks facing Japanese civilization. He felt that the logical development from one to the other would not be easy, because Kume felt uncomfortable with certain aspects of Western civilization—notably the peculiarly Western principle of interest-based politics.

According to Kume, a pillar of the individual autonomy that was the pride of the West and one of the guiding principles of Western politics was the relentless pursuit of private interest. "The people of Europe," Kume lamented, "make their livelihoods through competition with one another in seeking to satisfy their desire for profit."[66] Kume had discovered the role of interest politics in Western political culture—the conflict and competition of interests and the political institutions that served them.

This was antithetical to the traditional political thought of East Asia, in which politics was seen as the loftiest manifestation of virtue. Kume squarely faces this contradiction:

> The received idea of the [respective] characters of the two races is this: the white race has powerful desires, manifests zealotry in matters of religion, and is deficient in self-control. In short, it is a race of strong passions. In the yellow race, desires are weak and the ability to bend the character [by curbing impulses] is strong. In brief, it is a race of few passions. The principal concerns of government [in East and West] are therefore opposites. In the West, government concerns itself primarily with the protection [of life and property]; in the East, government concerns itself primarily with [the inculcation of] morality.[67]

This passage has often been cited as an example of Kume's "racial theory." Nishikawa Nagao, however, points out that what is being discussed here is a "matter of fact" not "a matter of values."[68] Kume is simply and objectively spelling out the fact that power politics in the defense of interests, completely different in spirit from the East Asian tradition of rule by virtue, is at the root of the strength and the prosperity of the West.

The clash of interests

Another principle of Western political culture is the separation of politics from morality. Kume speaks of this as something that put an end to social and political dependence on a patriarchal Other, enabling individual autonomy. An additional implication that I would like to point out is that the demand for the separation of politics and morality disregards considerations of morality, encouraging instead the people's pursuit of profit domestically and its protection from external threats. Social ills may arise out of competition in the pursuit of interests, but it is not a primary responsibility of politics to intervene or to impose regulations to prevent this. Politics stands as the servant not of morality but of practical interests. In Kume's view, other principal concepts of Western politics, such as "justice" and "society," have no moral coloration. Their social currency derives solely from their utility as the tools of interest politics:

> In any discussion of the linchpins of European government, it is invariably stated that they are "'justice'" and "'society.'" By "'justice'" is meant the

clarification of rights and duties. "'Society'" refers to the warm feeling that exists within a community. One might go so far as to say that these are the equivalents of the two words *gi* ['righteousness'] and *jin* ['benevolence']. "'Benevolence'" and "'righteousness,'" however, are concepts which are founded upon morality, while "'justice'" and "'society'" are ideas derived from the protection of property. Their meanings are therefore diametrically opposed. When observing the political culture of Europe it is of the utmost importance never to lose sight of this fundamental point.[69]

For someone steeped in the East Asian tradition in which virtue was the ultimate value of civilization, Western politics, with its pursuit of private interest and its use of power to legitimize that pursuit, was no doubt abhorrent.

> In the West the chief concern of government is protection [of the people and their property]. In the East, it is the inculcation of morality [in the people]. When we observe Western nations in the light of the usages of our own system of government, therefore, [we see that] even when circumstances appear to be the same the people's temperaments are shaped by different fundamental ideas.[70]

Here Kume seems to have arrived at the idea of an ethnic difference in the basic temperament of the Eastern and Western peoples. If East Asian civilization was a civilization of sheep nourished by the virtue of rulers, then Western civilization was a civilization of wolves bred out of the relentless and intense clash of private interests.

Surviving "war in peacetime"

What Kume saw being presented under the aegis of Western civilization was a simple choice of eating or being eaten. Through their negotiations for treaty revision with the Americans, the Japanese were made acutely aware of the cunning that underlay the politesse of civilization, as indicated in *Jikki*:

> In the course of diplomacy in Western countries, while amity and justice are displayed in the light, deceit and envy invariably reign in the dark. Whenever there is some incident, even a declaration of complete neutrality is only intended for show.[71]

As this civilization of wolves advanced eastward, East Asia had fallen under its sway. The East was being introduced to "war in peacetime"—the struggle for survival amid unceasing competition that came with entry into the sphere of Western civilization:

> Commerce is war in peacetime. Heaven cannot be relied upon, nor can Earth. The only thing that can be relied upon is the willingness of men to cooperate with one another.[72]

The members of the embassy, who had departed their country for America and Europe determined to become participants in the civilization of the West, had now had a glimpse of the realities of that civilization's "war in peacetime." The national mission that then fell to them was to discover how their country could survive it. They began to recognize that the best means to this end was "the willingness of men to cooperate with one another."

The institutionalization of nationalism

Kume grasped the essence of Western civilization as competition between autonomous individuals engaged in the pursuit of personal profit. In this context, the role of politics became the expansion of personal gain through the encouragement of such competition. Competition between individuals, by this logic, is raised to the level of social competition and, ultimately, of competition among nations. The "war in peacetime" in pursuit of profit becomes the essential nature of international politics, with people forming nations in order to emerge victorious in this struggle:

> However, people have a right to autonomy, and they live in a world of competing interests. Authority must not bow to, nor laws be shackled by, nor punishments be deterred by relationships among interests. The way to ensure that these are properly safeguarded is to create a society in which men join together to cooperate with one another in the competition among interests.[73]

Kume is preaching the necessity of increasing "the cooperative impulse" among autonomous individuals and of forming "united and cooperative associations" to engage in competition for profit. He sees the ultimate form of such cooperation as the nation-state, because the highest form of the "cooperative impulse" is found in the hearts of individuals as patriotism or nationalism:

> Although the countries of the world differ in size, each is dedicated to its way of life, and if a nation achieves independence, a spirit of patriotism inevitably wells up [in their hearts]. It is rather like loving oneself and one's home [above other places] . . . People born in a particular land naturally love that land, just as trees rely on their roots. Therefore, the patriotic mind naturally gives rise to humane feelings and becomes a source of loyalty. When the people of Europe and America talk about civilization, it is based on patriotism.[74]

The task Japan faced in achieving a spirit of cooperation among its people in order to join the ranks of the "civilized" world is restated as an effort to arouse and develop feelings of patriotism and nationalism. In other words, the task was to institutionalize this nationalism or spirit of national independence. According to Kume, the establishment of a constitution was an integral part of this process. Based on observations in Belgium, Kume writes:

> Belgians contend that if there are too few people who are [economically] self-sufficient, the country will grow weak and become difficult to preserve. The political and legal systems here are all set up with the aim of cultivating self-reliance, with everyone, high and low, participating to foster a culture of diligence and to nurture independent enterprise.[75]

The need to establish a constitution is clear. A constitution can nurture a spirit of national independence and unity among the people, encourage the growth of individual autonomy, and enhance the nation's power. It is the backbone of national integration.

In *Jikki*, a variety of factors—technology, industry, and so forth—are cited as making the civilized nations what they are. One of the most important, as we have seen, is a framework of national institutions fostering nationalism. And so the attention of the Iwakura Embassy began to focus upon the concept of a national structure organized around a system of constitutional government.

At the outset of this chapter, it was noted that the embassy's tour of Western civilization was a search for "civilized" national institutions.

Witnessing firsthand the institutions of the United States and Europe, the embassy's members began to develop a vision of the type of institutional structures suited to Japan. The institutionalization of nationalism has been discussed. Kume, however, stipulates another principle governing the national institutions of the civilized nations: gradualism.

"And so we move forward by degrees"
On September 27, 1872, the embassy visited the world-renowned British Museum. Kume records the following:

> When one looks at the objects displayed in its museums, the sequence of stages of civilization through which a country has passed are immediately apparent to the eye and are apprehended directly by the mind.[76]

The embassy thereafter made a point of visiting museums at each stop on its itinerary. In June 1873, its members toured the Universal Exposition in Vienna and were impressed by its magnificence.[77]

Indeed, for the Iwakura Embassy, all of America and Europe were a universal exposition. Kume writes of museums as follows:

> "Seeing but once is better than hearing a hundred times," said the ancients, and truly the sense of sight is more important than the sense of hearing in enabling people to absorb information.[78]

Jikki is a record of observations made in that great exposition hall of civilization: the countries of the Western world. These observations also led the embassy's members to reflect on the character of individual nations. The West, they saw, was not monolithic; its countries presented innumerable differences in terms of prevailing conditions, institutions, and so on. The embassy was touring a vast display of national systems and institutions, and Kume notes that

> on the surface of the earth there are a dazzling array of nations inhabited by various peoples with diverse customs and lifestyles who are joined together in a magnificent display like a hundred flowers in bloom. While countries in Europe resemble one another in their shared political roots, it is in their ways of life that the differences between them lie.[79]

The embassy was dispatched to discover the common structure and institutions essential to civilized nations. What confronted it when it reached the West, however, was not unity but diversity. As Kume writes, the Western nations may have originated in a shared political culture, but history had forged palpably different national characters. Faced with this reality, the embassy turned its attention to the "stages of civilization" that Kume cites in his impressions of the British Museum, given in full here:

> When one looks at the objects displayed in its museums, the sequence of stages of civilization through which a country has passed are immediately apparent to the eye and are apprehended directly by the mind. No country has ever sprung into existence fully formed. The weaving of the pattern in the nation's fabric is always done in a certain order. The knowledge acquired by those who precede is passed on to those who succeed; the understanding achieved by earlier generations is handed down to later generations; and so we move forward by degrees. This is what is called "progress." Progress does not mean discarding what is old and contriving something which is entirely new. In the forming of a nation, therefore, customs and practices arise whose value is tested by constant use, so that when new knowledge arises it naturally does so from [existing] sources, and it is from these sources that it derives its value. Nothing is better than a museum for showing clearly the stages by which these processes happen. "Seeing but once is better than hearing a hundred times," said the ancients, and truly the sense of sight is more important than the sense of hearing in enabling people to absorb information.[80]

Clearly, the British Museum tour inspires Kume to contemplate the laws of development. He sees that progress consists not of recklessly discarding the old, but rather in maintaining traditions and "moving forward by degrees." In short, he finds gradualism. Kume sees that Western civilization is founded on continuity of tradition. The tendency in Japan, however, was to praise Western civilization and its accomplishments and to abandon Japanese traditions. Kume recognizes that this is not an enlightened attitude and laments, "How can this be called progress? A large tree of a hundred years' growth does not mature overnight."[81] Instead, it was the following attitude that gave rise to Western progress:

Westerners strive for innovation, but at the same time they reflect upon the past and revere the ancient, retaining rather than discarding it. Always treating things in this manner might be said to be a custom of civilization.[82]

Western custom, therefore, is true to the old Japanese proverb: "Discover the new by studying the old" (*furuki o tazunete atarashiki o shiru*). Kume rebukes the shallowness of his countrymen who advocate radical modernization at the expense of tradition and offers gradualism as an antidote.

Fukuzawa Yukichi wrote that "the reason we have made Western civilization our goal is that we believe the spirit of civilization with which we wish to equip ourselves is to be found there."[83] For Fukuzawa, civilization was not merely a means to national prosperity and strength, it was a spiritual matter.

This might also be said to be Kume's conclusion. Amid the diversity of the civilized nations that he encounters, Kume saw that the lesson to be learned was the ethos of civilization, which embodied both nationalism and gradualism. This was also where a vision for civilized national institutions should be sought:

> The basic principle of government in Europe is to rule in accordance with the peoples' customs, rather than bend them [to the ruler's will] or suppress them outright.[84]

The spirit running consistently through Western political culture was of government based on the manners and customs of the people. Hasty imitation of Western national institutions by Japan was to be avoided in favor of their gradual adoption and cultivation on the basis of Japanese political customs and practices. Kume, it might be said, conceived of national institutions as the institutionalization of two aspects of the spirit of civilization: nationalism and political tradition.

This blueprint for the shape of the nation was certainly not an individual discovery on Kume's part. Kido and Ōkubo, the most important of the vice-ambassadors, submitted memoranda upon their return to Japan that detail their opinions on the issue of national institutions and are evidence of the value of their experiences in the West. We look next at the design each of them sketched out for the structure of the Japanese nation.

"Progress from the very marrow"

As we have already seen, the failure in the United States of the attempt at treaty renegotiation spearheaded by Itō led to a falling out between Kido and Itō. This was due in part to a mismatch of personalities between Kido and such advocates of "enlightenment" as Itō and Mori. But it also arose from Kido's distress at having to reassess the modernization policies that Japan had implemented since the Meiji Restoration.

Given that Kido had remarked that the trip overseas was "the biggest mistake in my life," it must have been all the more painful for him to be stuck in Washington waiting for Itō and Ōkubo. The unscheduled stopover, though, had unexpected results. Kido and his associates immersed themselves in studying the national institutions of the United States, and research into Western governmental structures became the dominant theme of the remainder of Kido's journey.[85]

Kido was a budding constitutionalist from the outset. A month after arriving in the United States he remarks in his diary on the need to "develop a more fundamental law" based on the Charter Oath of 1868, "so during this trip I want to give the highest priority to an inquiry into the basic laws and structure of each country we visit."[86] And he does. Assisted by close associates Kume Kunitake and Sugiura Kōzō in the United States and by Aoki Shūzō once the embassy reached Europe, Kido pored over the constitutions of each country visited and met with some of those nations' leading scholars, including Maurice Bloch (1816–1901) in France and Rudolf von Gneist (1816–95) in Germany. This allowed him to hear views on constitutional government firsthand. After visiting Gneist he noted in his diary, "I profited a great deal from our talk."[87] Though terse, the entry is testimony to Kido's ambitious research.

As a result, Kido came to share Kume's insight that the issue was not the superficial fruits of civilization, but its essential spirit—not its skin, but its marrow:

> If we do not set aside for a time the things that are merely skin-deep, and progress from the very marrow, then I fear for the damage today's "enlightenment" may wreak upon the future.[88]

This shift in focus was occasioned in part by the diversity of national institutions and political systems that confronted Kido as he studied the constitutions of the Western powers:

> Each country naturally differs in its manners and customs and the temperament of its people. Thus it follows that the realities of each country's form of government should also differ greatly.[89]

Kido recognized, moreover, that his insight warranted equally serious consideration in reforming national institutions. Kido had ample opportunity to observe in the farce surrounding the attempt at treaty renegotiations the laxness of judgment accompanying the superficial advocacy of modernization and arrived at the conviction that "the basis of the nation has not yet been established."[90] Progress toward enlightenment demanded a reassessment of the foundations of the nation, and this must be carried out in such a way as to foster "progress from the very marrow," adapted to the unique character of the Japanese people. Upon returning to Japan, Kido submitted a memorial advocating the establishment of constitutional government, the embodiment of his most fervent hopes for genuine enlightenment.

The most urgent task

On July 23, 1873, Kido returned to Japan before the main party of the Iwakura Embassy. He was confronted with a caretaker government that had broken its promises to its members who had been sent abroad and had pushed ahead with modernizing reforms. Saigo Takamori, moreover, was about to submit a proposal for a punitive expedition to Korea that would soon throw the government into turmoil. Overhasty reformism and adventurism were not unique to embassy members such as Itō. Kido must have felt acutely that "the basis of the nation has not yet been established."

Indeed, Kido had returned to a nation whose foundation was shaky. He immediately submitted a memorial to the emperor regarding a constitution. The substance of that memorial was published in October in *Shimbun zasshi* (News digest) under the title "Kido sangi kichōgo no enzetsu" (Speech by Councillor Kido upon his return to Japan). What he said is worth examining.[91]

Kido proposed that "the most urgent task at present is to supplement the foundation provided by the Charter Oath with additional articles and expand it into regulations for government."[92] By "regulations for government," Kido means a constitution, and he clearly sees an expanded version of Emperor Meiji's five-article Charter Oath of 1868 as the means to fulfill the nation's pressing need for a constitution. Why a constitution is so important is addressed by Kido in a passage that demonstrates the value of his experiences in the West:

> If we consider the nations of the world, whether great or small, similar or dissimilar, the key to their prosperity or failure, survival or ruin, lies entirely in what they have achieved or failed to achieve in terms of establishing a constitution [*seiki tensoku*: literally a code of regulations for governance].[93]

In other words, a country's survival hinges on the state of its constitution. A good constitution is the cornerstone of a nation's existence and the foundation of its prosperity.

> When a single sovereign is able to unite all the lesser lords and exercise authority over the entire country, then even if its territories are not vast, if all follow the same path and share common interests, this is sufficient to defend against any insult from neighboring lands.[94]

The independence, prosperity, and power of a nation are, according to Kido, guaranteed when the people are united under a single ruler. Like Kume, Kido conceived of a constitution as the backbone of national unity.

Kido's project

Among the various issues facing the nation, Kido places top priority on establishing a constitution. What he calls for to accomplish this "urgent task" is strong leadership on the part of the emperor and his government. The benefits of civilization were not yet commonly known throughout Japan. Bold decision-making by the emperor and implementation by his ministers was required to gradually lead the people to the citadel of civilization:

Very little time has passed since the Restoration, and naturally more will be required for our knowledge to advance to the point that we can create a popular assembly. Therefore, it scarcely needs saying that for the present, the leaders of the government should debate all matters thoroughly, with His Majesty the Emperor continuing to exercise absolute authority.[95]

Kido is endorsing absolutist rule by the emperor and his advisers. His determination to achieve the immediate goal of an "autocratic constitution" (*dokusai no kempō*) was unshakeable. In November 1873, shortly after Kido had submitted his memorial to the throne, Itō asked Kido's opinion on the form the government should take. Kido flatly stated that "the fundamental law of the state must be 'despotic.'"[96]

It may seem strange that Kido, a progressive, would so dispassionately support autocracy. But his ideas were grounded in his experience of the West. He knew that even autocracy requires the confidence and trust of the people, and that even even the emperor "cannot treat the realm as the private property of the imperial house."[97] An autocratic constitution, insofar as it was to be constitutional, must have as its central purpose not the maintenance of despotic rule but respect for the will of the people and the fostering of national unity. Government on the basis of the popular will was the fundamental point of a constitutional system:

> In the civilized nations, sovereigns *do not rule arbitrarily* [emphasis added in the *Shimbun zasshi* edition]. Rather, they achieve unity and cooperation among the people of the country and carry out their will by establishing regulations for the affairs of state, delegating responsibility for judgment upon them to an agency called the government, and staffing it with talented officials. These officials are entrusted by the united will of the people to bear the heavy responsibility of the affairs of state, and even in times of great emergency or crisis, they must not act irresponsibly, in ways that are not permitted by the united will of the people. The people hold them strictly to this by admonishing them if they exceed their authority, and their representatives carefully scrutinize all matters in order to prevent arbitrary decisions on the part of the officials.[98]

Kido continues:

> The people have individual rights and have duties. Asserting their rights, they preserve their innate liberty; taking up their duties they participate in the public affairs of the nation—this is the raison d'être of the people.[99]

Although Kido flirts with harsh terms, such as despotism and autocracy, what he has in mind is a people's constitution—a political structure that promotes the political enlightenment of the people and protects their rights.

The project Kido outlines for Japan's national institutions is intended to guarantee the nation's independence based on the political and social autonomy of its citizens, achieved as described. Beyond talk of an autocratic constitution, Kido's sights are set on the eventual establishment of a constitutional monarchy in which sovereignty is shared with the people:

> If His Majesty the Emperor will act decisively to welcome the will of the people, codify the affairs of state, and delegate their determination in such a way as to control arbitrary decisions on the part of the officials, thus making the public affairs of the nation a common concern, then what is today an autocratic constitution will certainly, at some later time, when deliberations among the people reach that point, serve as the seed of a constitution of shared sovereignty, which will become a great pillar of the happiness of the people.[100]

Kido, it is well known, opposed Saigo Takamori and others in their agitation for a punitive expedition against Korea. He argued that "at this time the proper management of internal administration must have first priority."[101] In his very real opposition to the Korean adventure, Kido again demonstrates his desire for national reform grounded in his observations of the Western nations. He understands that before anything else can be undertaken a firm basis for domestic government must be established. The manifestation of his political conviction was a constitutional form of government with two central pillars: the development of a patriotic citizenry and a gradual transition from autocratic rule to shared sovereignty. It was a vision for the shape of the nation shared by Ōkubo Toshimichi.

The sole fruit

During his time in Europe, Ōkubo spoke derisively of himself as being "like a wooden dummy" and spent his days sunk in gloom. A letter that he wrote in January 1873 from Paris says that the survey of the United States, Britain, and France is at an end and hints at his deepening pessimism: "Even if we manage to climb a few rungs up the ladder of civilization, there are a myriad of ways in which we cannot measure up [to these countries]."[102] Of Prussia and Russia, however, which the embassy had yet to visit, he writes, as if trying to buck himself up, "In my humble opinion there should be a great deal in these countries we might adopt as standards."[103]

The newly risen Germany and Tsarist Russia, located as they were on the periphery of the Western nations, must have been suggestive models for Japan. This was especially true of the new German empire. Its national prestige had expanded rapidly when, powered by the military might of Prussia, it had defeated France, regarded as being in the first rank of the civilized nations, in the Franco-Prussian War of 1870–71. It is not difficult to see why Ōkubo had hopes for what he might learn there.

These hopes were not unfounded. Ōkubo writes from Berlin to Saigo Takamori and Yoshii Tomozane in Tokyo that

> this country is very different from the other countries of Europe; it has a more rough-hewn and honest aspect. And particularly since it has produced such great teachers as the famous Bismarck and Moltke, who make me want to follow in their footsteps.[104]

It appears that contact with such nation-building heroes as Bismarck and Moltke on the eve of his return to Japan helped Ōkubo to at last dispel his gloom. The day before sailing back to Japan, he wrote: "I am inclined to say that meeting the great teachers Bismarck and Moltke alone was worthwhile."[105] For Ōkubo, his experience of Germany appears to have been the sole fruit of the embassy.

Realpolitik

What Ōkubo learned in Germany is suggested by the text of a talk given to the ambassadors by Bismarck that must have made quite an impression on Ōkubo.

The embassy left Japan naive in its faith in "the law of nations," an ide-alistic belief in what was thought to be a dependable international standard of civilization. But the Japanese reassessed their appraisal when faced with the realities of Western politics and diplomacy. Bismarck clearly support-ed their misgivings:

> Nations these days all appear to conduct relations with amity and courtesy, but this is entirely superficial, for behind this façade lurks a struggle for supremacy and mutual contempt.[106]

Bismarck then says this about the "law of nations":

> From the very beginning, the so-called international law, which was supposed to protect the rights of all nations, afforded us no security at all. In cases involv-ing a dispute, a great power would invoke international law and stand its ground if it stood to benefit, but if it stood to lose it would simply change tack and use military force, so that it never limited itself to defense alone. Small nations like ours, however, would assiduously abide by the letter of the law and universal principles, not daring to transgress them so that, faced with ridicule and contempt from the greater powers, we invariably failed to protect our right to autonomy, no matter how hard we tried.[107]

It is quintessential Bismarck and a legitimation of Realpolitik. Bismarck goes on to defend the "blood and iron" policies he has used to advance Prussia's fortunes:

> Aroused by this deplorable state of affairs, we summoned our strength as a nation and made a great effort to promote a patriotic spirit with a view to becoming a country that merited due respect in diplomatic affairs. In the sev-eral decades since then, right up to the present day, all we have ever set out to achieve has simply been to uphold the autonomous rights of each nation. Nevertheless, we hear constant expressions of horror from other powers at the way Prussia has used force on all fronts, and they censure us for rejoicing in our military prowess and depriving people of their sovereign rights. This, howev-er, is entirely contrary to the will of our country, for it is our hope that, moti-vated solely by respect for national rights, each nation may be independent and

conduct diplomatic relations on equal terms, living within its just territories without its borders being violated.[108]

In concluding his message, Bismarck urges the Japanese to see Germany as the best model for Japan. He tells them that "while Japan may now have amicable diplomatic relations with a number of countries, its friendship with Germany should be the most intimate of all because of the true respect in which we hold the right of self-government."[109]

For Ōkubo and the embassy as a whole, Bismarck's speech was eye-opening. Bismarck begins by asserting that civilization and the law of nations are at base nothing other than competition and the balance of power and ends by teaching that only naked force can be relied on to preserve national independence.

In May 1873, Ōkubo returned to Japan with Bismarck's teachings fresh in his mind. His answer to the question what must be done to increase the nation's power and preserve its independence is identical to Kido's—establish a constitution.

Advocacy of progressive constitutionalism

On November 19, 1873, the government ordered Itō Hirobumi and Terashima Munenori to investigate the form of government Japan should adopt. Ōkubo, meanwhile, had handed Itō a memorandum on constitutional government.[110]

Ōkubo begins his memorandum along the lines of thought of Kume and Kido. He acknowledges the diverse political systems in the United States and Europe, ranging from monarchies to democracies, and accepts that each has strengths, such that it is difficult to judge the best. "In the first place," Ōkubo writes,

> monarchies and democracies differ as forms of government, but generally speaking they arise naturally in response to factors that include geography, the customs and temperament of the people, and the movement of history, and as such they are not something that can be constructed overnight. Yet neither are they something that should simply be clung to stubbornly out of dependence upon the past.[111]

The political institutions of a nation arise organically and cannot be designed anew solely by human ingenuity. At the same time, it will not do to fall into a hidebound conservatism. Reform of national institutions must be considered, but this cannot be done in superficial imitation of the national systems of foreign countries, such as the United States, Great Britain, or Russia.

The issue, therefore, is how to establish a system of national government suited to Japan's environment and political culture. "At present, there is no more important and urgent task than to deliberate upon the shape of our nation (*kokutai*)."[112] Ōkubo emphasizes domestic administration, seeing Japan's most urgent task to be the strengthening of its foundations. He, too, stipulates that the first thing that must be done is to establish a "codified national law" (*teiritsu kokuhō*)—a constitution.

Ōkubo thus shares with Kido a grand plan for the establishment of a constitution. Differences, though, are apparent between the two men's view of what its content should be. In contrast to Kido's advocacy of monarchical absolutism, Ōkubo calls for shared sovereignty between the emperor and his people:

> In [re]constructing the land of our forefathers, how is it possible that we could exclude its people from [participation in its] governance? But if we create a government for the people, then how can we possibly abandon their sovereign and hope to preserve the nation? Thus a constitution should create a system of shared sovereignty between the monarch and the people, defining the rights of the ruler above, and the rights of the people below, achieving fairness and justice for both ruler and ruled and eliminating selfish interests.[113]

The prevalent image of Ōkubo is of a crafty, dictatorial political operator. But the content of Ōkubo's memorandum to Itō suggests instead a man whose political philosophy is a conscientious and progressive endorsement of constitutional government.[114] Compared, at the very least, with Kido's remarks on "despotism," Ōkubo's championing of dual sovereignty has a progressive ring.

Democracy and gradualism
Rather than picking apart the differences in their language, however, it is probably more fruitful to note the structural similarities in the two men's

positions. Certainly there are differences between the concepts of autocracy and dual sovereignty, but there was, in fact, little that separated Kido and Ōkubo in terms of where they positioned "the people" in their political discourse. Ōkubo asks, "How can we exclude the people from . . . governance?" He goes on to state that a constitution should define the mutual rights and constraints of the sovereign and the people to ensure that neither converts the public trust into a private possession.

For Kido, an autocratic constitution was only a temporary expedient for realizing the popular will. He joins Ōkubo in aspiring to a system of national politics that facilitates the enlightenment of the people. Nor were the two that far apart concerning how best to achieve this goal, as Ōkubo's words show:

> We should not blindly copy the systems of dual sovereignty between monarch and people that are found in the various countries of Europe. Our country has its own canon of laws based on an unbroken imperial line. There are still limits to the enlightenment of the people. So we must deliberate and carefully consider what is appropriate in terms what we have and what we do not, what will be of benefit and what would be harmful, and frame a constitution accordingly.[115]

Ōkubo is calling for the establishment of a constitution that protects Japan's ancient and unbroken imperial tradition and is calibrated to the degree of enlightenment possessed by the Japanese people. Itō Hirobumi, the recipient of this memorandum, described it as "a gradualist argument for constitutional government."[116]

Both Kido and Ōkubo's positions on constitutional government took democracy and gradualism as organizational principles. Both men hoped first to establish the overall framework of the political system with a constitution, utilizing it to develop the political and social energies of the people and to achieve national unity. And both saw it as essential to proceed gradually with the creation of this new order.

The Struggle for Rights

On March 11, 1872, as the Iwakura Mission was arriving in Washington, a lecture was being given in the Austrian capital of Vienna that would be discussed for generations to come. The lecturer was Rudolf von Jhering

(1818–82), among the greatest German legal scholars of his day. He titled his presentation "The Struggle for Rights."[117]

Jhering argues passionately that the struggle of individuals to assert and establish their rights is an indispensable factor in the formation and development of just laws. He maintains that this struggle is a sublime duty of mankind, a duty that is not merely personal, but an ethical duty to the nation.

The individual's struggle for personal rights, says Jhering, is a lofty undertaking, for it is also a struggle to defend the constitutional order of the nation and, as such, will contribute to enhancing the nation's position within international law. All people, he urges, should be "fighters, born to assert their rights in the interests of society." In a nation made up of individuals endowed with this fighting spirit, the constitutional rights won by the people in their struggle for liberty and the rights won by the nation in its struggle against foreign adversaries will be duly exercised. For Jhering, the essence of Western civilization was the achievement of order through conflict.

Yet it must be pointed out that Jhering also sounds an alarm for Western civilization. Capitalism had taken root in the West, and the birth pangs of industrialization had commenced. Austria's neighbor, Germany, was experiencing an economic bubble, with corporations springing up overnight. Jhering asserts the heritage of the European law in the face of the struggle for profit rampant in society at large. He appeals instead for a struggle for rights, accompanied by ethical self-restraint.

When the Iwakura Embassy landed in Europe, Western civilization was in an era of upheaval. The Japanese witnessed firsthand the factories springing up everywhere and the dazzling technological developments of the times. They also saw how the struggle for profit that provided the motive force for this activity was testing even the independence of nations.

But could they have concluded, as Jhering preached, that the historical significance of the struggle in Europe resided in an ethically tinged struggle for rights? Or was such an overview of Western civilization in an era of transition something possible only for a gifted scholar, such as Jhering?

What is certain is that the embassy's members had their eyes opened to a concept alien to them: conflict as a principle of civilization. For leaders such as Kido and Ōkubo, this occasioned a paradigm shift in their understanding of civilization and of the policies required to guide their nation.

Their goal had changed from an emphasis on the law of nations to the establishment of a constitution.

Toward the creation of a nation-state

As Yamanouchi Susumu so aptly notes, "The first European law that the Japanese encountered, and the first they labored to understand, was international law."[118] And the Japanese took this international law—the law of nations—to be another name for civilization itself. Initially, the Iwakura Embassy reflected this misconception. Its basic policy guidelines, the "Jiyusho," demonstrate that the embassy set sail for the homeland of civilization supported by a naïve trust in the "law of nations."

A year and a half into its tour of observation of the United States and Europe, however, and the embassy's members' faith in what they thought was an underpinning of civilization was pretty much shattered. Their glimpse behind the veil of civilization revealed the savage reality of Western politics: unrestrained competition and the escalation of national rivalries. Bismarck had pointedly shown them that a cold logic prevailed; a country's laws and rights were unsupportable without national wealth and power.

This new reality forced the ambassadors to change perspective. They abandoned their faith in the law of nations and aimed instead at bolstering Japan's international competitiveness through a buildup of national power. Rather than appealing to the morality of civilization in the form of the law of nations, they turned to the pursuit of power and the theory of Realpolitik.

Based on the Iwakura Embassy's Western experiences, the Meiji state sought to fundamentally strengthen Japan for survival in the harsh international environment. That the leaders of the embassy—Iwakura, Kido, and Ōkubo—were united in recommending that domestic administration and policy be given top priority reflected their understanding of contemporary civilization.

Essential to this understanding was the idea that a constitution was the fundamental legal principle upon which the Meiji state should be founded. The memoranda by both Kido and Ōkubo on constitutional government are political manifestos supporting this. They both propose building the domestic political structure of a nation-state, and know that the state's most urgent task is to establish its legal framework in the form of a constitution. The means for Japan to assimilate Western civilization, therefore, had shifted from dependence upon the law of nations to the creation of a constitutional order.

CHAPTER TWO

Itō Hirobumi's European Research

From Constitution as Law to Constitution as National Structure

1. The Political Crisis of 1881 and Itō's Return to Europe

Divided leadership, rebellion, antigovernment agitation

On September 13, 1873, Iwakura Tomomi landed at Yokohama, bringing to a close his nearly two-year tour of the United States and Europe. The Iwakura Embassy had completed its mission. There are a number of consequences this unusual national mission of cultural observation had for Meiji Japan, but from the perspective of legal history the most significant was its encouragement of the shift in the paradigm of Japan's nation-building policies from the law of nations toward a constitution, as discussed in the preceding chapter. fl

Even so, work on the drafting of a constitution did not commence immediately upon the embassy's return to Japan. The approach to the establishment of a constitution that Kido and Ōkubo had learned in the course of their travels in the West was gradualism. The wholesale importation of Western legal models exemplified in Etō Shimpei's slogan, "Don't worry about translating it correctly, just translate it quickly!," was rejected in favor of a search for a legal structure tailored to the nation's character and temperament. For the leaders of Meiji Japan, the most pressing issue was how to strengthen their nation to the point that it could support constitutional government. One of the principal tasks they faced in this regard was establishing a truly national politics in the sense of unifying the political and social energies of the people and bolstering the country's capacity to compete in the international arena. A constitution was conceived of as a symbol of this, but to prepare the way for constitutional politics, domestic order must first be achieved.

The political climate at the time certainly did not encourage a concerted effort to create a constitution. Despite its promises to the leaders who participated in the Iwakura Embassy, Japan's caretaker government had implemented radical initiatives in domestic and foreign policy in their absence. The ambassadors were greeted upon their return, for example, with a proposal for a punitive military expedition against Korea, a policy of overseas expansionism that was scarcely cognizant of the Japan's actual strength. The conflict over this issue soon drove councillors Saigo Takamori, Itagaki Taisuke, and Etō Shimpei out of the government. The resulting disarray made the leaders of the coalition of southwestern domains who dominated the Restoration government acutely aware of how shaky its the foundations were.

Before long, disorder escalated into open revolt, beginning with the Saga Rebellion. Armed uprisings by disgruntled former samurai who looked to the men who had been driven from the government for leadership ensued at locations throughout the country with increasing frequency. They climaxed in the Satsuma Rebellion of 1877—a full-blown civil war.

Opposition to the government was not confined to armed insurrection. The Freedom and Popular Rights Movement had considerable overlap with the samurai revolts, but it used the ideology of constitutionalism as a weapon for attacking the government. After Itagaki Taisuke and his associates published what became known as the Tosa Memorial in January 1874, that document's demand for the establishment of a popularly elected national assembly became a rallying cry that stirred public debate. The leaders of the government were open to the idea of a parliamentary system, but they believed that it was too early to institute the type of nationwide assembly called for in Itagaki's memorial. As expressed in the imperial proclamation of April 1875, their policy was first and foremost the *gradual* implementation of a constitutional system.

The period from the embassy's return to the early 1880s, therefore, was one of domestic strife ranging from dissension within the government to armed uprisings and antigovernment political agitation. For the members of the Iwakura Embassy, who had returned home with vivid images of the power of the Western nations, the political priority was ensuring domestic stability. Even when they finally began to draft a constitution, it was almost as if they had been reminded of the idea by the popular rights movement and the numerous private constitutional proposals then circulating, and this remained little more than a secondary concern of those within the government.[1]

The shock of Ōkuma's memorial

It was the Political Crisis of 1881 that forced the government to reconsider its stance.[2] The crisis was touched off by a memorial Ōkuma Shigenobu submitted in March 1881 to Prince Arisugawa Taruhitō, then serving as minister of the left (*sadaijin*). In this memorial, written in consultation with a group of former students of Fukuzawa Yukichi's that he had brought into the government, Ōkuma took the radical approach of advocating the convening of a national assembly as early as 1883 and making it the core of a British-style system of gov-

Ōkuma Shigenobu

ernment featuring a cabinet determined by parliamentary majorities. His proposal shocked the other leaders of the Meiji government. In response to Ōkuma's memorial, which flatly stated that "constitutional government is government by political parties," Itō Hirobumi wrote with alarm to Iwakura Tomomi that it was "quite unexpectedly radical" and "something a poor fool such as myself couldn't possibly keep pace with." He ends the letter by saying that if such a policy were to be adopted, "after much thought I have concluded that there would be nothing left for me to do but tender my resignation."[3]

At the same time, Councillor Kuroda Kiyotaka was proposing the sale of the assets of the Hokkaido Colonization Office (which had been established with public funds) at an absurdly low price to a private-sector company headed by his friend Godai Tomoatsu. Before this subterfuge could take place, news of it was leaked to the public, inflaming the popular rights movement. The mass media of the time—newspapers, magazines, rallies—launched a superheated antigovernment campaign, driving the government into a corner.

Ōkuma, whose radical memorandum on constitutional government had shaken the government, was in a delicate position. Because he advocated party politics and had earlier embraced the Fukuzawa wing of the popular rights movement, rumors circulated that he had teamed up with popular rights activists to overthrow the government. This notion was even given some credence in the corridors of power, where there was talk of an "Ōkuma plot."

On October 11, the government suspended the sale of the Hokkaido Colonization Office's assets and at the same time forced Ōkuma out of the government. A mass exodus of Ōkuma's associates from the bureaucracy followed.

The Political Crisis of 1881 thus ended with a purge of the Ōkuma faction, with immense effects on the political situation. In particular, the movement to establish a constitution, temporarily shelved, started afresh and gained speed.

On October 12, the day after Ōkuma was forced out, an imperial rescript was issued. Caught between the challenges of the external antigovernment campaign and Ōkuma's pressure from within, the oligarchic government, still dominated by men from the coalition of domains that had overthrown the shogunate, was making a public declaration. In the name of the emperor, it promised that a national assembly would be convened in 1890. It was no longer possible, in the name of gradualism, to make vague claims that the time was not yet ripe for a national assembly and the constitution that must precede it. An official schedule had been established for both.

Itō, the ambivalent leader

It was then proposed and quickly decided to send Itō Hirobumi to Europe for constitutional research. The choice of Itō "was obvious, as he had been proposed as the man to take responsibility for drafting the constitution" by other powerful figures within the government since the preceding year.[4] Although there was a general consensus that Itō should be central to the process of drafting a constitution, Itō must have had mixed feelings, for he did not as yet have a clear vision for it.

That Itō should be seen by himself and others as a leader in establishing constitutional government was only natural. Upon his return from the embassy to the United States and Europe, he had shared Kido's concerns about the dispute brewing over the proposed punitive expedition to Korea, and the chilly relationship between the two thawed. Itō, in fact, recommended an even more gradual approach to the constitutional question than Kido.[5] And it was to Itō that Ōkubo entrusted his memorial on constitutional government, mentioned in the preceding chapter. In a sense, therefore, Itō linked the constitutional thinking of the other two men.

Itō would henceforth be central to the government's reforms of the national political system. Soon after the return of the Iwakura Embassy, he was assigned responsibility for researching forms of government. At the Osaka Conference that led to the promulgation of the imperial rescript on the constitution, and other venues, Itō played a major role in steering government policy in the direction of a constitutional system and a national assembly. If he fancied himself the de facto leader of the Japanese movement toward constitutional government, it is not surprising.

Itō Hirobumi

In the early Meiji years, Itō's relationship with Ōkuma had been quite close and he had been among the most important participants in the political debates and discussions at Ōkuma's residence in Tokyo's Tsukiji district, which had been dubbed the Tsukiji Ryozanpaku (an illusion to the meeting place of heroes in the popular Chinese novel *Shuihu Zhuan*).[6] At the Atami Conference from January into February 1881, Itō and Ōkuma teamed with Inoue Kaoru to form a sort of three musketeers of constitutionalism, winning over Kuroda Kiyotaka of the Satsuma faction and giving a real boost to the prospects of convening a national assembly. As it turned out, however, Ōkuma, who at Atami had seemed to be in complete agreement on the course constitutional policy should follow, would draft his own plan for a constitution and attempt to secretly petition the emperor with it through the good offices of Prince Arisugawa. Itō,was profoundly shocked, and not merely because Ōkuma had submitted his memorandum in an apparent end run around him. The scope and detail of Ōkuma's proposal stunned Itō, who had rested complacently in his notions of gradualism.

The resourceful Inoue Kowashi

Itō had to admit that Ōkuma's proposal had left him in the dust. Ōkuma, though, was not Itō's only competition; another specter loomed from within the government: the man who had drafted Iwakura's counter-memorandum to Ōkuma's proposal, Inoue Kowashi.[7]

Inoue is renowned as one of the more resourceful figures in the Meiji government and perennially gets high marks from many historians, who consider him the true author of the Meiji Constitution. In June, Iwakura gave him a copy of the

Inoue Kowashi

Ōkuma memorial and ordered him to study it. At the end of the month, he submitted a memorandum (now known as the Iwakura memorandum) to Iwakura, complete with a draft constitution.[8] Inoue counters Ōkuma's advocacy of British-style party politics with a constitutional concept built on the Prussian model, placing a transcendental monarch at the center of government. He also expresses some fundamental principles later incorporated into the Meiji Constitution: the bestowing of the constitutional system by the emperor, the creation of an Imperial Household Law and its legal separation from the constitution, and the ability of the government to apply the budget of the previous year in the event of a deadlock in parliament over approval of the annual budget. So Itō found himself sidelined as Ōkuma and Iwakura defined their visions for constitutional government without his involvement.

Iwakura's and Inoue's support of Itō as the man to draft a constitution was window dressing. The glory Itō had enjoyed as successor to Kido and Ōkubo in leading constitutional matters was fading. Caught between the Ōkubo faction and Iwakura and Inoue, leadership eluded him. His friend Inoue Kaoru reported that "recently Itō has been fretting himself into such a nervous state that he has insomnia every night and has to down a large bottle of saké before he can get to sleep."[9]

Last chance

It was at this time that the idea emerged to send Itō to Europe to study constitutions. Inoue Kowashi had made meticulous progress with such research in Japan, and many in the government questioned the value of sending Itō to Europe for an extended period to pursue similar studies. Iwakura and Inoue assented to sending Itō, but not because they expected much from his research. After Itō departed for Europe, Inoue wrote to him as follows:

> I believe the cleverest way to prevent any leaks is to have you do most of the drafting of the constitution over there. I am taking the liberty of sending you the draft I myself have prepared, so you may use it for reference.[10]

In other words, it was hoped that overseas, insulated from domestic politics and intrigue, Itō would use Inoue's research to put the finishing touches on a draft constitution. With the basic principles of the constitution established in detail, using the Prussian model for reference, there was little need for Itō's investigations, so what Inoue was in effect saying was relax, enjoy Europe, and while you are at it polish up my draft. As far as Inoue was concerned, the process of writing the constitution had reached its final phase.

Itō, however, must have viewed this trip to Europe as his last chance to regain leadership of the constitutional process. The decision to implement a Prussian-style constitution had been made, but Itō no doubt sought to gain an advantage over his rivals by conducting firsthand research on Prussian soil that might help him regain the authority he had lost. He probably hoped that he could declare the progress in creating a constitution under the aegis of Iwakura and Inoue a false start and retake the initiative. So it was that a decade after the Iwakura Embassy, Itō would revisit Europe.

Clandestine journey

On March 14, 1882, Itō arrived at the port of Yokohama to commence his second journey to Europe. Until his return on August 3, 1883, he would commit himself to constitutional research in the homeland of civilization. Boarding the ship, he no doubt recalled the Iwakura Embassy. But much had changed since that earlier journey.

The scale of Itō's present trip suffered greatly by comparison with that of the Iwakura Embassy, which, with forty-six official members and their entourages totaled more than a hundred people. In contrast, the government dispatched a mere nine men to assist Itō in his constitutional research.[11] Even with accompanying personnel the party consisted of only fourteen members. Small though it was, however, this was an elite research team headed by Itō, still a powerful figure.

The team's departure also differed from the Iwakura Embassy's. There was no formal bon voyage ceremony, no artillery salute. Sanjō Sanetomi had seen off the Iwakura Embassy with a gallant poem exhorting them to "Go! Over the seas on wheels of fire . . . ," but there was no such excitement on Itō's behalf. At his farewell party, Itō spoke matter-of-factly, saying, "I do not think of this trip as being of special significance or importance," because he had always thought of any imperial command as significant and important. As his present mission was by imperial order, he would simply endeavor to carry it out to the best of his ability, as he would any imperial command, large or small.[12] Itō and company thus boarded ship without fanfare. In contrast to the great national pageant of the Iwakura Embassy, it seems an almost clandestine journey.

Fukuchi rubs Inoue the wrong way

In certain respects, it was a clandestine journey. Strict confidentiality was maintained regarding Itō's mission so that details would not leak to the public. Rumors of the trip to Europe nevertheless spread quickly among young bureaucrats. For these promising young men, a trip to Europe with a study group headed by Itō was a way to deepen their international experience and to better their chances of being selected as key staff members in the national reforms that would be carried out after their return, with Itō as the nucleus. Ōmori Shōichi, who would later serve under Yamagata Aritomo at the Home Ministry and make a major contribution to the institutionalization of local government, was working in the Sanjiin along with Itō Myoji, who had been selected for the trip, and hoped to be included as well. But one day he was summoned by Inoue Kowashi "and told that since I was needed to stay and work for Yamagata, it was unfortunately necessary to drop me from this trip to Europe."[13]

The intensely competitive atmosphere around the choice of personnel to accompany Itō naturally caused friction with the government leaders who were trying to keep the trip confidential. A letter from Fukuchi Gen'ichirō to Inoue Kaoru, sent in February, the month prior to Itō's departure, gives a glimpse of the turbulence behind the scenes. Fukuchi had personally requested that Inoue persuade Itō to allow Fukuchi to accompany the mission. But this had somehow become public knowledge, and Inoue relayed his intense irritation to Fukuchi. In response, Fukuchi writes:

> I have just had the honor of reading your letter. I must say I am completely shocked. The request I made privately to you with regard to accompanying the mission, since it bears on other matters, is something of which I would never speak openly. Even at the company [Fukuchi was at the time editor in chief of *Tokyo nichi-nichi shimbun*, a newspaper sympathetic to the government] only three of my closest associates know of it. These men are not the sort who would leak something like this. The fact that this is circulating among the public has to be the result of complete speculation on the part of rival newspapers. Since yesterday there have been seven or eight of them who have come to our paper requesting information. In each case they have been told that these wild rumors about my accompanying the mission are utterly groundless, and I have maintained the strictest confidentiality.[14]

Fukuchi's excuses did not temper Inoue's anger, and the rumors that he would accompany the mission did not die down. Instead, they were "becoming common knowledge at every newspaper," with each of them "sending representatives or showing up to question Gen['ichirō] personally," further infuriating Inoue. Fukuchi's request to meet with Inoue to explain was rebuffed, so Fukuchi, alarmed at Inoue's displeasure, penned another imploring letter:

> Your honor, losing your favor would not only mean the end of my ambitions to accompany this mission, it is also of utmost significance in terms of my future success or failure on my chosen path, so I cannot help but pour my feelings out to you in this way.[15]

Itō's mission to Europe had initially been greeted with skepticism by high-ranking government officials, beginning with Iwakura. It was Inoue Kaoru who played the key role in forestalling this criticism and making the mission a reality. He had visited each of the leaders who had expressed misgivings and had carefully laid the groundwork for Itō's constitutional research trip. This may have made him particularly sensitive to the rumors about Fukuchi accompanying the mission, and his reaction tells us something of the tensions within the government on the eve of the mission's departure.

Inscrutable intentions

So, strict gag rule in effect, Itō's trip to Europe took on an air of secrecy. The fragmentary information getting out occasioned public suspicion, primarily since it was unclear why a politician of Itō's stature would go abroad for more than a year.

Tokyo nichi-nichi, the leading pro-government newspaper of the day, reported in its edition of February 28 that Itō was going to Europe. "However," it wrote, "the nature of his mission is unclear. There are rumors to the effect that it may be for the purpose of securing foreign loans, but their veracity is difficult to assess." The March 1 edition added that "it appears that he has been entrusted with other important diplomatic matters" but cast doubt on the idea that the purpose of the trip was for constitutional research, noting that "another newspaper has reported speculation that he might be embarking upon a tour of the European nations in order to prepare for the national assembly that will be convened in 1890, but there are indications he was ordered to depart immediately on urgent business, and this would seem unnecessary haste in preparing for an assembly that is still eight years in the future."

The *Asahi shimbun* concurred. An editorial in its March 8 edition, "On Councillor Itō's Overseas Travels," dismissed the theory that the trip was "to investigate the realities of European constitutional systems" as "extremely wild speculation." The editorial continued, "For these past fifteen years and more there should have been more than adequate opportunity to observe at firsthand the constitutional governments of the European nations. Why bother with the futile labor of adding further detail to something that is already known so exhaustively?" The article concludes that "Councillor Itō must have some other extremely pressing business on this trip."

The public really was at a loss as to the real motives for Itō's mission. An editorial in the *Yūbin hōchi shimbun* (March 9) mused, "This is a most opportune time for politicians, as our country undertakes great political reforms and begins the transition from our present political system toward a constitutional order." In view of the monumental issues facing Japan both at home and abroad, "now is not a time at which one of the key officials in the government can readily leave the country." Could Itō have possibly "seen in this trip abroad something of such superior value that he would throw away this important opportunity"? The general consensus was that it defied logic for such a major player as Itō to choose this particular time to take off on a long European tour for such questionable pursuits as "constitutional research" or "preparations for a national assembly" or the "investigation of constitutional systems," and that therefore he must have some other more important purpose in mind. The documentary research for the preparation of a constitution was best left up to legal experts in the bureaucracy, anyway, and scarcely seemed the sort of thing that Itō should be involving himself in personally.

The veil of secrecy cast over the purpose and the personnel of Itō's mission only heightened the consternation of government officials and the public. Things did not sit well on the eve of Itō's departure.

The Ono connection

On March 14, Itō boarded the British mail steamer *Garrick* at Yokohama on a venture that, though less grand than the Iwakura Embassy, was for Itō a much greater personal gamble. There is, as noted previously, every reason to believe that his ambition was to use this trip to Europe recapture the leadership in constitutional matters that he had forfeited to the Ōkuma faction and to Iwakura and Inoue. Amid the sober atmosphere of his departure, he must have felt tense yet determined. Juxtaposed with the grand national pageant that was the Iwakura Embassy's departure, Itō's return to Europe had more the air of an intense personal drama.

Indeed, an element of drama was in store for the day. A man named Ono Azusa boarded to bid farewell to a friend traveling to Europe on the same ship. Ono was one of the men who had been forced out of office along with Ōkuma Shigenobu in the Political Crisis of 1881. He was also, along with Inoue Kowashi, among the most learned men of the time and had been instrumental in helping Ōkuma draft his memorandum on the constitution. After his expulsion from the government, Ono dedicated himself to cultivating the talent that might eventually bring about a constitutional system along the lines of Ōkuma's proposal. He exerted his energies in founding a political party (the Rikken Kaishintō, or Constitutional Reform Party) and a university (Tokyo Semmon Gakkō, now Waseda University).[16]

In a sense, Ono, had been an indirect cause of Itō's journey to Europe, and Itō could hardly have been unaware of this. When Itō spotted Ono, he approached him and, with a polite bow, shook his hand and then took his leave.[17]

2. Melancholy in Berlin: Heavy Weather for the Parliamentary System

Itō and his party reached Naples on May 5. It was nine years since Itō had set foot on European soil. But this was no grand tour. His destination was Germany. Responding to the consensus within the Meiji government that Prussia should serve as Japan's model, Itō was bound for Berlin "with scarcely a sidelong glance," as Yoshino Sakuzō put it.

Things, however, did not go smoothly. Aoki Shūzō, the Japanese chargé d'affaires in Berlin, secured an interview with constitutional scholar Rudolf von Gneist, of Berlin University, who had so impressed Kido, and arranged for Itō to have private instruction from Gneist. But Gneist's first words to Itō were as follows:

Rudolf von Gneist

> I am most grateful that you have come all the way to Germany on this mission, but a constitution is not a legal document; it is the [embodiment of] the spirit and capacities of a nation. I am a German, and therefore a European. I know something of the countries of Europe, Germany best of all. Unfortunately, however, I know nothing of Japan. If I studied it, I might understand it, but first I must ask you about Japan, and ask you to give me a clear account of the nature of the relations between ruler and ruled, the customs and temperament of its people, its history, and so forth. I will think about all this, and then give you my advice. But I have no confidence that what I can tell you will actually be of use to you, or provide a basis for your drafting of a constitution.[18]

Gneist's remarks are a blunt expression of the historical school of jurisprudence. This school of legal thought, established by the great German jurist

Friedrich Carl von Savigny (1779–1861), held that law is not something that can be arbitrarily legislated by the state; it is created organically out of the spiritual capacities of a people, in much the same way as language and customs. Legislation should be something that retroactively ratifies what has arisen organically.

Savigny used this perspective to critique the position of Heidelburg University professor Anton Friedrich Justus Thibaut (1772–1840), who was calling for the immediate creation of a unitary civil code for all the German states and principalities. In 1814, a debate on this issue, famous in modern German legal history, transpired between the two men. According to Savigny, the spirit of the German people was not mature enough to produce a unitary legal code. If this reality was ignored and such a code hastily enacted, it would simply not receive popular acceptance. Instead, jurists must represent and guide the national spirit, creating a shared legal understanding and a common body of law. Only on the basis of such unified jurisprudence could a unitary legal code for the German people be compiled.

Savigny practiced what he preached, striving to systematize and unify German law by authoring such masterpieces as *System des heutigen Romischen Rechts* (The system of contemporary Roman law) and using the University of Berlin as a base for developing his own school of jurisprudence. Savigny's historical school would later not only spread throughout the universities of Germany but also extend its influence from continental Europe to Great Britain and cross the Atlantic to the United States.[19]

Gneist was positioned squarely within this philosophical tradition. He was, moreover, Savigny's successor as a lecturer on Roman law. His remark that "law is not a legal document, it is a spirit" was clearly intended to open the eyes of his listener to the principles of Savigny's historical jurisprudence.

"Gilding a bronze pot"
What really crushed Itō, however, were these words from Gneist:

I have a story for you. Four or five years ago, after the Russo-Turkish War and the Berlin Conference, when the Balkan states achieved independence or autonomy, Bulgaria approached Germany for assistance in framing a constitution. At that time, none of the legal scholars in Germany had the confidence to come forward with advice on the Bulgarian constitution. Why? Because even though Bulgaria is nearer to us than your country, and we have a general knowledge of its history, a number of different peoples have mingled together to form what is now Bulgaria, and no one has really studied this in detail. So everyone hesitated. In the end a jurist who is a friend of mine agreed to go, and said he would show us all by creating a constitution in six months' time. Everyone laughed, but in fact he created a constitution in six months. Upon his return, he provoked everyone's laughter once again by saying, 'It's not much trouble, after all, to gild a bronze pot!'[20]

It is apparent that Gneist thought Japan was about a century too early for a constitution and that producing one would simply be gilding an inferior vessel. The party was dumbfounded, then angered by the condescending sneer behind Gneist's remark. Itō had taken it on the chin at the outset, a taste of the difficulties that lay ahead.

Beware the power of the purse

Itō's research in Berlin did not produce fruitful results, serving only to deepen his distress. He received private instruction from Gneist, but what he heard was not to his liking. Soon after attending one of Gneist's classes, Itō wrote to Matsukata Masayoshi in Japan:

> Three or four days ago I met the famous scholar Professor Gneist, and from what I have been able to gather of his opinions so far, in light of Japan's current situation he advocates a terribly autocratic line. He says that even if we were to create a national assembly, the wisest policy would be to make it a weak one, for if we allow it to stick its nose into military and budgetary matters it is inevitable that this would soon become a catalyst for disorder. Of course I cannot grasp the profundities of what he has to say in only one meeting. In the days to come I hope to meet with him repeatedly, acquaint him thoroughly with the state of affairs in our country, and then once again hear his opinions.[21]

Legislative authority over the budget—the power of the purse—was one of the most important powers within the parliamentary systems of Western Europe. This was well understood even in Japan. Yet here was Gneist, one of Germany's leading authorities on constitutional law, telling the

Japanese to strip their legislature of this basic but vital function. Taken in conjunction with Gneist's other remarks, this must have left Itō with a deepening sense that Gneist was skeptical of Japan's capacity for adapting to the Western parliamentary system. Itō, however, had no one else to look to other than Gneist. He could only hope that if he could help Gneist understand Japan, Gneist might change his mind.

Gneist's position, though, remained consistent, particularly on the power of the purse. On September 9, Itō wrote again to Matsukata, saying of Gneist's teachings that "Gneist argued against including unnecessary matters in the constitution, saying that anything with regard to the reading of the budget before the national assembly or the ability of the national assembly to deliberate upon the budget should be left out." Itō amplifies Gneist's points as follows:

> If consent of the national assembly was not made completely unnecessary and instead misguided policies conferred full fiscal powers on the assembly, the government would become incapable of collecting revenues or providing for government expenditures. Its hands would be tied, and it would have to follow the lead of the assembly, which would open the way to the decline and stagnation of national administration. Meanwhile, the assembly would always be greedy for more power and would not stop until it had dispensed with the sovereign and instituted a republic. This was, he said, a general rule that applied to every country.[22]

Gneist was not the only one with this point of view. On August 28, Itō was honored by a banquet with Kaiser Wilhelm I (1797–1888) and was treated to a "quite unexpected remark" by the kaiser: "For the sake of the Japanese emperor, I hope you do not create a national assembly." According to Itō, the kaiser added that

> if it should become unavoidable in the course of Japan's development to do so, take good care in establishing your nation's laws so that no matter what situation may arise, you do not pursue the foolish policy of making it impossible to manage the nation's finances without consent of the assembly, for you should know that delegating such power to it is a recipe for civil war.[23]

Like Gneist, Kaiser Wilhelm was vehemently opposed to granting the legislature the right to deliberate on the budget and exhorted Itō "quite earnestly that this was a misguided fashion of contemporary Europe." It would appear that neither Gneist's nor the kaiser's opinions on the budgetary power of the legislature were simply casual remarks stemming from skepticism regarding Japan's capacity for constitutional government, but were rooted in a more fundamental and deeply held conviction. To understand this, we will take a brief look at the state of constitutional government in Germany in this period.[24]

The realities of constitutional government

The background to the advice Itō was given lay in the difficulties Germany's leaders were confronting in constitutional government.

Bismarck, the famous "Iron Chancellor," had instigated a constitutional crisis in Prussia by forcing through an expansion of the military budget in 1862 without the approval of the Prussian Diet, and by managing the affairs of state for five years thereafter without securing further budgetary approval.

With the unification of the German Empire in 1871 and the promulgation of the imperial constitution, however, such strong-arm tactics were no longer possible. The imperial government was confronted with the additional headache of the growing power of political parties in the Diet. While Itō was in Berlin, a bill that Bismarck had introduced to establish a state-owned tobacco monopoly was being debated in the Diet, but, Itō reported, this was "extremely unpopular" and "unlikely to pass" and Bismarck was "disgruntled and has shut himself up in his residence."[25]

Yet even Bismarck was not blindly hostile toward the parliamentary system from the outset. He saw it as desirable for the Diet to function as an institution representing the interests of the people, serving as a conduit for communication between the government and the people. For Bismarck, who sought the essence of politics in compromise and flexibility, political parties were more than just the manifestation of factional interests. Ideally, through dialogue and cooperation with the government, they could become partners in support of the nation's interests.

This was why the German Imperial Constitution of 1871 (commonly known as the Bismarck Constitution) provided for universal suffrage for adult males. By empowering a broad spectrum of the empire's citizens with the vote, Bismarck hoped to make them agents of national unification and overcome the fragmentation characteristic of the empire's federal structure.

The economic depression that began in 1873, however, worked to undermine Bismarck's aims. The introduction of universal manhood suffrage seemed to intensify class interests and conflict between political ideologies instead of marking the advent of citizens' politics. Achieving parliamentary consensus became increasingly difficult as squabbling parties representing special interests dominated the Diet and coalesced into an antigovernment force.

As a result Bismarck's domestic initiatives began to run aground. His principal concern was to secure the autonomy of imperial authority from the federation of states making up the empire. Doing so called for expanding the empire's fiscal base, for which Bismarck submitted legislation calling for new taxes and the establishment of state monopolies over the sale of certain goods, such as tobacco. The Diet, however, rejected all this legislation. Frustrated with struggling to develop a strategy for dealing with the Diet, Bismarck decried "the disease of factionalism" and proclaimed that his party had only two members, "the kaiser and myself."

During Itō's visit, Germany thus faced the breakdown of a politics of compromise based on the spirit of parliamentary conciliation. It was this political reality that manifested itself in the advice Itō received from Gneist and Kaiser Wilhelm. Given the difficulty the Germans themselves were having with the parliamentary system, it is hardly surprising that they were pessimistic about the ability of the Japanese to make it work.

Lectures from Mosse, "The Little Monk"

A considerable gap obviously existed between the Japanese and the Germans in their perceptions of parliamentary government. The Japanese, who had yet to introduce a parliamentary system, were enthusiastic, whereas the Germans, who were struggling with unruly parliamentary politics, had become disillusioned. Having arranged, within this context, to study with Gneist, it is no wonder that Itō was unhappy with the results. Perhaps most disappointing for Itō was Gneist's complete lack of warmth.

Gneist, it appears, agreed to hold "informal talks" with Itō three times a week. But he passed responsibility for these sessions to his student Albert Mosse (1846–1925), who would later go to Japan as a legal consultant to the Japanese government. Japanese notes on the contents of Mosse's lectures have been preserved.[26] Itō struggled to understand what Mosse was saying, as he indicates in a letter to Inoue Kaoru:

> In my investigation of constitutional and administrative matters, there are a great number of technical terms, and I am quite distressed because often the most I can do is refer to their English equivalents in trying to understand them.[27]

Albert Mosse

No matter how "enlightened" Itō fancied himself, he could not understand German and was a neophyte in German legal theory. Mosse's lectures, moreover, were a clause-by-clause march through the German constitution and its institutions, and this plodding exegetical approach was not to Itō's liking, moving him to refer to Mosse derisively as "the little monk."[28] Itō's discontent comes through in his writing:

> One can imbibe neither the spirit nor the reality [of the constitution] simply by understanding the language of each of its clauses. A scholarly analysis that does not delve more deeply into these matters is a superficial thing indeed. What I am intent on is discovering its fundamental structure, and learning something of how it works.[29]

Generally speaking, for Itō Berlin yielded little satisfaction and was largely a waste of time.

Miyoshi's admonition

Itō's ongoing distress, however, was not solely the product of his unsatisfactory studies. He was also having difficulties supervising the members of the mission, which had lost its unity of purpose. Mission member Kiba Sadanaga recalled their Berlin days as follows:

> As far as the mission's research was concerned, we weren't under any specific instructions or orders from Itō, and aside from Itō going to listen to the

lectures, it seemed like everyone pretty much sat around the hotel reading the European newspapers and books, or else busied themselves with a lot of field trips and sightseeing excursions. There wasn't a lot of intellectual discussion. Every once and awhile you'd see Itō Miyoji—and only him—doggedly taking part in some debate with [Itō Hirobumi], but as for the rest, we took life pretty easily.[30]

In fact, however, some in the party were not taking things as easily as Kiba suggests, and voiced discontent with the slow pace of the research. Miyoshi Taizō, for example, wrote a memorandum in Berlin remonstrating with Itō:

> Your Excellency has come to Europe by order of the emperor to study, first of all, the German constitution. To this end you have been personally consulting with leading authorities and have set the members of the party accompanying you to their own investigations, dividing up the work and assigning to each his duties.[31]

However, as alluded to by both writers, Itō alone was attending lectures on the constitution. The others were left out of the loop, and on unfamiliar ground. According to Kiba's memoir, "There were only two people among the party who could speak and read German," so there was probably little they could do other than kill time. Yet, as Miyoshi goes on to state with some passion, Itō was not alone in taking pride in participating in a research mission for Japan's constitution:

> One might say that each member of the mission is part of a single body accompanying Your Excellency, to serve as your arms and legs, eyes and ears. Thus, each member of the mission is attempting to embody that ideal, taking as their goal the comprehensive study of the constitution under Your Excellency's direction, with the expectation that after we return home they will put their talents to work as members of the committee researching our nation's constitution.

Miyoshi does not mince words in criticizing Itō. He tells him that by distancing himself from the mission's other members and being the only one to attend constitutional lectures, the research of the others will lack coherence, their morale will suffer, and in the end he will become the object of discontented grumbling and damage his reputation. Miyoshi also goes on to say that he cannot understand Itō's fixation on Germany:

> When I think of this in terms of the feelings of the people involved and the realities of the situation, and carefully weigh the advantages and disadvantages, pros and cons, it would seem that assembling all the mission's members in Germany to do piecemeal research may not be the wisest policy.

Miyoshi proposes instead that the mission's members be divided up and assigned to a comparative study of the four nations of England, France, Germany, and Austria:

> Depending upon what orders you have may have received from the emperor or what instructions were given you by the government, it may not be possible to give this your consideration, but from the statements Your Excellency has made, it has been understood that your orders were to investigate the constitutions of the European nations and to report the results to the throne.

Behind this seemingly reasonable proposal is an indication that the members do not even have a shared understanding of the mission's purpose. From Itō's perspective, of course, the accompanying members were little more than clerical staff, and it is likely that his intent was to monopolize the real work of the mission. His private desire was to reestablish his primacy in bringing constitutional government to Japan, an aim that he could not share.

Itō's distress during the mission's sojourn in Berlin, therefore, combined his dissatisfaction with his research and his growing awareness of the discontent brewing among his companions. In the letter to Matsukata cited earlier he laments that the size of his entourage makes it difficult to control and that its members have not escaped "the common disease of our countrymen"—they all "fancy themselves leaders" and prefer big talk and grandiose debates to doing "their real work."[32]

Itō's response to this situation was to request an extension of the mission's stay in Europe, probably out of a deepening sense that the mission was in danger of failing. A visit to Vienna in August, however, brought a sudden change in Itō's mood.

3. Resurrection in Vienna: Awakening to "National Structure"

The constitution and administrative law

Although Itō's research in Berlin was not delivering results, he still had hope for the mission. He was gradually becoming convinced that confining his research solely to the study of constitutions was a mistake.

Itō had been pointed in this direction by Aoki Shūzō, the Japanese chargé d'affaires, soon after arriving in Berlin. According to Aoki, constitutional research would not be that difficult. One had only to grasp the basic framework of the texts of the various countries' constitutions, and then do a bit of research into the historical events leading up to them. More important was administrative law; this was the real foundation upon which constitutions rested. If, metaphorically speaking, the constitution was a flower, then administrative law was its roots and stem. This was a very broad field and not easy to research. In every country, though, the norm was to have established a complete corpus of administrative law prior to writing a constitution. Because of this, the mission should not confine itself to researching constitutions alone—studying the related administrative laws was absolutely essential.[33]

Aoki proposed that Itō himself should concentrate on constitutional research and divide responsibility for studying the various aspects of administrative law among the other members of the mission. This plan, however, did not bear fruit. The mission's members, "fancying themselves leaders," felt that being delegated the drudgery of examining administrative law rather than doing constitutional research was beneath their dignity. As Aoki wrote, at this point "the mission's research had not produced a single thing worth looking at in days to come."[34]

Connecting the constitution with administration

Aoki's advice was nonetheless significant, because through it Itō gained an awareness of administrative law as complementary to the constitution. The most extensive of the Western nations' constitutions contained perhaps a hundred articles, much of which consisted of proclamations of ideals. A constitution could not be the last word on how to administer a nation, especially in terms of concrete polices. It made sense that a constitution would need a variety of supplementary institutional arrangements.[35]

Itō was perceptive enough to see this. "The myriad affairs of government," he wrote, "must be taken into consideration," and the complexity of this undertaking compelled him to ask his colleagues in Japan to extend his sojourn in Europe. In a document presumably written in Berlin prior to his departure for Vienna, moreover, he remarked that "it is not that difficult a task to translate the text of a constitution, but it is impossible to understand how a country is organized without looking at this in tandem with its administration."[36] Clearly, constitutions and their supporting administration were very much on Itō's mind, and it is fair to say that his attention had turned to a conception of the state in which the two were united.

Aoki's suggestion, however, of assigning members of the mission to investigate discrete aspects of constitutional provisions and administrative law was not something Itō found congenial. Instead, he sought to form a blueprint in his own mind for a comprehensive set of national institutions encompassing both administrative law and a constitution. Achieving this would provide him with a unique constitutional philosophy that would allow him to regain his leadership in the process of creating Japan's constitutional order. Itō would find what he sought in Vienna.

Meeting "Dr. Stone"

Itō's sessions in Berlin with Gneist and Mosse entered summer recess in August. In a letter to Japan, he writes that "right now Berlin is at the height of the summer season, everyone is away on holiday, and I can do no further investigation, so I am making a brief visit to Vienna, where I have an appointment to meet a scholar of some renown, a Dr. Stein."[37] Far from simply a jaunt to Vienna to dispel the boredom of Berlin, there was method in Itō's movements. As soon as he arrived in Vienna on August 8, he made his way to the address of Lorenz von Stein (1815–90), professor of political economy at the University of Vienna. Itō's visit with Stein, undertaken with barely enough time for Itō to change out of his traveling clothes, was described by Yoshino Sakuzo as "marvelously prompt action."[38]

Another member of the mission was doubtless significant in inspiring this promptness on Itō's part. Kawashima Atsushi served in the Japanese legation in Vienna from 1879 to 1881 and during that period arranged for private instruction with Stein. After returning to Japan in January 1882, Kawashima submitted to the government a memorial on governmental reform based on what he had learned from Stein.[39] In it, Kawashima writes that "having had the opportunity to meet with the great Dr. Stein a number of times, and listen carefully to his teachings, there were many points I felt were both pragmatic and full of the wisdom of experience."

Lorenz von Stein

It is unclear whether this memorial was connected to Kawashima's selection, not long afterward, as a member of Itō's mission. But it is almost certain that at some point Kawashima informed Itō of Stein's existence and his teachings. Testimony exists to indicate that Kawashima influenced Itō to visit Stein. According to mission member Yoshida Masaharu, Kawashima was angered by the cold and contemptuous reception Itō and company had encountered in Berlin by Gneist and proposed that they go to Vienna to see Stein.[40] Another person accompanying the mission, Kiba Sadanaga, speaks even more directly of Kawashima's role:

> The person who most looked up to Stein, and in fact was a frequent visitor to his home, was Kawashima Atsushi. They were acquaintances from the days when Kawashima had served as attaché at the legation in Vienna, and he frequently served as intermediary between [Itō and Stein].[41]

Kawashima, though, was not alone in preparing the way for the encounter between Itō and Stein. Stein was highly regarded at the Japanese legation in Vienna. Many of the legation's staff had gone to hear Stein's lectures, and a succession of Japanese envoys had enjoyed personal relationships with him. In fact, Stein was something of an unofficial adviser to the Japanese legation. When news of Itō's voyage to Europe to study constitutional systems reached Vienna, the staff of the legation appear to have seen this as a rare opportunity to introduce their longtime friend and teacher to a wider Japanese audience. Ida Yuzuru, former Japanese envoy in Vienna, wrote to the legation suggesting that if Councillor Itō should have the opportunity to meet with our "Dr. Stone" [Stein meaning stone in German], one can scarcely imagine what an interesting exchange of ideas they might have. I think such an event could well be the most significant benefit of the councillor's European tour.[42]

Ida, meanwhile, also wrote directly to Itō, hinting that Stein should be invited to Japan:

"Dr. Stone" is truly a teacher for our nation. At the time of last winter's political crisis [the Political Crisis of 1881], I even went so far as to suggest to Foreign Minister Inoue that he be given an invitation to [Japan] to consult on the organization of the government.[43]

Spreading Stein's gospel

There is reason to believe that Stein was eagerly awaiting Itō's visit. In Japan, Stein is frequently characterized as a world-famous scholar. He was a man of encyclopedic intellect who, under the rubric of *Staatswissenschaft* (political economy), had achieved impressive results in fields spanning the entire range of the social sciences, from law, economics, and political science to sociology and education. In an era of increasing academic specialization and empiricism, however, his scholarship was given the cold shoulder by his colleagues as a relic of an older generation. Possessed of a voracious appetite for research, yet receiving scant attention for his scholarship in his own country, Stein had grounds for resentment. In addition, failed business investments had left him with substantial debt.

It is likely that his contacts with the Japanese are what helped him out of these straitened circumstances. No doubt he saw in Japan's rapid advance along the road to modernization fertile ground in which to propagate his academic theories. His ambitions did not stop at becoming an adviser to the Japanese legation in Vienna. Since his primary interest was in spreading his gospel to distant Japan, he had been working for some time to gather information about the country. This is attested to by a letter from Stein to Fukuzawa Yukichi. Stein was a subscriber to the *Japan Weekly Mail*, published in Yokohama, and a notice concerning a recent work by Fukuzawa, *Jiji shōgen* (Brief comments on current affairs), had caught his eye. Impressed by its contents, Stein contacted Fukuzawa. His letter was published in the June 2, 1881, edition of *Jiji Shimpō* (News of Current Affairs), the newspaper that Fukuzawa had founded:

> I take the liberty of sending you this letter through the kind offices of my dear and respected friends Mr. Ida Yuzuru and Mr. Homma Kiyoo, formerly envoy and secretary of the Japanese legation in Vienna, who overcame my reticence with their offer to deliver it to you personally. Recently I have been engaged in researches into the history of Japanese law and of the Japanese political system. Nothing would make me happier than if this might make a small contribution to spreading the word of the great enterprise upon which the Japanese people have embarked. The Japanese people have made immense progress in the course of the past seventeen years, and will no doubt in future become a great civilized nation of the Pacific; permit me to express my admiration in this regard. I am a fellow of the Austrian Academy of Science, and present you with one of the academy's recent works. A mere glance should be enough for you to see the serious attention our academy has devoted to Japanese history. If you would receive this volume and my letter as a token of my respect and of my desire to learn more of your own writings, you shall have my deepest gratitude.[44]

In short, prior to Itō's visit Stein had already established something of a relationship with Japan, a relationship for which he was highly motivated.

Itō in many ways was just what Stein had been waiting for. The pair seems to have hit it off immediately. On August 11, three days after his first visit to Stein, Itō reported to Iwakura that he had "found a logic and a means to restore" the country from the excesses inflicted upon it by the gang who had been deluded by the "writings of radical libertarians in England, America, and France." He asserts that "I feel that if I were to die now, I could rest in peace."[45] In a letter of August 27 to Yamada Akiyoshi, Itō writes, "Fortunately, I have found a good teacher" and notes that he has sounded out Inoue Kaoru on the idea of inviting Stein to Japan.[46] Itō was in an ebullient mood; he was rid of the melancholy of Berlin. As a result of meeting Stein, Itō's confidence in his research mission returned. Vienna, thus, was a crucial turning point for his constitutional research. But what was it that Stein conveyed to Itō?

Stein's unique theory of the state

Manuscript notes from Stein's lectures to Itō permit a fairly detailed recon-
struction of Stein's discourse on several topics directly related to the introduction of a constitutional system of government to Japan, Itō's principal concern.[47] First, however, we must understand Stein's conception of
the state.

Characteristic of Stein's view was a unique organic theory that construed
the state as a distinct human personality. He defined the state as "the
community (*Gemeinschaft*) raised to the level of an independent personality." Itō appears to have gotten this slightly wrong. His notes on this lecture say that the state "is a society that possesses the nature of the human
body,"[48] expressing an anthropomorphic view of the state based on a comparison to the human physical form. For Stein, the human personality
possessed self-awareness and volition and acted accordingly. The state,
like the autonomous individual, also embodied these three elements, of
awareness, will, and action. The self-awareness of the state is embodied
in the institution of the sovereign, the formation of the state's will in
the legislative branch, and the conduct of the state's activities by the
executive branch. In Stein's view, the constitutional system was a form
of government that gave shape to a unified and harmonious relationship
among these three independent but mutually restraining institutions.
Stein said that if the sovereign alone controlled the government, one
had despotism; if the legislature dominated, one had absolute democracy
(the Japanese phrase used to render this might be translated as "tyranny
by popular government"); and if the executive branch was in control, one
had a dictatorship. He characterized all of these as antithetical to constitutional government.

Defending against both legislature and sovereign

Stein urged the greatest vigilance against the second of these three institutions. Excessively democratic government invited the tyranny of the
majority and the undermining of the state from below, he said. Democracy
was "nothing more than majority rule," which meant "important matters
of state would be determined solely by the weight of opinion." Stein did not
think that democracy could be equated with constitutional government,
and in fact stressed the tension that existed between the two. Stein's teaching was that democracy could easily lead to absolutism on the part of the

legislative body, which should constitute no more than one branch of the government, and thus contained the dangerous potential for undermining the constitutional order altogether. The same could be said of an imbalance favoring either of the other two branches, but it should be emphasized that what repeatedly comes up in Stein's lectures are references to the dangers of radicalized democracy and critiques of republicanism and parliamentary politics. Here again Itō heard a less than enthusiastic endorsement of a parliamentary system.

Stein's lance, though, was not directed at the legislature alone. His theory of the state just as firmly rejected despotism on the part of the sovereign. This is clear from lecture notes taken by Mutsu Munemitsu, who received personal instruction from Stein in 1884 thanks to an introduction from Itō. The notes reveal boldly stated limitations on the political status of the sovereign:

> The King or the Chief of the State gives the character of unity to the Ministry as a whole, just as well as to the whole State, but he has no right to order anything, on his own account, to the Ministers or to interfere with them in any degree. If such be the case, there will be no responsible Ministry. That the King has no power over the legislative body, is quite clear.[49]

The sovereign is seen as having no special powers over either the executive or legislative branches of the government. He is not conceived of as having any real powers in the determination of national policy. In Stein's view, the sovereign's role as head of state stops at approving or ratifying decisions made through the executive and legislative processes, thus serving to symbolize the nation's unity of purpose and action.

> "The King can do no wrong" is an old phrase, and it admits of various shades of meaning. But in the Constitutional sense it cannot signify otherwise than this, that the King shall stand completely outside the pale of the legislative and executive powers; in other words, the Chief of the State is bound not to do anything material as to either the legislative or the executive functions; he must not meddle with any matter that is going on as the working of the State. What he does, ought not to be an actuality but only a formality. Therefore he can do no wrong.[50]

Stein's position is that "the sovereign should not involve himself in any of the affairs of the state," legitimizing broad restrictions on his powers. In Stein's theoretical framework, the sovereign is no more than an organ of the state, charged with the symbolic function of representing the unity of the nation. Stein is known to have expressed to Itō the opinion that the sovereign "represents the nation using the pronoun 'I.'"[51]

The Meiji constitutional order is commonly viewed as a variety of Prussian absolutism, and Stein as being partially responsible for its emperor-system ideology. It must be emphasized, however, that this line of thought is not to be found in his theory of the state. He subscribes instead to the principle that "the sovereign reigns but does not rule."

Administrative autonomy as a theme for nation building

With the sovereign's retreat into the background of national politics, the bureaucracy takes center stage, serving in the sovereign's place as bearer of the state's governing functions. Even in a constitutional monarchy, bureaucratic appointments continue to be made by the crown. Yet the bureaucracy eventually acquires a greater degree of autonomy from the sovereign, and to see itself as responsible for governing the nation. Stein believed that the executive power "should possess its own motive force and constitute its own independent structure." He sought the autonomy of the executive branch, so that it would not simply be an agent executing "the will of others." Stein felt that placing constraints on the activities of the executive branch would likely reduce the state's range of action.[52]

When Stein speaks of "the will of others," he is implying either the will of the legislature or the will of the sovereign. Stein was critical of the British parliamentary system because the government was completely dependent upon maintaining a parliamentary majority, meaning the will of parliament dominated the executive. For Stein, "this should be called parliamentary politics and still does not deserve to be called constitutional government." The same could be said of the relationship with the sovereign power, and Stein was equally critical of the German bureaucratic system for its servility to the crown: "In Germany, the executive branch is held to be simply the ministers and agents of the sovereign, possessing no powers beyond that of executing his will."[53]

In criticizing the situation in Germany, Stein argued that the executive branch must establish its independence from both the legislative branch and the sovereign. He stressed that securing a high degree of autonomy for the executive was a new theme in the process of nation building.

An evolutionary theory of the state

Stein's unique worldview explains why he felt an autonomous executive was necessary. "Human affairs," he observed, "are in a constant and extreme state of flux, and because of this laws cannot continually remain the same," adding that in the constantly changing environment of human endeavor "one can certainly not expect all the laws to change of their own accord and adapt themselves adequately to the way things are."[54]

In other words, the laws passed by the legislative branch are insufficient to cope with continually changing social realities. The human social order must be capable of responding flexibly to the unceasing changes in its environment. It is the executive that should respond to these changes, deal with everyday problems, and contribute to shaping the social order. Attempting to resolve the various conflicts and contradictions arising on a daily basis in the real world by relying on the judgment of the sovereign power carries the danger of arbitrary abuse of power, whereas the parliament's legislative powers are frequently inadequate to the task.

Stein defines the executive as "the institution responsible for governing the life of the nation,"[55] and he entrusts it with a prominent place in the system of national institutions—the national structure. Only through the executive is the national structure capable of resolving or adapting to issues arising out of myriad external and internal environmental factors, from the impact of events in the natural world or in foreign relations to domestic political factors, such as the movement of public opinion, class conflict, and social problems.

Stein thus sees the state as an organic institution able to evolve in response to historical change through a ceaseless process of interaction mediated by the executive. His concept of the state can be characterized as evolutionary. Itō accepted the idea of the evolution of the national structure, but only after recasting its implications. We will return to this point later.

A vision for the reform of national institutions

It is obvious that from Stein's lectures Itō gained an overview of the constitutional order that went considerably beyond the simple drafting of a document, and learned much about the role of the executive. The result was a more clearly defined image of the state than Itō had been pondering in Berlin.

As a result, Itō was able to embrace a broad vision for the reform of Japan's institutions that saw the constitution as but one element in a comprehensive structure. In a letter written to Inoue Kaoru from Vienna on October 22, Itō writes with assurance, "As far as the constitution alone is concerned, I will soon have quite enough."[56] He sounds like a different person from the man who wrote from Berlin. In a memo from Vienna immediately after the conclusion of Stein's lectures, he writes, "There is no utility in concentrating on investigating the constitution alone." He adds that "since the constitution deals only in generalities, it is not worth that much expenditure of mental effort," further displaying his newfound conviction and self-confidence. He then speaks of the necessity of administrative reform in the following manner:

> No matter how good a constitution one establishes, no matter how good a parliament is convened, it goes without saying that without proper administration, there will be no results worth considering. If we desire good administration, we must first establish organizational guidelines for it. Among these organizational guidelines, the most indispensable concern the powers and responsibilities of the chief ministers; the structure of the government ministries; the regulations to be followed by government officials and the provisions for their appointment and dismissal, promotion and demotion; the procedures for [civil service] examinations and provisions for retirement benefits . . . If these are in place, it will be possible to preserve the authority of the imperial house and enhance the powers of the throne. In Stein's lectures, three things are absolutely essential for constitutional government: an imperial house law and organizational rules for the executive and for the legislative branches. If any one of these is lacking, then you do not have a constitutional monarchy, he says. What ensures that organizational regulations are properly established and maintained for these three institutions, forming the axis unifying them and preventing them from interfering with one another, is none other than the

constitution. Thus it follows that laying the groundwork for the organization of government and administration is truly something of the gravest importance.[57]

Thus, Itō defines the constitution as just one element in a broader "political organization" and advocates study of the general life of the nation from a perspective that includes politics and economics. "The two aspects of politics and economics are intimately connected with the rise and fall, prosperity and decline of nations, and are matters to which the people of our country must pay the deepest attention," Itō writes. He goes on to insist that the theme of his studies must not stop with "the items previously selected for investigation" but expand to a "major research effort into administration, economics, etc."[58]

Not afraid of "scribbling savants"

It is fair to say that Stein's lectures enabled Itō to relativize the constitution and grasp the issue of a nation's political structure within a broader context. A constitution and a national assembly were, after all, no more than one aspect of the life of the nation; their functions could not be fulfilled without the complementary workings of administrative or executive institutions. Itō's broad insight into national structure was what equipped him for leadership in Japan's adoption of constitutional government. It also gave him self-confidence in confronting the popular rights advocates and other intellectuals. He could take pride in his expert knowledge of constitutional systems and dismiss his intellectual opponents as "scribbling savants" (*hebokure shosei*):

> It would be a happy thing indeed if the scribbling savants of Japan were not misinforming the ignorant public by simply translating phrases out of books without any understanding of the realities behind them, and claiming this is the constitution of such-and-such a country, this is how its government is organized, and so on; and that instead we could hear a clear discussion of these matters, based on thorough knowledge of what place they have in the nation's history, and an informed judgment regarding the fundamental pros and cons of debate on these issues.[59]

Itō, confident that he had bested the popular rights advocates in the realm of theory, was now sufficiently restored in spirit to harrumph about Ōkuma Shigenobu: "Our 'Mr. Progress' is putting on quite a pathetic show."[60] This may be the birth of what Sakamoto Kazuto has termed Itō's "constitutional charisma." Hitherto without sufficient knowledge of constitutional matters, Itō had been unable to seize the initiative in the drive to establish the constitution from amid the scrum of political intellectuals that had suddenly formed in late nineteenth-century Japan. Now, however, he would return to Japan confident that he had surpassed them all.

The intellectuals Itō had in mind were first and foremost those outside the government, specifically, the activists among whom Ōkuma was the most prominent. But he was no doubt wary, too, of the intellectuals within the bureaucracy. Within the government, Inoue Kowashi had been the prime mover in ensuring that the adoption of a Prussian-style constitutional system had become something of a certainty. Itō's failure to climb aboard this bandwagon prior to leaving for Europe was paralleled by his inability to adopt anything more than a passive stance toward the conception of the constitution being advanced by Iwakura and Inoue.

So Stein must have been an answer to Itō's prayers, offering him a way to make up for lost time. It is probably not reading too much into things to sense the glee with which Itō, who had discovered another font of German wisdom from which to drink, wrote from Vienna to cast doubt on the government's one-man German brain trust, Hermann Roesler, saying, "I have uncovered ample evidence that Roesler's thinking is overly inclined toward liberalism."[61] At this point Itō had equipped himself with both the principles and the methods with which to take on the German political thought that had already established itself in Japan.

But while it is true that Itō was enormously influenced by Stein's teachings and drew considerable inspiration from them, it would be a mistake to assume that he swallowed them whole. Take, for example, Stein's thinking on the national assembly. Stein, like Gneist and Kaiser Wilhelm I, saw the growth of the parliamentary system as a threat to the national order. Itō, meanwhile, had left Berlin to distance himself from such opinions. Yet in Vienna he found Stein, whom he trusted, offering the same teaching. To address whether Stein was able to change Itō's mind, we must look at the political situation in Vienna as Itō might have seen it.

A carnival of ethnic conflict

In Berlin, Itō had the opportunity to observe firsthand the dysfunctional reality of the parliamentary system under the new German empire. Similar problems were latent in Austria, which consisted of an unusual confederation of states. The Ausgleich, or Compromise of 1867, had established a dual monarchy in which the Hapsburg emperor of Austria was also coronated the king of Hungary and ruled over it and an array of smaller kingdoms and principalities that had been part of the former Austrian empire. But the complexities of this new Austro-Hungarian Empire went far beyond the dual-state structure. Its territories were vast, extending into all or part of what is now the Czech Republic, Slovakia, Poland, Romania, the Balkan states, and Ukraine, making it a complex cultural amalgam encompassing a variety of ethnic groups, languages, and religions.[62]

The parliamentary system introduced for this multiethnic, multicultural society was naturally fraught with difficulties.[63] In 1865, the Austrian Empire temporarily suspended its constitution, following this with the establishment of a parliamentary system under the newly revised legal framework of 1867. The parliament, however, was not an institution representing the popular will through direct elections. Instead, it tended to represent specific interest groups, since a fixed number of representatives was drawn from each of four electoral blocs: landholders, urban areas, chambers of commerce and industry, and rural communities. Bismarck's ideal of parliament as an institution for unifying the national will was abandoned from the start, and given the multiethnic character of the empire it is not difficult to understand why.

Parliament's role as the representative of interest groups gradually shifted toward the representation of ethnic groups. By the end of the nineteenth century, ethnic issues flooded parliament, paralyzing the system. Czech representatives intent on asserting their independence clashed with their German-speaking counterparts, with one side or the other disrupting the activities of parliament on numerous occasions and turning it into a carnival of ethnic conflict.[64] Parliamentary politics reached a dead-end, and the business of government was increasingly conducted through a succession of emergency edicts issued in the name of the emperor—a situation that eventually led to the suspension of parliament.

The linchpin

If Austrian parliamentary affairs could be described as carnivalesque, then the period of Itō's stay in Vienna might be described as an intermission of sorts, when parliament was working with uncharacteristic smoothness. But this was not because parliamentary government had gotten itself on course. In 1880, prior to Itō's arrival, discontent was building among the ethnic German population of Bohemia at the adoption of Czech as the official language of the area, making it mandatory in government offices. Ethnic issues that would flare up in later years were already smoldering. Ethnic cleavage was being forestalled only by the authority of Emperor Franz Joseph I and his government's success in manipulating parliament.

Indeed, the linchpin holding the ungainly multiethnic empire together was Franz Joseph I, in his dual role as emperor of Austria and king of Hungary. He was fully aware of this and regarded hands-on rule over the empire as his personal mission.[65] He rose at four o'clock every morning to be in his office by five, a habit he kept up until just before his death. It was said that he alone knew what was happening at all levels of his complex empire. Under his authority, the government ministers were no more than instruments of the imperial will, the prime minister was literally the emperor's chief servant, and the cabinet devolved into a purely bureaucratic institution. He and he alone stood at the apex of the passive bureaucracy and had the power to deploy it at will to manage the empire's affairs. This image of the sovereign is in complete contrast to that envisioned by Stein, who may well have had Franz Joseph in mind as a negative example.[66]

Franz Joseph seems to have left a strong impression on Itō as well. In the draft of a letter composed during his time in Europe, Itō writes, "There is nothing for which this country does not have a rule or regulation; it is like a giant machine." He goes on to observe that

> in constitutional terms the emperor may appear to be simply one of the parts of this machine, but this is definitely not the case; he is the one who presides over it, controlling its operation and making sure everything runs without a hitch. So from time to time he must make some adjustments to it, oiling it here, or tightening a bolt there.[67]

Plainly, the country referred to here is Austria, and the emperor, Franz Joseph I. For Itō, who was setting about the deliberate creation of the machinery of a constitutional system, there were certainly lessons to be learned in Austria about the nature and significance of the sovereign power.

These lessons did not necessarily lead, however, to his affirmation of Austrian-style constitutional government, where direct rule by a powerful sovereign overwhelmed parliament. Despite repeated warnings in Germany regarding the dangers of parliamentary government, there is nothing to indicate that Itō ever hesitated over the introduction of a parliamentary system—even though he had accurately observed Bismarck's difficulties with regard to the issue of the tobacco monopoly. It is possible to see Itō as having maintained a consistent commitment to the concept of governing in partnership with a parliament. We also might assume that Itō's primary concern in transplanting the parliamentary system to Japan was determining which surgical procedures to use to avoid weakening the immune system of the patient. In observing the realities of parliamentary politics in Austria, Itō must have spent a good amount of time pondering the principles and methods for creating a constitutional government equipped with a healthy parliamentary system. His conclusions likely centered on the following two points.

Adaptation

First, a parliamentary system cannot function in a nation without citizens. Patriotism must serve as the backbone of national unity so that parliament is not torn apart by various political ideologies arising out of class and ethnic differences. Cultivating patriotism is a precondition for constitutional government.

Second, parliament must be augmented by a system external to it. During Itō's time in Austria, he witnessed this role performed solo by Franz Joseph, and was impressed by its functionality. But as a result of Stein's lectures, Itō's eyes had been opened to having the executive branch play this role. Made aware of the instability of parliamentary politics, Itō had learned how an executive system could carry out the work of government despite this, and how a constitutional monarch could, when parliamentary politics broke down, come to the rescue as sovereign.

Itō's vision was to carefully prepare the internal and external conditions supporting a parliamentary system and to then allow parliamentary government to gradually take root in Japan. This was Itō's variation on Stein's teachings on the evolution of national structure. In contrast to Stein, who emphasized executive power as the agent of evolution, Itō's interest was in instituting a parliamentary form of government to promote the development of the nation.

4. Later Research

Prelude to the Stein pilgrimage

Itō stayed in Vienna from August 8 to November 5, 1882, and attended lectures by Stein for all but a two-week excursion to Berlin and Paris. His encounter with Stein revived his spirits, and not simply because he had acquired a clearer theoretical grasp of constitutional government. Through Stein, Itō was also able to regain control of the mission. He had experienced difficulty with the other members in Berlin, but thanks to Stein, they had come together as a group in Vienna. Stein gave them pep talks, such as the following, as recalled by Kiba Sadanaga:

> One day Stein called me over to a globe, and pointing to it with his finger, said, "European civilization and the countries that belong to it developed around this Mediterranean Sea, and as a result my lectures cannot escape being centered upon it as well. We must expect that your future development will take place here, on the other side of the globe, centering on the Sea of Japan and the China Sea. And in the same fashion, your scholarship will reflect this."[68]

The difference between this and what Gneist had to say to the mission is immediately apparent. Stein's attitude helped the members regain their sense of purpose as a research team. After Itō departed Vienna on November 5, some of them, including Yamazaki Naotane and Saionji Kimmochi, would engage in independent travel and research, but this, too, can be seen as an indication that Itō had reasserted his leadership of the mission.[69] Having acquired a firm grasp of the big picture of constitutional government from Stein's lectures, Itō was confident enough to delegate more detailed investigation in specific areas to his associates.

Also noteworthy is that the members of the mission maintained contact with Stein.[70] The most notable example was Itō's arrangement to have two students accompanying the mission, Kiba Sadanaga and Sueoka Seiichirō, remain in Vienna for additional instruction from Stein. Among the mission's regular members, Kawashima Atsushi revisited Stein on December 22 and, according to a letter to Stein from Itō Miyoji, Itō and the rest of the mission's members hoped to study with him again.

After Itō's return to Japan, Stein would indeed enjoy a steady stream of Japanese visitors in what came to be known as the Stein pilgrimage. But there were already clear harbingers of this. Prince Arisugawa stopped in Vienna in October while on a European tour and joined Itō at one of Stein's talks. Gotō Shōjirō met Itō in Paris at year's end and at Itō's insistence also visited Stein. After petitioning Itō as described earlier, it appears that Miyoshi Taizō did not accompany Itō to Vienna and remained in Berlin to pursue research. But he, too, ultimately went at Itō's recommendation to hear Stein lecture, and was hugely impressed. Itō also wrote to Aoki Shūzō, the Japanese attaché in Berlin, encouraging him to meet Stein. The prelude to the "Stein pilgrimage" that would begin in earnest after Itō's return to Japan was already being played.

Letter to Gneist

After leaving Vienna, Itō returned to Berlin, where he received further instruction from Gneist and Mosse and had conversations with Bernhard Fuisting (1841–1908), privy councillor to the German emperor.[71] In this second round of research in Berlin, Alexander Freiherrn von Siebold (1846–1911) was Itō's indefatigable aide.[72] He was the son of Phillip Franz von Siebold (1796–1866), famous as one of the major figures in the introduction of Western learning to Japan in the late Tokugawa period. Alexander, who worked tirelessly in the service of Japanese diplomacy as an interpreter and in other capacities, was also an old friend of Itō's. With his support, Itō took Mosse's lectures much more seriously than previously and applied himself enthusiastically to his research.

It appears that Itō also sought more actively to draw out Gneist's opinions. From Siebold's diary and from correspondence between Itō and Gneist, it is clear that Itō, accompanied by Siebold, visited Gneist frequently and had Siebold produce English translations of some of Gneist's lecture notes.[73]

Most of the information that has come down to us regarding Gneist emphasizes his high-handedness and leaves an unclear picture of his influence on Meiji Japan. He seems, though, to have been of some importance within Meiji government circles. This reassessment is based on the letters from Japanese correspondents preserved as part of the Gneist Papers in the collection of the Geheimes Staatsarchiv Preußischer Kulturbesitz (Secret Central Archives, Prussian Cultural Heritage Foundation).

During a visit to the archives, located in Dahrem on the outskirts of Berlin, I discovered while browsing the catalog of the Gneist Papers entries for sixteen letters from Japanese correspondents, including Aoki Shūzō, Itō Hirobumi, Prince Komatsu, Hirata Tōsuke, and Yamagata Aritomo.[74] These are evidence that throughout the 1880s, Gneist was in regular contact with Japan. Unfortunately, most of these letters were lost during the World War II, but two from Itō, one dated May 18 and the other December 26, 1883, and one from Hirata, dated March 20, 1885, survive.

The first letter from Itō was written as he prepared to depart Berlin at the end of his constitutional research. After informing Gneist that he was leaving that evening and bidding him farewell, Itō introduces Mori Arinori, who happened to be in Berlin at the time, and requests that Gneist instruct him regarding the German educational system.

The second of Itō's letters was written after his return to Japan. He mentions hearing of a visit to San Francisco by Gneist, saying that had he known of it earlier, he would have urged Gneist to visit Japan as well, since it was close enough to have made a pleasant extension to his travels, but alas had discovered this only after Gneist's return to Germany.

Both letters reveal an unexpected level of familiarity. Itō's introduction of Mori

Letter from Itō Hirobumi to Rudolf von Gneist, dated 26 December 1883. Only the beginning and the conclusion are reproduced here.

and request for help with Mori's research in particular suggest a relationship of trust and amity between Itō and Gneist.

The Hirata letter preserved in the archives enlists Gneist's opinions on the famous Prussian constitutional dispute of the 1860s. Hirata is particularly interested in increases in military spending and hopes to use information from Gneist to support expansion of the Japanese military budget. "Your name," Hirata writes, "is held in great esteem here, and your authority in matters regarding the state has been widely acclaimed."

These three letters alone suggest more positive connections between Gneist and the Meiji state than previously thought. It is unfortunate that the additional letters from Japanese correspondents—including those from Yamagata and others from Itō—have been lost. However, we know that two members of the imperial family, Prince Fushimi and Prince Komatsu, visited Gneist with Yamagata and heard him lecture, more evidence of close communication between Gneist and the Japanese government. I will return to this point in the following chapter.

"The confessions of a beautiful soul"

Meanwhile, according to the diary of Alexander von Siebold, Itō confessed to him something "that made my hair stand on end":

> When he was a young samurai, Itō was involved in the assassination of a high government official and scholar whose name began with the syllable "Ha" (whose son, I am told, presently serves in the Foreign Ministry). At the behest of the *taikun's* [shogun's] government, he was investigating the idea of dethroning the emperor. When the *ronin* [here, antigovernment samurai] got wind of this, they sent Itō to pay a call on this personage, in order to see him first hand and be able to identify him later . . . They decided to lay in wait for him at Kudanshita, and when he appeared, they attacked him and his retinue and cut them down. Itō then went the following day to the man's residence to ascertain whether he was actually dead. There he was told the man was ill, and that his son had gone to see the Council of Elders [the equivalent of cabinet ministers in Tokugawa Japan]. The retainers of the house invited Itō in, probably in order to seize him, but he did not linger there. Later, he realized that his sword was still caked with blood.[75]

The man cut down by Itō and his associates was Hanawa Jirō, son of the famous scholar of Kokugaku (National Learning), Hanawa Hokiichi, and himself a Kokugaku scholar.

Siebold must not have known how to react to this grisly confession. His confusion comes through in his diary entry, where he can only conclude, somewhat awkwardly, that this is "the confession of a beautiful soul."

What was it that induced Itō to recount this bloody tale from his past? He is reported to have told the same story to some of his companions during the Iwakura Embassy's travels through America and Europe.[76] Perhaps, as before, being abroad emboldened him to let down his guard. Or maybe his success in his mission to investigate the constitution left him in an expansive frame of mind.

On February 19, 1883, Itō left Berlin, passing through Belgium on his way to London. During his two months in England, he met Herbert Spencer (1820–1903), the famed theorist of Social Darwinism, and apparently heard lectures by an individual named Grigsby, but no details of this exist.[77] According to Itō Miyoji, Itō Hirobumi contracted in London to have a number of documents collected in Germany translated into English and worked on putting in order the results of the mission's research. It seems safe to say, then, that the actual research phase of the mission had been completed in Germany and Austria.[78]

In May, Itō Hirobumi traveled to Russia to attend the coronation of the tsar, and on June 26 departed from Naples for the voyage home.

A secret letter to Ōkuma

Preserved among the Itō Papers in the National Diet Library is the draft of a letter that Itō began composing during his sojourn in Europe but never completed. The content suggests that its intended recipient was Ōkuma Shigenobu and that it was written following Itō's research in Vienna. This unfinished letter to an old comrade turned political rival reveals a reflective side to Itō that contrasts with the impression he gave of being drunk with success in Vienna and overplaying that success to the audience back home. It attests to the introspection behind his comment in an earlier letter to Iwakura that "I feel that if I were to die now, I could rest in peace." The unfinished draft includes this passage:

It has now been more than a year since I have seen you, my esteemed friend, and now we find ourselves at opposite ends of the earth. Nor is this just a matter of physical distance. We also differ in myriad ways on the course that we would chart for our nation. When I think back on last spring when we bathed together in the hot springs at Atami and discussed grand plans for the future, the scene still comes vividly to my eyes. Yet the meetings and partings of life are like this. Nor is this true merely of our usual meetings and partings; it is also seems true of our changes in course. Is this something that results from the workings of nature, or from the choices that we make ourselves? What would be accomplished if I should try to discover what separates that which is nature's part and that which is man's? Even if I were to do so, it would not profit the nation. If one were to take the country . . . [the manuscript breaks off here][79]

Only the previous spring the two men had discussed national politics at the Atami Conference. Yet, in the short time that had passed, the world of politics had shifted significantly, and the respective position and status of the two had been radically altered. They now were at opposite ends of the earth in a literal sense and poles apart politically.

Yet there was no difference between them in their grand goal: the establishment of Japan as a modern nation-state with a parliamentary system and the renegotiation of Japan's unequal treaties with the Western powers. Far from Japan, where the dust had still not settled after the Political Crisis of 1881, Itō was able to think objectively and systematically about where he felt the nation should be headed. He could draw the distinction between his views and Ōkuma's radicalism on the one hand and between the instinctive rejection of parliamentary politics by Iwakura and other government leaders on the other. His course would be to harmonize and unite these two conflicting positions. His unfinished letter exudes his confidence in his ability to do so.

CHAPTER THREE

Yamagata Aritomo's European Tour

A Different Kind of Constitutional Research

1. The Promulgation of the Meiji Constitution

Institutional reform through "constitutional charisma"

On August 3, 1883, Itō Hirobumi returned to Japan and put what Sakamoto Kazuto has called his "constitutional charisma" to work. Using the authority and confidence he had gained in Europe, Itō took the lead role in a reform of national institutions intended to lay the groundwork for the introduction of a parliamentary political system.[1]

In Hong Kong, while he was still en route home, word had reached him that Iwakura Tomomi had conveniently died after a lengthy illness. This guaranteed that upon Itō's return to Japan he would have complete authority, both in name and in fact, to preside over the process of formulating a constitution.

Yet after his arrival, Itō did not immediately begin work on the constitution. As we have seen in the preceding chapter, in Europe Itō had become convinced that the constitution as a written document was insufficient in and of itself. What was needed was a constitution in the sense of the deeper structure undergirding the state. Constitutional government could not be achieved simply by writing a constitution. It would have to be premised upon a complete overhaul of national institutions, beginning with the administrative system, as well as a remaking of the consciousness of both officials and the people in accordance with this institutional transformation. This was the lesson that Itō had brought back with him from Europe.

Knowing that a major revision of the country's system of government had to be undertaken before writing the constitution itself, Itō took steps to achieve this end. In March 1884, he was appointed director of the Bureau for the Investigation of Constitutional Systems in the Imperial Household Department. From this command post, Itō carried out a variety of institutional reforms. He was concurrently made minister of the Imperial Household Department, and immediately initiated a series of palace reforms, reorganizing the structure of the department itself and working to establish the financial autonomy of imperial house. These efforts were directly related to Itō's concept of the state, which called for establishing a clear separation between the imperial house and the government.

In the late 1870s, as Emperor Meiji, born in 1853, came to maturity both physically and mentally, rising sentiment favored his personal rule. However, Itō labored to prevent the emperor or his advisers from willfully meddling in the affairs of state or, conversely, from being drawn into political involvement against his will. Itō did so by attempting to create an autonomous space in which the palace could exist independent of politics and to sever the direct link between the emperor and the government. This was the first step toward turning the emperor into a constitutional monarch.

A system for building a bureaucracy

In December 1885, a major restructuring of the government abolished the Dajōkan, which had served as Japan's governing body since shortly after the Restoration. In its place, a modern cabinet system was introduced. This ended the nominal control of the government ministries by members of the nobility, formally opening positions of national leadership to a broad spectrum of the nation's citizens. It also signified the establishment of an executive branch of government that, while still responsible to the emperor, was also autonomous.

In Europe, Itō had his eyes opened by Stein to the significance of the executive in supporting constitutional government. Indispensable to this was the existence of a modern bureaucracy and a recruitment system to staff it. In March 1886, the Imperial University Order was issued, creating the Imperial University (later Tokyo Imperial University). Article I of the order stated that "the Imperial University has as its goal the teaching of, and the fundamental research into, arts and sciences necessary for the state," indicating that this was an institution of higher education and research established with a strong awareness of its ties to other state institutions. The Imperial University Order, along with the Regulations for Civil Service Examinations and Probationary Civil Officers and the Civil Service Code issued in 1887, constituted a system for fostering a bureaucracy that could provide the administrative support for constitutional government. This interrelated set of institutions is what Nakano Minoru has called the Imperial University system.[2]

Institutional constraints on the emperor: the Privy Council

The Sūmitsuin, or Privy Council, was established in 1888, with Itō as its first president. The Privy Council was initially created to deliberate upon and ratify proposals for basic national laws such as the constitution and the Imperial Household Law, giving it a pivotal role in the new constitutional monarchy. Itō explained its significance to Inoue Kowashi in the following terms:

> In my humble opinion, we cannot imitate the British and immediately establish parliamentary government, and in light of the state of affairs in our country, it would be extremely dangerous to leave matters to the vicissitudes of politics and the survival of the fittest, as the Prussian chancellor [Bismarck] suggests; we must of course not allow His Majesty to be troubled by such matters. This can be dealt with by a completely new invention of my own devising. When you inquire into the basic principles of our Constitution, you will see that sovereignty resides firmly in the imperial house, and that in a crisis His Majesty's judgment is to be the basis for the final decision. In the event that the government and the Diet find it impossible to come to agreement, then in accordance with the imperial will either the cabinet must resign or the Diet be dissolved; there is no other alternative. In such a case, there must be conscientious imperial advisers who can clearly ascertain the state of the nation and the sentiments of the people, and in the end secure what is in their best interests. I am convinced that only a Privy Council can provide the place where such advisers may be found . . .[3]

Itō points to the decision-making authority of the emperor in the event of a deadlock between the government and the national assembly and conceives

of the Privy Council as an advisory body to the emperor in such circumstances. He was proud of his "completely new invention," seeing it as a
unique institution for Japan's parliamentary system that was in no way
beholden to the English or Prussian models. It is unlikely, though, that
Itō would have proposed such an idea without the knowledge he acquired
through his study of European statecraft, especially under Stein.

In February 1887, Prince Komatsu attended lectures by Stein in Vienna
in which Stein spoke of the role of the sovereign as a mediating force in
politics. According to Stein, for the sovereign "to stand above both the
executive and legislative branches, overseeing all affairs of state" he must
always employ "people personally loyal to His Majesty" as advisers to
"broadly and fully comprehend the situation of the nation at home and
abroad" and "determine affairs of state."[4]

In any case, the Privy Council was intended as a consultative body for
political action on the part of the emperor. Even if the emperor were to be
accorded the honor of "overseeing all affairs of state," it would not do to
overestimate his actual political sovereignty. Rather, the creation of the
Privy Council was intended as a check on the emperor's intrusion into
politics. It drew the imperial political decision-making process forth from
the shadowy recesses of the palace and placed it openly before the members of the Privy Council, to be carried out on the basis of their deliberations. The separation of the imperial household and the government
forestalled the emperor from becoming a political ruler, and the establishment of the Privy Council institutionalized any political activity on the
part of the sovereign. The emperor was thus encouraged to develop into a
constitutional monarch.

Along the tracks laid by Itō

The period from Itō's return to Japan to the promulgation of the Meiji
Constitution, therefore, involved more than merely drafting a document.
The entire framework of the nation's institutions was being overhauled to
shape the Meiji state into a constitutional order.

This effort owed much to Itō's forceful leadership. He followed a blueprint of his own devising to turn Japan into a constitutional monarchy and
skillfully directed Inoue Kowashi and other legal bureaucrats under his
command to reform Japan's institutions. This was the practical application
of what Itō had learned from Stein during his studies in Europe. Faithful

to Stein's teachings, Itō vigorously constructed an administrative system to undergird the constitutional order.

In Europe, Itō deepened his insight into the pitfalls of constitutional government through the examples of Germany and Austria. Yet this did not lead him to reject the parliamentary system; his faith in it remained unshaken. He realized that parliamentary politics were inevitable under a constitutional system, but had to be backed by a strong concern for the collective national good within the popular consciousness, or they could easily disintegrate into factionalism. This led to the insight that the introduction of a parliamentary system would not be finished with the establishment of a constitution; for it to fully take root, patient political effort was required. Itō had taken Stein's hint, and recalibrated his political aims from an immediate concern with the soon-to-be-enacted constitution to the more protracted task of implementing a viable national structure.

Itō's political leadership after the opening of the Diet was consistent with regard to this point. The first parliamentary government in Asia was fraught with difficulties from the very start. Conflict between antigovernment forces based in the Diet on the one hand and the government and its bureaucracy on the other produced a series of crises in which suspension of the constitution loomed as a real threat. That they were overcome was in no small part due to the suppleness of Itō's policies in dealing with the Diet. He constantly and carefully strove to maintain a parliamentary majority through a shifting series of alliances and by whittling away at the largest opposition party, the Jiyūtō (Liberal Party), all the while working to overcome conflicts between the government and the Diet as amicably as possible. Only when the situation reached real crisis would he call on the emperor to intervene, as a limited version of the activist monarch he had seen in Franz Joseph.

In 1900, Itō himself organized a political party from the remnants of his erstwhile rival and negotiating partner, the Jiyūtō. Called the Rikken Seiyūkai (Friends of Constitutional Government), it represented his entry into parliamentary politics as a party politician. Itō passed away in 1909, but parliamentary politics in Japan continued its development. The first genuine party cabinet, achieved in 1918 under the leadership of Hara Takashi, could not have come into being if not for the tracks laid by Itō.[5]

An "immutable fundamental law"

The culmination of Japan's reform of its national institutions was the promulgation on February 11, 1889 (Meiji 22), of the Constitution of the Empire of Japan (the Meiji Constitution). The day also saw the promulgation of a variety of supplementary laws and the enactment of the Imperial Household Law (which, because it pertained to the private affairs of the imperial house, was not publicly promulgated). The supplementary laws included the Law of the Houses, the Law of Election of Members the House of Representatives, the Law of Finance, and the Imperial Ordinance Concerning the House of Peers. Along with the Constitution of the Empire of Japan, they constituted the collective body of laws fundamental to the Meiji state. It is this integrated whole that should be considered to be imperial Japan's real constitution, establishing the institutional features of the modern monarchy, legislature, and cabinet and initiating Japan's development into a constitutional state.[6]

There is a considerable gap, therefore, between the Meiji Constitution and the actual constitution of Meiji Japan. The written constitution was only one among a number of basic laws structuring the state, though it was accorded a different normative status from these ordinary laws and ordinances, having been promulgated as the nation's "immutable fundamental law."[7] Yet it was impossible for this document of only seventy-six articles to define every aspect of national life. To truly constitute Japan's political order, other legislation, and the mediation of the political and administrative process, would be required.[8]

Unity and symbolism

Limitations aside, the constitution's significance lay in it being the most fundamental law among the nation's fundamental laws, the *primus inter pares*. Its abstract language expressed the fundamental guiding principles of the Japanese state. But how these principles were to be interpreted remained open to question.

It is well known that the Meiji Constitution established sweeping imperial powers, proclaiming the emperor to be "the head of the Empire, combining in himself the rights of sovereignty." Yet the aims of its principal architect, Itō Hirobumi, lay elsewhere, in the concept of a limited monarchy in which the government and parliament cooperated in conducting the affairs of state. What, then, did the Meiji Constitution signify?

The focus of this book, as stated earlier, is on the unifying and symbolic roles of the constitution. And, indeed, the Meiji Constitution was a cohesive force uniting the various institutions of national government and the nation as a whole. Of particular significance was its codification of the country's highest normative values. The diverse ordinances previously issued ad hoc as responses to the pressure of events would now have to be drafted in compliance with the constitution. The nation could now erect a consistent legal system with the constitution at its apex.[9]

The constitution's symbolic function had two aspects: domestic and international. In the international context, Japan's promulgation of the constitution signified more than anything else its intent to join the ranks of the "civilized" nations. At the time, treaty revision was still a fervently desired goal, and the constitution was regarded as the symbol of a civilized polity.

At home, it was hoped that the promulgation of the constitution would serve as a public expression to the Japanese people of the desired shape of their nation and thereby politically invigorate the citizenry and serve as a force for national unity. Under the constitution, the political energies of the people could be channeled and incorporated into the process of national government, meanwhile guaranteeing them the prospect of influencing that process. The constitution, in short, symbolized the modern nation-state.

Japanese spirit, Western learning

Episodes surrounding the promulgation of the constitution, beginning with the ceremony itself, give us a glimpse of its symbolic power.

The promulgation ceremony was held in the new imperial palace, completed in January, a month before the promulgation. In May 1873, the former imperial palace within the grounds of Edo Castle was destroyed by fire, and for more than a decade the former mansion of the daimyo of Kii in the Akasaka district of Tokyo served as the emperor's provisional residence. The promulgation ceremony was thus also the first formal exhibition of the new palace.

Immediately before the promulgation ceremony, a different ceremony in observation of Kigensetsu, the date commemorating the founding of the nation, was conducted by the emperor in the Kashikodokoro, a shrine within the palace dedicated to the imperial ancestors.[10] Before the assembled members of the nobility and high government officials, the emperor appeared, clad in "ancient court dress," and then retired behind a ceremonial screen, where he read a text informing his ancestors of the promulgation of the constitution. Like the Charter Oath of 1868, which had also been presented to the imperial ancestors, the promulgation of the constitution was thus situated, first and foremost, within the framework of a "restoration of antiquity" (*fukko*).

This is reminiscent of the events surrounding the Iwakura Embassy's departure presented in chapter 1. The embassy was also sent on its way with ceremonies deliberately ancient in nature. This "restoration of antiquity," however, was left behind almost as soon as the embassy left port. Much the same could be said of the ceremonies surrounding the promulgation of the constitution.

When the ceremony in the Kashikodokoro had been concluded, the assembled dignitaries moved to the Seiden, the palace's public hall of ceremonies, for the promulgation ceremony itself. The proceedings now threw off the air of a secret rite with which they had begun and became a majestic display of pomp and circumstance. Ottmar von Mohl (1846–1922), a foreign expert employed at the palace, gives the following account:

> Afterwards, the emperor changed into Western-style military uniform, and accompanied by a solemn procession of courtiers, and entered an ornate throne room expressly prepared for this occasion. In it, the empress and the imperial princesses were already arrayed to the right of the throne; the imperial princes and members of the foreign diplomatic corps to the left.[11]

In other words, the emperor, after presenting the constitution as an offering at the ancestral shrine in the inner recesses of the palace, immediately changed into Western dress to preside over a ceremony in which he presented the constitution as a gift to his people. As the emperor's Western clothing suggests, the promulgation ceremony itself was conducted in the Western manner. Indeed, as the day approached, there were so many orders from participants for new Western formal attire that it is said that all the Western tailors, hatters, and cobblers in the capital were sold out.[12] The following lengthy quotation gives a clear impression of the promulgation ceremony:

From the dais, in a loud, clear voice the emperor read the rescript bestowing the constitution on the Japanese people. The hall presented a solemn spectacle. Facing the emperor stood ranks of Japan's high officials and notables, and the members of both houses of the soon-to-be-convened Diet.[13] To the right of the emperor, on a slightly elevated dais stood the empress and the imperial princesses, together with their ladies-in-waiting. The empress wore a Western-style crown studded with diamonds, and her rose gown was set off by accessories such as one might see on the Riviera, also laden with diamonds. The empress and the princesses at her side all

"The Promulgation of the Constitution" by Wada Eisaku.

wore Japanese medals. This party of the women of the imperial house and the throng of other elegant women in attendance made a most favorable impression. The men serving in the palace were arranged in a line along the rear wall of the hall, behind the emperor and empress. The members of the diplomatic corps were all in attendance—this in itself a rarity—and their colorful military uniforms and formal dress lent an undeniable liveliness to the celebration.[14]

Again, unlike the earlier private and very ancient Japanese rite before the imperial ancestors, this took on all the coloring of European court ceremony. "Japanese spirit" was concealed within the recesses of the palace, and the constitution was displayed to the world in the full regalia of "Western learning."

The presence, therefore, of the members of the Western diplomatic community is profoundly significant. Moreover, the foreign presence was not limited to diplomats; large numbers of foreigners in the employ of the Meiji government also attended. Their presence at the birth of the constitution clearly conveyed a specific message to the West that Japan, now possessed of a constitution, was also a civilized nation. The constitution thus assumed its aforementioned role in foreign affairs as the symbol of Japan's civilization and enlightenment.

Determined to enhance the prestige of the constitution, the emperor gave it his all that day. Following the promulgation ceremony, he reviewed the troops at the Aoyama Parade Grounds at 1:00 p.m., returning to the palace at 5:00 p.m. with scarcely time to catch his breath before the formal banquet at 7:00 p.m., to which more than three hundred people had been invited (mostly participants in the promulgation ceremony) and which would continue well into the night. As the evening wore on, the emperor was unable to conceal his fatigue, and the ballroom dancing, which did not start until 10:00 p.m., had to be temporarily halted.[15]

Unforeseen events

The promulgation ceremony centered on the emperor, but the highest officials of the government were feverishly at work in the wings. Three unanticipated events arose on the day of the ceremony to add to the behind-the-scenes commotion.[16]

The first was the assassination of Mori Arinori. Mori, who was serving in the cabinet as the minister of education, was cut down by a swordsman as he left his residence that morning on his way to the ceremonies at the palace. The other officials, waiting impatiently for his arrival, were shocked at word of this tragedy. Concerned about the confusion that would arise if the participants were to learn of this event, the government suppressed the news of Mori's death until after the ceremony.

The second incident involved Itō Hirobumi's misplacing the constitution itself. He appeared haggard and empty-handed before the other officials on the morning of the ceremony, and not just because he, too, had been unable to sleep for all the excitement. When Kaneko Kentarō, who along with Inoue Kowashi and Itō Myoji had assisted Itō in drafting the document, asked Itō where the constitution was, Itō, who had the previous day received the official copy, carefully wrapped in purple brocade, had to confess that he had left it behind at his official residence. A messenger was hurriedly dispatched to retrieve the precious document, but the episode was "one of the biggest blunders in Prince Itō's life."

And, finally, there was Inoue Kowashi's mistake with a date. In the text of the rescript the emperor read aloud at the ceremony and in the text published in the government's official gazette, the incorrect date was given for the imperial rescript of 1881 promising that a national assembly would be convened in nine year's time. The declaration had been published on October 12, but this was incorrectly given as October 14. It was a slip of the pen in the eleventh hour by Inoue, who had worked heroically and anonymously as one of the chief architects of the constitution. What most might dismiss as a minor error compelled Inoue to submit an offer to resign, and a request for "appropriate punishment." So great was his torment that he began to feel "death is the only way to atone for this." Inoue took pride in his precise and meticulous mind and had enjoyed the unconditional trust of others because, in the words of Kaneko Kentarō, "any proposal of Inoue's was bound to be free from slips or errors." So this oversight must have, to quote Ōishi Makoto, "felt like snatching defeat from the jaws of victory."

Behind the scenes, the government leaders were truly shedding blood, sweat, and tears. It seems more than mere coincidence that the "constitutional charisma" of both Itō and Inoue was so thoroughly punctured. What is revealed by the incidents involving these two men is the striking differences in their temperaments. In contrast to Inoue—"loyal samurai," diligent in every word and phrase—Itō comes across as nonchalant, forgetting the constitution on the very day of its promulgation.[17] Perhaps this was the distinction between a high-minded bureaucrat so immersed in the minutiae of the constitution that he identified himself with it, and a politician who saw the constitution as no more than an instrument to be wielded as skillfully as possible in realizing his vision for the nation.

A cynical view

How did the Japanese people respond to the promulgation of the constitution? Erwin Baelz (1849–1913), a physician employed by the Japanese government, remarked on the celebratory spectacle in the streets: "Yet the amusing thing was that not one of them had any idea of what was in the constitution."[18] A letter written by another German in the employ of the government, Karl Rathgen (1856–1921), a professor of political science at the Imperial University, goes further. Rathgen writes that when people first heard about the promulgation they had no idea what this meant.

When the news spread that the constitution was to be promulgated on February 11, the people were quite indifferent. The rejoicing that the government clearly anticipated was nowhere to be seen. Yet the government thought that the people should be happy. Local officials and newspapers received their orders, and immediately articles such as the following began to appear: It is the duty of all loyal subjects to dress up, drink saké, and celebrate this day. Officials summoned the local notables and let them know that the emperor desired them to celebrate this day in the manner of a local temple festival. Anyone who did not join in would not be allowed to participate in any future festivals. Opening shops or working on this day was forbidden. According to my cook, the entire neighborhood is most depressed by this.[19]

We can see that the people were initially discomfited by the demands for celebration. The government's persistence in fomenting a celebratory mood, though, seemed to take hold, and popular excitement grew.

Over the past several days, the people, each after their own fashion, have put some energy into preparations for the celebration, and things have acquired a bit more colorful an air. With the festive decorations that have been put everywhere, the town is looking quite lovely. Crowds have gathered in surprising proximity to the imperial palace. They probably have no clear idea what all the fuss is about. It was totally impossible for the police to control such extraordinary crowds, and yet, strangely enough, there have been no incidents at the narrow gates to the castle, on the bridges, or elsewhere. This is thanks to the

Festivities for the promulgation of the constitution in the Ueno district of Tokyo.

Japanese national character, which possesses a discipline, patience, and gentleness that defy our comprehension. The major responsibility for the numerous accidents that have occurred lies with the mob who drove heavy oxcarts up to the palace and then circled it in an endless procession. The majority of the carts were extremely gaudy, eye-catching affairs. Yet it is difficult to understand what such foolishness has to do with the constitution or political maturity.[20]

Rathgen also reports that "I witnessed the first genuine brawl I have seen since coming to Japan" and makes note of free saké being dispensed, fireworks day and night, the decorative illuminations in the streets, and torchlight processions of students. Overall, Rathgen and Baelz view the proceedings cynically. Rathgen concludes his letter by writing that "despite all the uproar and boisterous celebration, it was all for show; no one really shared in this sentiment from the depths of their heart."

O Constitution, you are born at last!

Seen through the cool eyes of a foreign resident, the carnival atmosphere in the streets attending the promulgation of the constitution was an embarrassment. The people who would be involved in the political and governmental system that would emerge from this constitution, however, saw things differently.

The newspapers and magazines of the Freedom and Popular Rights Movement, for example, which had long clamored for a constitution, on the whole welcomed the constitution's promulgation.[21] Takada Sanae, polemicist for the Kaishintō (Progressive Party), opined "I think the Constitution of the Empire of Japan is a good constitution; a better constitution than we were led to believe." This view, common among Kaishintō members, was expressed by newspaper reporter Koezuka Ryū in the *Mainichi shimbun*, "In general, it is truly a praiseworthy constitution." Another party member said upon reading the constitution that "I was filled with a spirit of great joy" and relates that "we were not the only ones who felt this way; among the people of the entire nation I think there was not one who voiced any dissatisfaction."[22]

Contributing no doubt to the positive reception of the constitution by Kaishintō supporters was the appointment to the cabinet the preceding year of their leader Ōkuma Shigenobu. But their emotion for the constitution was genuine. Ōoka Ikuzō, who would later serve in the House of

Representatives and who was a representative in the Tokyo Metropolitan Assembly at the time, reminisced as follows:

> On the day the constitution was promulgated, you can scarcely imagine my surprise when I heard the news that even members of the prefectural assemblies had participated in the ceremony at the palace. Up to that point, one frequently heard that even people of considerable status had not been permitted to enter the palace, and had to content themselves with prostrating themselves in the gravel outside the palace gates. What an immense change it was when on that day even commoners such as the prefectural assemblymen were given the honor of attendance at the palace.[23]

In fact, only the chairmen of the prefectural assemblies were permitted to attend. But it is significant that a rumor that all of the assemblymen had been granted access spread so rapidly, and seized the popular imagination. It was captivating to think that the doors of the palace had been thrown open to anyone involved in politics, even to assemblymen who had been hostile to the government. The newly renovated imperial palace, as the setting for the emperor's gift of the constitution to his people, made its debut as a venue where entrenched political conflicts could be ameliorated. Even the imperial pardon of the popular rights activists being held as political prisoners can be seen as part of the message of political reconciliation conveyed from the palace to the people with the promulgation of the constitution.

Popular rights activists embraced the notion that the establishment of the constitution legitimized their existence within the system and opened a path to their participation in national politics. They accepted the constitution as a political symbol without hesitation. A newspaper piece, reportedly by Ueki Emori read, "O Constitution, you are born at last! At this I rejoice. And if I am to celebrate your birth, I must also pray for your growth. Grow strong, I beg of you!"[24] In this unfeigned excitement we can sense Ueki's hopes for the convening of the national assembly mandated by the constitution, where at the very least the struggle for rights could be continued.

Undeniably, Japan had entered a new era in politics. The personal networks and associations that people form to pursue political ends and the political space that people create or activate through them were termed "the public sphere" (*Öffentlichkeit*) by the German political theorist Jürgen Habermas.[25] Borrowing Habermas's term, it can be said that the promulgation of the Meiji Constitution was a historic event announcing the formation of such a public sphere in the nation-state of Meiji Japan. In Japan, however, this public sphere arose not from the grassroots, as envisioned by Habermas, but was created by imperial fiat from within the palace walls.

Tension over the creation of a public sphere

The constitution was an established fact, but this did not immediately result in popular participation in politics or in the participation of the opposition parties in the government. Suffrage was restricted to adult males over the age of twenty-five paying more than fifteen yen in direct national taxes per annum. Unless one was a large landholder, it was difficult to acquire the franchise.

In addition, the government's deep-rooted antipathy for the popular rights movement and its parties had not been dispelled. Several days after the promulgation of the constitution, its architect, Itō Hirobumi, admonished a gathering of prefectural assembly chairmen:

> Now that the Diet is about to be convened and the affairs of government opened to public debate and discussion, we must avoid the quite dangerous temptation of hastily organizing a parliamentary government—in other words, a cabinet formed by political parties. Though there are many who preach the advantages of political parties, we must still cultivate the strength necessary to place the nation on a secure enough footing to allow the affairs of state to be determined by public debate. If we should fail to recognize this necessity, and engage lightly in something that could shake the foundations of the nation, who knows what harm might be done? This is something about which I am personally quite concerned.[26]

Itō is not rejecting party politics out of hand. He sees the domination of the Diet by political parties as inevitable but is nevertheless apprehensive lest the nation's governance fall prey in its infancy to partisan forces. So he argues that despite the implementation of the constitution it is still too early for parliamentary government and party cabinets.

The day after the promulgation of the constitution, Prime Minister Kuroda Kiyotaka likewise delivered a famous speech stubbornly rejecting party government and defending the so-called transcendental cabinet system. That he and Itō felt inclined to make such remarks shows that government insiders feared the prospect of the formation of a public sphere that included their rivals in the popular rights movement. The constitution had been established, marking the culmination of an era of vigorous nation-building that had commenced with the Meiji Restoration, but the leaders of the government were unable to summon the enthusiasm and excitement of the popular rights activists, much less lose themselves in the drunken revelry in the streets. They were already facing the difficulty of how to engage the forces of the political parties and continue to run the country after the Diet convened in 1890.

An elder statesman visits Europe

At the time of the promulgation of the constitution, one of Japan's *genrō*, or elder statesmen, was contemplating the problem of popular politics from a solitary vantage. Yamagata Aritomo was on a fact-finding tour of Europe, the goals of which he defined as follows:

> At this time I am intending to spend a period of about eight months touring the European nations in order to inspect their coastal defense batteries. In addition, since preparations are under way for the anticipated introduction of a new system of local administration throughout the country in
>
> *Yamagata Aritomo*
>
> April of next year, I plan to observe at first hand how the local government system has been implemented in Prussia, and expect to find it instructive in numerous ways.[27]

Wherever he went on his tour, Yamagata explained that his visit was "to observe the actual workings of local administration, and to study military affairs in general."[28]

There was, however, a deeper significance to his journey. Yamagata would become Itō's principal rival, and the two would divide Japan's political world between them.[29] Unlike Itō, who would advance party politics as the head of the Rikken Seiyūkai, Yamagata would weave a web of influence from his base in the Home Ministry that extended into the bureaucracy, the army, the House of Peers, the Privy Council, and even the imperial palace. He would vigorously employ this Yamagata clique in an effort to contain the power of the political parties. The subsequent constitutional history of the Meiji era essentially unfolds through the conflict and rivalry of these two men.

Yamagata's journey, which he embarked upon despite having to miss the birth of the Meiji Constitution, was yet another constitutional inquiry, following in the wake of the Iwakura Embassy and Itō's mission. What concepts of national structure would Yamagata learn on this visit to distant Europe?

2. Yamagata Aritomo's European Study Tour

"Like visiting Arima and not bathing in the hot springs"

On December 2, 1888, Yamagata Aritomo, then home minister, entrusted his office to Matsukata Masayoshi and set out on a journey to Europe and the United States.[30] For the next ten months, until October 2, 1889, Yamagata put Japan behind him. It seems somewhat odd that key figures in the government, such as Yamagata and Itō before him, should absent themselves from their country for such extended periods of time. Political factors, however, underlay Yamagata's decision to this trip.[31] It should also be recalled that since Itō's trip to Europe in 1882, it had become *de rigueur* for high-ranking officials of the Japanese government to travel to the West.

The "Stein pilgrimage" was emblematic of this. Itō's return to Japan touched off an avalanche of Japanese visitors to Vienna to meet his mentor Stein—a chronology of which I have published elsewhere.[32] These included Prince Arisugawa (October 1882) and Prince Komatsu (February 1887) of the imperial house; government leaders, such as Ōyama Iwao (November 1884), Tani Tateki (July 1886), Saigō Tsugumichi (1886), and Kuroda Kiyotaka (January 1887); bureaucrats, among them Kaneko Kentarō (November 1889); and even political figures who were out of office at the time, such as Gotō Shōjirō (December 1882) and Mutsu Munemitsu

(June 1885). Other major figures either consulted with Stein
in writing or dispatched representatives to hear his lectures
and opinions. These included
the *genrō* Inoue Karou and
Matsukata Masayoshi and even
Emperor Meiji himself.

Stein (second from left) lecturing to three uniden-tified Japanese visitors.

The truly diverse list of Japanese who knocked upon Stein's
door continues with the mili-
tary men Torio Koyata (November 1886) and Nogi Maresuke (January
1887); the scholars Ariga Nakao (July 1887) and Kanei Noboru (December
1889); the religious leader Kitabatake Dōryō; entrepreneurs such as Shōda
Heigorō; and the occasional anonymous student. An observer mockingly
remarked that "to go on a study tour of Europe without meeting Dr. Stein
was like visiting Arima and not bathing in the hot springs."[33]

In 1887, Yamagata, too, made the pilgrimage to Stein in Vienna, though
meeting Stein was not the be all and end all of Yamagata's voyage. Let's
retrace Yamagata's itinerary and assess the significance of his tour.[34]

"Teutonic madness"

On January 9, 1889, the ship carrying Yamagata and his entourage arrived
in Marseilles—beginning an eight-month tour of Europe. Their first destination was Paris, where Yamagata met unexpected difficulty.

Yamagata met on January 16 with the French foreign minister René-
Marie Goblet (1828–1905). In this meeting, his first official call in Europe,
Yamagata received a surprisingly cold reception:

> It appears that your country has recently become uncommonly friendly with a
> certain country other than France and has thus not continued to employ the
> military advisers my country has sent you, creating a difficult situation on both
> sides, and something I find most regrettable.[35]

The other country with whom Japan was deepening its friendship was
Germany. With the Political Crisis of 1881 as a watershed, the government
had shifted decisively toward adopting the German model as a ruling

ideology. Goblet's remarks to Yamagata were an admonition against this tendency in Japan, delivered with characteristic French irony. To fully understand Goblet's statement, we must take a bit of a detour and consider the trend of "Germanification" in Meiji Japan.

A major impetus behind this "Germanification" was the Political Crisis of 1881. On the day that Ōkuma was driven from the government, an imperial rescript was issued. It promised to convene a national assembly in nine years, a declaration that the movement toward constitutional government would gradual, not radical. What the leaders of the government had in mind was a Prussian-style constitutional monarchy. To supply the ideological weapons for this endeavor, the government promoted German scholarship, especially the teachings of the German statecraft school. Inoue Kowashi, a behind-the-scenes engineer of the bloodless coup culminating in the crisis of 1881, wasted little time in submitting a position paper to the government in November of that year. He proposed "the encouragement of German studies," arguing that "if we wish to create a somewhat more conservative mood among the hearts of the people, we should encourage only Prussian [constitutional] theory . . . and silence the headlong rush toward the British model."[36]

As Inoue proposed, German theory was introduced at a sufficiently vigorous pace to "silence" British and French alternatives. In September 1881, immediately before the crisis, the German Studies Association (Doitsugaku Kyōkai) was formed. Organized and managed through the efforts of Inoue, the association had a membership that included the majority of the Meiji *genrō*: Itō Hirobumi, Yamagata Aritomo, Inoue Kaoru, Matsukata Masayoshi, and Saigō Tsugumichi. It embodied the ruling ideology. The association published and distributed a steady stream of works on German jurisprudence and political science and in October 1883 established the Academy of the German Studies Association, an institution for the reproduction of this ideology. The academy provided a venue for advancing the association's goal of disseminating German thought among the ruling strata. The institutionalization of this ideology was further advanced through the creation of seminars on German political economy directed at members of the bureaucracy and through publication of an official journal of the German Studies Association.[37]

The ascendancy of the German model was not confined to government circles. An article in a leading opinion magazines had this to say:

O blow thou German wind! Your approach is felt in scholarship, in the military, in students' caps, in beer—though why you blow, I do not know. A professor of sociology pronounced you to be the wind of madness, but when I asked him why, he simply smiled, making no reply. [38]

This German "wind of madness" was blowing at gale force through Japanese society and culture. Was it just a passing gust, blowing in concert with the political interests of Japan's rulers? Or did it foreshadow the shallow intellectual fads and fancies that blow through Japan so frequently today? Also to be asked is whether what Itō and the other leaders had in mind was simply the Germanification of Japan, but I have written on these matters in another book and will not pursue them here.[39] For present purposes, the significant issue is the "German wind" that blew through Japan's armed forces—for this is what led to the dismissal of the French military advisers dispatched to Japan and Goblet's complaint to Yamagata.

Discord between Japan and France

From the waning years of the Tokugawa shogunate through the early Meiji period, Japan modeled the development of its army on France's. At least initially, the Meiji government simply inherited the military system developed through the close relationship that had developed between the shogunate and the French government.

Germany's rise as a military power, however, was obvious—especially after Prussia's victory over France in 1871 and the subsequent use of its military might to unify Germany. Soon a movement was under way within the Japanese army to make Germany the model for military affairs. In 1885, the government invited Klemens Wilhelm Jacob Meckel (1842–1906) of the Imperial German Army's general staff as an instructor at the Army War College, decisively signaling the Japanese Army's shift to the German model. The problem was the French officers employed in Japan as military advisers. It is not difficult to imagine why the French authorities might have felt that they had lost face when Meckel was invited.

French efforts to save face did not end with a simple protest from the French legation. Nakamura Takeshi's research gives a fascinating account of the deepening rift between Japan and France over the issue of the French military advisers. The following account is based on his work.[40]

In March 1888, with Meckel's contract coming to an end, the question of his replacement became an issue. The Army Ministry once again entrusted the selection to the German government. No sooner was this done than on April 11 the Army Ministry received yet another protest from the French legation. This time as well the Japanese brushed aside the French complaint, but there is little doubt that they were both shocked and disturbed by the depth of the French anger over this issue. On December 4, 1888, Prime Minister Kuroda Kiyotaka sent the following private instructions to Army Minister Ōyama Iwao:

> Since your ministry's employment of military advisers through the good offices of both the French and German governments is something that also has bearing upon our foreign relations, I am advising you privately to see to it that all of these officers, with the exception of technical personnel, are terminated upon the conclusion of their present contracts.

Bowing to the French pressure, the Japanese government decided not to extend the contracts of its present military advisers from either France or Germany or to employ any new advisers from either country. When the term of the contract with Meckel's successor Wildenbruch ended in April 1890, he was sent home.

In January 1889, however, just as Yamagata arrived in France, three French military advisers were on their way home from Japan. One of them had not even completed his contractual term, and though the Japanese government had requested that he stay until he had, the insulted French legation sent all three back to France at the same time. The French were playing for keeps now that they believed Japan had given up on France and was cozying up to Germany. The situation was such that Hara Takashi (Japanese prime minister from 1918–21, at the time serving with the Japanese legation in Paris) confessed that "relations between Japan and France are in complete disharmony."[41]

So this was the reason behind the cold demeanor that Foreign Minister Goblet showed to Yamagata. From the way that the Japanese government had handled matters so far, he probably believed that all French advisers would soon be purged from the Japanese Army. Yamagata had picked a poor time to visit France.

An awkward effort to mend things

It is unlikely, though, that Yamagata was completely unprepared for this eventuality. Presumably he approached his interview with foreign minister with a degree of resignation. As a member of the cabinet, Yamagata was aware of diplomatic drama at the Army Ministry.[42] Although no longer directly involved in administering the army, he was also a military man turned politician who had served as the first minister of the army and who contributed enormously to the institution of a nationwide system of military conscription. It is no exaggeration to say that the army was his home base.

That Yamagata, unlike Itō, chose to visit France before visiting Germany was probably for diplomatic reasons. It is reasonable, in other words, to assume that Yamagata intended to meet personally with the French leaders, sound out their feelings, and attempt to wash away the bad blood between Japan and France over the issue of military advisers.[43]

Even the formidable Yamagata, however, was taken aback by the brusque treatment he received at the hands of Goblet. In a letter to Matsukata Masayoshi in Japan, he wrote:

> Today I had a meeting with the foreign minister, which was influenced by the business about the sending home of the military advisers, as I was addressed in quite cold language regarding my request to inspect units of the French army. Later I am to meet with the minister of war, and am currently pondering what that might be like.[44]

Yamagata obviously sensed stormy weather ahead for his mission following his encounter with the foreign minister. One can imagine him mulling over how to deal with the minister of war. Five days later, a tense Yamagata met with Minister of War Charles Louis de Saulces de Freycinet (1828–1923). After they sat down, Freycinet said to him, "The people of my country have great affection for the people of your country. We would be happy to do anything we can to help you. That is, if our people can expect the same type of treatment in return from your country." At this point, Yamagata was probably thinking "Here we go . . ." He responded by saying, "I would like to have a word with you about why the contracts of the instructors were not renewed. Please bear with me for a moment and hear what I have to say." He continued,

With the support of your country, our army has now been able to train, in both Japan and France, a cadre of officers that it feels are ready to be assigned as instructors on a trial basis. For this reason, the government decided last year that contracts for all foreign instructors, from whatever country, would be terminated when the term of the contracts was fulfilled. I am giving you a plain account of the facts with regard to why the contracts were not renewed. I can only hope that your excellency will honor us by understanding our position in this matter.[45]

This was a labored explanation, since the government decision to suspend its employment of all foreign military advisers, as we saw in the private instructions from Kuroda to Ōyama mentioned earlier, had arisen for diplomatic reasons.

Freycinet's response to this awkward effort to mend things was something of an anticlimax. He expressed the opinion that there was no reason to doubt that French officers could continue to be a useful presence in Japan but added that "since the measures taken by your government were determined according to what it saw as the best interests of your nation, there is no reason for me to harbor the slightest dissatisfaction in this regard."[46] Yamagata must have been enormously relieved. At one point, he had probably resigned himself to the idea that his mission in France might be in vain. The war minister's generous attitude no doubt restored his spirits.

Once Yamagata was able to get on with the job at hand, the French authorities appear to have been quite helpful. In a letter to Japan, Yamagata described how his tour was proceeding:

I have been able to study at first hand the actual workings of local government offices, and in terms of military affairs I have toured and inspected an academy and a variety of other facilities; I have received extremely cordial treatment and the results are really considerably better than anticipated.[47]

When Yamagata met with Charles Floquet (1828–96), who served concurrently as France's prime minister and minister of the interior, he was told, "simply let me know what it is that you want and I will do whatever is in my power to arrange things for you" and was given introductions on the spot for inspection tours of the work being done at prefectural and municipal governmental offices.[48] Yamagata's worries had been ground-less, and his study tour began in earnest.

Popular hysteria

During Yamagata's visit, France was in the midst of a political crisis touched off by an antigovernment populist movement known as Boulangism. The movement centered on the charismatic general Georges Boulanger (1837–91).[49] He came to embody a number of powerful currents in contemporary French politics—popular discontent with the scandal-ridden Republican government, hostility to Germany, and a yearning for major reform. The result was his elevation into an iconic figure, the anticipated savior of the nation.

Riding on a wave of sentiment, Boulanger displayed an appetite for political power, running in by-elections in different constituencies with the slogan "Dissolve the National Assembly, revise the Constitution, create a new Constituent Assembly." Boulanger would be elected to office, only to resign and stand for election again elsewhere. It was an odd strategy, but it won him the support of the French masses. On January 27, the hysterical tide of Boulangism swept into Paris while Yamagata was there. In the election held that day Boulanger won a seat in the Chamber of Deputies by a landslide. That night, elated mobs pressed him to storm the presidential palace and effect a coup d'état. Paris was about to explode. Boulanger, however, rejected the coup d'état, and the movement rapidly deflated. Abandoned by the masses, Boulanger fled to Belgium and two years later killed himself with a pistol.

The French Third Republic had narrowly escaped a crisis that had threatened to destroy it. But the drama of Boulangism had exposed weaknesses in parliamentary democracy, which the sharp-eyed Yamagata certainly did not overlook. Pointing to the politically overheated masses and the reshuffling of the Floquet cabinet that came resulted, Yamagata expressed the opinion that "this is what comes out of the pernicious practice of leaving central power in the hands of a national assembly."[50] It is likely that Yamagata was more deeply impressed by the popular hysteria surrounding the French national assembly than by anything that he saw on his official inspection tours of local government. And his thoughts must have turned to the parliamentary system that was to be introduced in Japan the following year.

The Pink Pamphlet Incident

Yamagata left France on February 27 for a month of inspections in Italy, and then set out for Germany. Reaching Berlin on March 18, Yamagata and his entourage threw themselves into the study of the workings of local government that was the official purpose of their mission. They also toured the Reichstag, taking careful notes on the interior structure of the building.[51]

On April 16 they met with Bismarck, and on May 13 they were granted an audience with Kaiser Wilhelm II (1859–1941), who had just succeeded to the throne the previous year. In another year, the headstrong young kaiser would clash with the aging Bismarck and force him to resign. From that point, the kaiser himself would hold the reins of government and eventually lead Germany into World War I. Was it possible that Yamagata glimpsed how the kaiser would soon monopolize national affairs through his personal rule?

The highlight of Yamagata's time in Berlin was the personal lectures he received from Gneist. From May 3 to May 15, for two hours each day, Yamagata received private instruction from the noted jurist.

In contrast to the showy popularity of the Stein pilgrimage, a quieter Gneist pilgrimage was under way. Yamagata and others from Japan sought out Gneist's teachings. Among them were Prince Fushimi and Prince Komatsu of the imperial family, who received private instruction from Gneist from October 1885 to March 1886 and from January to September 1887, respectively.[52]

A copy of Prince Fushimi's notes was leaked to a Jiyūtō (Liberal Party) member and clandestinely published in October 1887 as *Seitetsu yume monogatari* (Tale of a dream of Western philosophy) just as Itō and others in the government were drafting the constitution under a veil of the strictest secrecy. This came to be known as the Pink Pamphlet Incident, from the color of the publication's cover, and it sent the government into a panic. At the time the government was deeply divided over the issue of renegotiation of the unequal treaties, and the popular rights movement was at fever pitch. The movement was subjecting the government to intense public questioning, and the coup of being able to publish the lecture notes, essentially a classified government document, and thus lift the veil somewhat on the process of drafting the constitution, was a tremendous boost to morale.

The pamphlet starts off in classic Gneistean style with the statement "I understand that Japan is planning on convening a national assembly, but you absolutely must not give it a voice in the three matters of diplomacy, military affairs, and the economy." This inflamed the popular rights activists. That same month, the "Sandai jiken kempaku sho" (Memorial on three great issues) was submitted by movement leaders to the Genrōin (Chamber of Elders). It was harshly critical of the government's policies on treaty revision, the land tax, and freedom of speech and assembly.

Seitetsu yume monogatari (Tale of a dream of Western philosophy)

With the antigovernment movement at a crescendo, the government, gripped by a sense of crisis, issued the Hōan Jōrei (Peace Preservation Ordinance of 1887) and set about suppressing the popular rights movement. The publication of *Seitetsu yume monogatari* was thus a major incident in the history of the establishment of the Meiji Constitution.

Gneist is usually mentioned in discussions of Meiji constitutional history almost solely for his haughtiness at the time of Itō's mission to Europe and for his role in the Pink Pamphlet Incident. As suggested in the previous chapter, however, there is reason to surmise that Gneist had a more fundamental relationship with the Meiji Constitution. Yamagata's contact with Gneist, as he followed in the footsteps of the imperial princes to Berlin, is revealing in this regard.

Creation of a political order from the bottom up

The record of the lectures Yamagata heard from Gneist is preserved in the archival materials left by Nakayama Kanrokurō, who accompanied Yamagata as his secretary.[53] Under the constraints of time, Gneist concentrated on a handful of topics, presenting Yamagata with an overview of Prussian historical progress, the ideal forms for local government and imperial household finances, and warnings of the danger of administrative courts and parliamentary politics. I will focus on Gneist's theories on local government and imperial household finances and consider their influence on Yamagata.

Gneist's first lectures, beginning on May 3, concerned local government. Yamagata, who was attempting to rethink the question of the best forms of local government and administration for Japan, had specifically requested this topic. Gneist had been informed in a letter from his student Mosse, then in Japan, of the newly implemented local autonomy laws (the Municipal Code and the Town and Village Code, both promulgated in 1889). Gneist started with some general remarks in which he said that those laws appeared to incorporate much of the German system, including the effort to give local autonomy to cities, towns, and villages regardless of size. But he pointed out that a possible problem with the new laws was that they seemed to have been devised almost exclusively for larger cities and towns.[54] According to Gneist, the essence of the local government system was to be sought in the smaller towns and villages:

> In German administration, the works of the nation are founded in the lowest order of the people; the beginning of the works lies in the lowest order. But in the French administration, the works begin in the upper order. To work from the lower order is by far the more difficult, but creates the strongest foundation.[55]

Gneist emphasized that "the foundation for the organization of the Japanese government should be local people, in other words, the lowest order." What he is discussing is the theory of how a national political system should be constituted. For him, the ideal way to construct this system is the bottom-up structure of Germany, not the top-down model of France.

Noteworthy is the "democratic" aspect of Gneist's lectures. He rejects bureacrat-led government from above and extols the virtues of locally based self-government. This, he argues, is what provides the foundation for national order and national power. What Gneist emphasizes is local voluntarism centering on landholders and local notables. Citing the maintenance of roads and bridges, preservation of public order, and charity to the poor as examples of the issues to be addressed, he advocates voluntaristic and unique administrative solutions carried out by local communities, with the town or village as the basic unit of administration.

Developmental dictatorship

As vigorous as he was in his advocacy of local autonomy, Gneist's thoughts on the national assembly are strongly conservative.

> It is much too early to convene a national assembly at the present time. Rather than reforming your government, you should seek to give it the freedom to speed your nation's progress and complete the development of its legal system.[56]

In a reversal of the antibureaucratic approach to local government he had expounded, Gneist is advocating an extreme form of bureaucratic rule. This is another characteristic of Gneist's lectures to Yamagata: approval of this role for the government and for giving it the strong powers necessary to carry it out. Gneist's position is that Japan is in a critical period of rapid development, during which the government should be given as much freedom as possible, rather than being constrained.

Gneist is not approving a dictatorial government alienated from popular sentiment. He goes on to speak passionately of the need for morality in government, saying that in carrying out its job of leading the people, government must set their minds at ease. If instead it oppresses them and establishes harsh punishments, it betrays its basic purpose.[57] The mission of government must be good government.

Gneist's conviction that "it is much too early to convene a national assembly" is evidence of his adamant rejection of popular participation in the affairs of state. His priority was on the efficient and expeditious implementation of policy by a government armed with strong executive powers. Gneist was consistent in preaching the efficacy of this type of government. His praise for town and village self-government in the context of local administration should also be understood in this perspective. He advocates that Japan follow the French rather than the German model of metropolitan and prefectural administration. In Germany, he explains, detailed legal provisions limit the power of the prefectural governors, whereas in France "prefectural governors are given ample authority to issue ordinances."[58]

Gneist's lectures to Yamagata are a classic argument for developmental dictatorship—administrative efficiency is to be achieved by giving the government vast powers. Japan now had a constitution and the following year would convene a national assembly, but Gneist continues to stress the failings of parliamentary politics and advocate the management of the country by an executive given broad freedom of action. The impression this left on Yamagata will be discussed later in this chapter.

The sphere of interests as essential to national independence
In the middle of May, Yamagata temporarily suspended his meetings with Gneist and set out for Vienna. He inspected the Austrian systems of local government and military organization, particularly the War College, and then Yamagata, like many Japanese visitors before him, contacted Stein. The teachings Stein conveyed to Yamagata are recorded in a document entitled "Sutei-shi ikensho" (The Opinions of Professor Stein), dated June 1889,[59] which has been examined in detail by Katō Yōko.[60] Katō makes the important point that the roots of the famous doctrine regarding lines of sovereignty and lines of influence that Yamagata developed in his policy speech as prime minister before the first session of the Imperial Diet are to be found in "The Opinions of Professor Stein," in which Stein makes the following remarks:

> No matter the country of which we speak, and no matter the reason, it uses military force to defend itself against its enemies, and the area it defends we call its 'sphere of power' (*Machtsphäre*). The political and military situation in foreign countries that bears upon the survival of this sphere of power, we call its 'sphere of interests' (*Interessensphäre*).[61]

The parallel with Yamagata's later speech is obvious, as when Yamagata states: "There is probably no country which does not possess a line of sovereignty and a line of interests . . . For a country to maintain its independence, simply defending its line of exclusive sovereignty cannot be said to be sufficient. The line of interests must also be protected."[62]

Another thought of Stein's later reflected in a Yamagata policy was that "the chief doctrine with regard to the protection of Japan's sphere of interests, now and in future, is the preservation of the status quo in Korea." Yamagata used this to sanction his efforts to link the independence of Korea with Japanese national interests.

It should also be noted that the sphere of interests concept that Stein passed on to Yamagata encompassed Stein's own unique theory of the state, which was rooted in a vision of international relations as driven by power politics. Stein saw the establishment and maintenance of a sphere of power and a sphere of interests as an essential condition for national independence. "A sphere of interests," he said, "must be created that is equivalent to or extends beyond the sphere of power.") He asserted that a country with an established sphere of interests acquires the right, in international law, to intervene to prevent another country's foreign policy encroachment into its sphere. In other words, the existence of a sphere of interests is a determining factor in foreign policy ("Without possessing some sort of sphere of interests, it cannot have a true foreign policy"). Stein adds that

> if a nation's political strategies are not clearly defined from the beginning and a fixed policy is not adopted and adhered to in determining the nation's actions, whether in peace or war, it will never win the respect of other nations. Nor will it be able to exert any power over other nations.[63]

In Stein's view, only by monopolizing a sphere of interests could a nation be recognized as an independent actor in the realm of international politics.

With previous Japanese students, Stein had focused almost exclusively on teaching the theory and mechanics of domestic administration. So it is interesting that with Yamagata, he took an entirely different tack and spoke of strategies for maintaining Japan's independence in international affairs.

The influence of "Opinions on the Diet"

Stein was not the only expert influencing Yamagata. Johann Freiherr von Chlumecky (1834–1924) was another Viennese who left an imprint on the development of the Meiji state.

Today, Chlumecky is little known even in his native Austria. During the period of the dual monarchy of Austro-Hungaria, however, he was a prominent political figure. He served in the Austrian government as minister of agriculture and minister of trade and, later, as vice-president and then president of the Austrian parliament. Ōishi Makoto has drawn attention to Chlumecky's role in establishing the Meiji constitutional system, securing him a permanent place in Japanese constitutional history. What follows is based on Ōishi's work.[64]

The story begins in December 1887, when Kaeda Nobuyoshi, a member of the Genrōin, visited Vienna on the "Stein pilgrimage." Kaeda befriended Chlumecky, then vice-president of the parliament, and was influenced by him. In his communications with Japan, Kaeda sang Chlumecky's praises. He also commissioned a position paper from Chlumecky that caused "an about-face" (Ōishi) in the process of formulating the Law of the Houses for the Imperial Diet, which was taking place concurrently with the drafting of the constitution.

Johann von Chlumecky

Chlumecky offers a host of recommendations in "Kokkai iken" (Opinions on the Diet).[65] Especially noteworthy are the following: (1) appointment of the president of the Diet by the emperor, (2) strengthening of the punitive powers of the president of the Diet, and (3) legal codification of legislative procedure.

Based on this advice, the leaders of the Meiji government dropped the selection of the president through public election that had been part of earlier drafts of the constitution. They also made detailed provisions in the Law of the Houses for sanctions against members, including suspension and expulsion. The latter were adopted in the final version of the law, which also specified that each house of the Diet would put forward a limited number of candidates for the post of president, with the final selection and appointment made by imperial decree.

The legal codification of legislative procedure—in other words, constraints on the Diet's power to establish its own house rules—was established policy among the Japanese leaders. But it was obviously of great significance to them to receive the seal of approval from a prominent European parliamentarian. So Chlumecky's advice left its mark on both the Meiji Constitution and the Law of the Houses.[66]

Chlumecky's papers are preserved in the Chlumecky Family Archive in Brno, in the Czech Republic. I visited the archive to see whether there were any materials pertaining to Japan in it. What I found was a total of forty-three letters from Japanese correspondents, including Itō Hirobumi.[67]

The letter from Itō was dated November 24, 1888. It recounts how impressed Itō was by Chlumecky's position paper and expresses gratitude for the advice given, based on Chlumecky's long years of practical experience as vice-president of the house of representatives. Itō confirms that it has provided a most profound and useful perspective in the shaping of Japan's parliamentary system. His letter thus is a valuable indicator of the impact of Chlumecky's paper on the leaders of the Meiji government. Itō also writes, "It is one of my greatest regrets that I was unable to have the pleasure of meeting you when I was in Europe." This gives an obvious sense of the high esteem in which Chlumecky was held by the most important figures in the Japanese government.

Letter from Itō Hirobumi to Johann von Chlumecky, dated 24 November 1888. Only the beginning and the conclusion are reproduced here.

Chlumecky's practical wisdom

Such was the context in which Yamagata requested an interview with Chlumecky. And something came of that meeting. In a letter from Yamagata to Chlumecky, dated August 13, 1889, and sent from New York City after Yamagata had left Europe, there is mention of a new opinion paper that Yamagata has received from Chlumecky. Yamagata calls it the most important gift he will bring home to Japan from his time in Vienna.

A second letter from Yamagata is dated October 13, immediately after his return to Japan. In it, Yamagata writes, "The position paper you have so graciously given me I have since had opportunity to read in its entirety and in it I have found many valuable observations. I must express my deepest appreciation for your kindness in preparing it and giving it to me."

What the contents of this second Chlumecky position paper are is unknown; unfortunately, I have been unable to locate any such document. There is, however, another document of interest: "Ōchirii kokkai daiichi fukuchō fuon Kurumetsuki-shi danwa" (Conversation with First Vice-

President von Chlumecky of the Austrian parliament). Dated May 27, 1889, it records a meeting that Yamagata had that day at the Chlumecky residence.[68]

Chlumecky covers a wide range of topics with Yamagata, but everything he says involves detailed, practical administrative guidance on government policy geared toward the anticipated opening of the Diet. The following are the more important points: (1) create "friends of the government" among the representatives; (2) to accomplish this, fine-tune the electoral system and leave a period of time between the elections and the convening of the Diet, using it to win over as many representatives as possible; (3) seek out factional bosses among the representatives who can serve as conduits to the government; (4) work at making sure that the members selected for the presidency and committee chairmanships are ones over whom the government has influence; (5) prepare a full legislative agenda, since leaving the representatives without anything to do "will be the beginning of them plotting mischief"; (6) establish detailed rules of legislative procedure; (7) give disciplinary authority to the president of the Diet, not to the representatives; (8) give the government the right to demand that interpellations by members be submitted in written form; (9) see to it that the government can repeatedly exercise the power to suspend or dissolve the assembly.

The first three points are measures to keep the Diet from turning against the government. Points four onward are means of ensuring government control of the Diet through political strategy (4 and 5) and legal structures (6 through 9). By undertaking these measures, the government could hope to tame and control the Diet. In Chlumecky's view the government must "be in collusion with the Diet" but must also work to ensure "that the 'reins' of the Diet are always firmly in the government's hands."

Chlumecky's advice was immensely enlightening to Yamagata, who was sharply attuned to the issue of the yet-to-be-convened Diet. Impressed, Yamagata handed Chlumecky copies of Japan's recently promulgated constitution and supplementary laws and requested him to write an opinion paper on them. Yamagata's request met with a favorable reply from Chlumecky, and when Yamagata eventually returned to Japan, he carried a paper by Chlumecky as a souvenir of his European tour. This second opinion paper (after the one given to Kaeda) is now lost, but the record of

Yamagata's meeting with Chlumecky probably hints at what it contained. Chlumecky's practical wisdom was precisely what Yamagata had been praying for.

On June 1, 1889, Yamagata and company left Vienna for St. Petersburg. They returned to Berlin on June 13 for more instruction from Gneist before leaving Berlin again on June 28 and then passed through Belgium on their way to England, which they reached on July 13. After three weeks in England, the party crossed the Atlantic to the United States, where they spent a month traversing the continent, arriving at last in San Francisco. The available materials are inadequate for a clear picture of the research Yamagata conducted in Great Britain or America. It would appear that he and his companions continued to focus on the workings of local government, as is suggested by a field trip to the London city council, but unfortunately further details are not forthcoming.[69]

On September 11, Yamagata and his party set sail from San Francisco. Their safe return to Japan on October 2 concluded Yamagata's tour.

3. The Other Constitutional Investigation

Trouble ahead

Yamagata's journey was, in a sense, the other constitutional investigation. It is true that its official purpose, as Yamagata repeatedly stated, was to inspect local government administration and military organization, and he made a point of visiting a number of such facilities at each stop on his trip, lending a willing ear to the opinions of resident experts. But we have seen that Yamagata's investigations went beyond the stated mandate.

Yamagata's interests spanned every aspect of national government, from dealing with a national assembly to foreign policy. His research can be seen to revolve around the overarching theme of how government should be approached after the opening of the Imperial Diet. Yamagata's European tour was unquestionably for research on the constitution in the deeper sense of the fundamental structure of the nation. In the following pages, I will flesh out the evidence for this.

First, let us return to the promulgation of the Meiji Constitution. As noted, Yamagata was not in Japan for this historic event, news of which reached him in Paris. In the midst of a banquet at the Japanese legation to celebrate the event a telegram arrived from Japan announcing that the constitution's promulgation and was displayed to the assembled guests.[70] Far from Japan though he may have been, Yamagata must have found himself caught up in the festivities. He lost little time in writing to Yoshikawa Akimasa, a colleague in Japan: "I share the joy at the news of the success of this great event, the promulgation of our Constitution."[71] Yet at the same time he looked askance at those who were overly enraptured by it and added, "There is no way of knowing what heavy responsibilities and many troubles await us both in future."[72]

Even at the first news of the promulgation, Yamagata retained a sober demeanor, for what flashed into his mind was less the glory of the constitution's birth than the difficulties that lay ahead for the new governmental and political order it had brought into being. His experiences on the remainder of his voyage only confirmed and consolidated this tendency in his thinking. To appreciate this, we must understand Yamagata's impressions of Europe.

The shadows of Western civilization

This was Yamagata's second trip to Europe. Early in the Meiji period, in 1869 and 1870, he spent more than a year on a study tour of the Western nations, focused primarily on France and Prussia. Like many others, Yamagata was clearly overawed by Western civilization and by the gulf separating it from Japan. For some time thereafter, he would inquire of his companions, "Are we going to be all right? Are we up to this?"[73]

When eighteen years later Yamagata again set foot on European soil, what met his eyes was the undiminished gap between the two civilizations. On his previous visit, Yamagata had been astonished by the air of prosperity in Paris, where Baron Haussman's plan for the renovation of the city was well under way. Revisiting the city nearly two decades later only made him feel Europe's differences with Japan more acutely:

> Compared with the time of my previous visit here the way things have changed, the pace of cultural development, the prospect of such innovation in every field, all make me painfully aware of what a terribly long road we have ahead of us.[74]

Yamagata's lament is reminiscent of Ōkubo's despair during the Iwakura Embassy.

For Yamagata, though, the West had ceased to be a model to be followed without question. In Paris, he had encountered the political unrest of the Boulangist movement and the collapse of a government as the result of parliamentary politics. Yamagata's assessment was that "this is what comes out of the pernicious practice of leaving central power in the hands of a national assembly." His apprehension with regard to parliamentary politics was only deepened and strengthened by what he observed elsewhere in Europe.

> In the course of my tour, I have witnessed at first hand the situation in the upper and lower houses of twelve assemblies, and their electoral methods, and from this I can tell you that of course restrained and mature discourse wins no applause; the influence of the noisy mob of radicals who are gradually making names for themselves by spouting their empty-headed theories appears to be increasing in tandem with the progress of civilization.[75]

Yamagata's gaze is fixed less on the glories of Western civilization than on its shadows. Not every aspect of "civilization" is worthy of emulation. With regard to the parliamentary system, Yamagata states bluntly that

> parliamentary government is held to be the fruit of civilization and the ideal of the politician, but its abuses and the ways in which it can trivialize the affairs of state are truly deplorable.[76]

Parliamentary government was indeed regarded as a symbol of Western civilization, but Yamagata feared that it might lead to the overthrow of the state. With Gneist he shared concern that it might be too soon for Japan to be convening a national assembly. He warned his colleagues that "extrapolating from the current situation in Japan, I think the establishment of the Diet will produce many more problems than anticipated."[77]

The more Yamagata traveled the more he viewed the West as a negative example. "The state of affairs in Europe is one of extreme unrest,"[78] he writes in a letter to Mutsu Munemitsu, one of many similar reports he sent from his travels. For him, it was important not to unquestioningly sing the praises of Western civilization but instead to "accurately perceive the situation in present-day Europe, and carefully reflect upon the source of its ills."[79] Yamagata saw the source of Europe's ills in "the system of laissez-faire." When news reached him from Japan that there was a move-ment afoot to revise the Ordinance on Public Assembly (Shūkai Jōrei), one of Japan's internal security laws, Yamagata immediately voiced his oppo-sition to this idea:

> While it may be the case that the present Ordinance on Public Assembly has not achieved a proper balance with either the Publication or Newspaper Ordinances, if its restraints were removed a hundred abuses would immedi-ately arise, and could develop into an uncontrollable force.[80]

Yamagata's fear was that if the ordinance was revised and relaxed the pop-ular rights movement might flare up again, gaining a momentum that might become impossible to control. "Why not," he proposed instead, "subject the political parties to even more stringent controls?"[81] He had seen that the countries of Europe approached political activity with too much of a laissez-faire attitude and as a result all of them were experienc-ing difficulties in dealing with it. In France "abuses by the newspapers have grown so egregious that the establishment of an ordinance [control-ling them] has become necessary."[82]

In Yamagata's eyes, laissez-faire was an evil infecting Western civiliza-tion, a pathology from which Japan should protect itself. He was also hear-ing "bitter remarks concerning the European situation" from the powerful figures in Europe who were having to deal with the issues of parliamen-tary politics and who were "counseling vigilance and caution when they speak of our nation's future."[83] Yamagata's skeptical attitude toward the political mores of the West appears to have hardened into an unshakable conviction.

Countermeasures against the "mob of noisy radicals"

The wave of Western political enlightenment was nevertheless steadily beat-ing against the shores of Japan. While overseas, Yamagata received a con-stant steam of communications from his subordinates, chiefly in the Home Ministry, giving him blow-by-blow reports of developments in the local assemblies and the political parties across the nation. His reaction was to denigrate the popular rights activists as being "like a bunch of madmen running about aimlessly."[84] He lamented, moreover, that if the situation in the assemblies "grows any more heated, it will end in complete and utter mayhem."[85]

If things went on in this vein, Yamagata foresaw that the convening of the Diet might simply put Japanese politics, like those of Europe, at the mercy of "a mob of noisy radicals" making their nest within the national assembly. Deeply concerned, Yamagata developed various countermeasures. One of them was more stringent control of the popular parties using the internal security laws, but he also offered the following proposals.

The first was to bolster Japan's system of local government. While highly critical of parliamentary politics in Europe, Yamagata was impressed by the moderation he saw in the local assemblies: "We must do our utmost to cultivate a similar atmosphere within our own local assemblies."[86] He wrote this after touring Italy and Germany, and when he later visited the London city council he was also full of praise for the "genial and harmonious" appearance of the members and the "completely matter-of-fact manner of the proceedings."[87]

In contrast, the prefectural assemblies in Japan had been turned into political battlegrounds by the activists of the popular rights movement. Even before he went to Europe, Yamagata had argued eloquently for the need to convert local government from a stage upon which idealistic political activists "debated the great issues of how to govern the land" into a place where "mature, reliable gentlemen" set about the practical tasks of local administration.[88] His European tour only deepened this conviction.

His second proposal was for the creation of a powerful cabinet. In a letter to Inoue Kaoru dated March 21, he writes:

> Now that the overall course for our Empire has been established, our first priority must be ways to make the unity and cooperation of the cabinet even more solid and unshakable. There is also no better policy for establishing a long-range, hundred-year plan to maintain the Empire in perpetuity.[89]

That said, he declares that "the key to administering even the most brilliant laws and golden rules lies in the men administering them." Even an everlasting covenant, such as the constitution, is useless if mistakenly applied. It is administered by "men"; it is they who determine whether it lives or dies. And foremost among these "men," for him, are the members of the cabinet, who must approach their work with a unity of purpose and spirit of cooperation.

Yamagata's ideal "men"

Yamagata's thoughts in his letter to Inoue Kaoru were only interim observations made during his study tour. But they nicely distill the essence of Yamagata's experience of the West and convey it openly and unambiguously to Inoue, who along with Itō was one of the most powerful and stalwart supporters of the drive toward constitutional government. Since we have covered what that experience was in some detail, there is no need to repeat it here. It is worth touching briefly, however, upon what might at first seem a minor episode recounted in the letter.

After leaving France, Yamagata next visited Italy, where he was reunited with Sufu Kōhei, who was serving in the Japanese legation as an attaché. Sufu's father was Sufu Masanosuke, who had displayed great shrewdness in engineering the reforms carried out in the Chōshū domain in the waning years of the Tokugawa shogunate. The younger Sufu asked Yamagata, an eminent leader from his ancestral home, to help him obtain leave to return home to visit his mother, who was on her deathbed.[90] Sympathetic, Yamagata immediately includes a strongly worded request on Sufu's behalf in his letter to Inoue, asking Inoue to influence the foreign minister for the sought-after leave. In it he writes of how Sufu, who lost his father at an early age (Masanosuke committed seppuku on the eve of the shogunate's first punitive campaign against Chōshū) and is now confronted with the news of his mother's final illness, "cannot rest easy ten thousand miles away" and solicits Inoue's "sympathy for the love between parent and child." He then continues in an even more impassioned vein:

> And if, having read civilized books and learned civilized ways, anyone should start blathering nonsense, questioning why we should persist in such foolish Asian customs, I implore you, in your wisdom, to demolish their arguments with a single stroke.

What particularly struck Yamagata in Sufu's concern for his dying mother was that in it he saw the embodiment of Japan's traditional virtues, a bulwark against the rising tide of Western civilization. Sufu represented the type of men upon whom Yamagata pinned his hopes for the future of the nation.

At the end of his letter, moreover, Yamagata expresses his condolences over the assassination of Mori Arinori: .

> On the very day of the promulgation of the constitution, Mori encountered this unexpected tragedy and has passed from this world. I am truly filled with the deepest regret. I pray that you remember the greatest enemy is a lack of vigilance, and will pay careful attention to your own safety.

We can only wonder if Mori's unfortunate end overlapped in Yamagata's mind with his concern for the fate of the nation. Mori had, from the time of the Iwakura Embassy, made a name for himself as a radical proponent of Westernization—he was certainly someone who had "read civilized books and learned civilized ways." Perhaps the fact that someone like Mori had fallen victim to terrorism caused Yamagata to wonder about the future of the Meiji state, which also eagerly sought "the fruits of civilization." Certainly there is nothing strange in thinking that this calamity on the day the constitution was promulgated must have struck Yamagata as an inauspicious sign that perhaps the next victim of the assassin's knife would be the nation founded upon this constitution seen by so many as the very emblem of civilization.

In any case, Yamagata returned from Europe with a private resolve: though the constitution itself might now be an established fact, "men" could do whatever was in their power to diminish its effects.

The Meiji Constitution Seen from Abroad

The new constitution makes its overseas debut

In July 1889, Kaneko Kentarō, who played an active role in drafting the Meiji Constitution and its supplementary laws as an assistant to Itō Hirobumi, set off on a study tour to Europe and the United States. Its purpose, in anticipation of the convening of the Diet in 1890, was to investigate "the actualities of constitutional government . . . from the internal organization of the parliaments of these nations to their procedural rules, the legal jurisdiction over parliamentary buildings, the right to police their interiors, preparation of minutes of parliamentary proceedings," etc.[1] For a year, Kaneko would investigate the legislative systems of Europe and the United States from a practical administrative perspective.

Kaneko Kentarō

Kaneko's voyage had another important mission. He carried with him English versions of Japan's new constitution and of *Commentaries on the Constitution*, the official interpretation of the document, edited by Itō Hirobumi. Kaneko was to elicit the opinions of politicians and scholars on these two texts in the countries he visited. The Meiji Constitution had been crafted as a symbol of Japan's status as a civilized nation, the culmination of the national quest since the time of the Iwakura Embassy to join the ranks of the other civilized nations. The question of whether or not the constitution would be accepted by international society—Western society —was a crucial touchstone.[2] Kaneko's mission was thus in part to debut the new constitution before a Western audience.

Kaneko made the rounds of a number of the figures who have become familiar names in this book: Gneist and Jhering in Germany and Stein and Chlumecky in Austria. In England, he called on some of the most noted scholars of the day, from Herbert Spencer to constitutional expert Albert Venn Dicey (1835–1922) and ethicist Henry Sidgwick (1838–1900). And in the United States he met with Oliver Wendell Holmes (1841–1935), later chief justice of the Supreme Court, and others.

Details on the reactions of these eminent Westerners to the Meiji Constitution are recorded in Kaneko's journal of his travels, which has recently been republished through the efforts of Ōbuchi Kazunori.[3] Salient points from their assessments follow.

"A truly wise approach"

Almost everyone to whom Kaneko presented the constitution noted the strong influence of the German constitution. The Englishmen made this particularly clear, though without criticism for not having adopted a British-style constitutional monarchy. Dicey, best known for having made the English "rule of law" a cornerstone of constitutional scholarship, expressed the opinion that in modeling their constitution on the German one the Japanese had taken "a truly wise approach."[4]

> Germany is a country whose fortunes are presently on the rise, and upon whom the greatest hopes may be placed for the future. Moreover, in today's world there are few monarchs who possess authority as great as that of the German kaiser. It may be that if you desire to maintain the monarchic form of government in perpetuity, you cannot but give the emperor vast sovereign powers. The British monarchy is peculiar to Britain, and not something easily emulated in other lands.[5]

Dicey supports Japan's decision to model itself on Germany, a rising power with strong imperial powers, rather than on Britain, whose institutions are the result of a lengthy and unique historical process that makes it difficult for other countries to use them as a model. The uniqueness of the British monarchy to which he refers is what has been called "the king in parliament"—a limited monarchy with authority centered on parliament rather than the throne.

Sidgwick went even further than Dicey in rejecting the utility of the British model of parliamentary government. "At present, he says, "constitutional monarchies across Europe are in decline, gradually devolving into the sort of parliamentary politics practiced in Britain." By contrast, he saw that the Japanese constitution guards against such a decline in its articles 63, 67, and 71. I am, Sidgwick said, "in agreement with the way you have restricted the very important powers of the Diet with regard to budgetary proposals."[6] Sidgwick would later send Kaneko an even lengthier statement advising Japan "to defend against the tendency, as exists in Britain, for a constitutional monarchy to shade into parliamentarianism."[7]

Parliamentarianism as an aspect of the Meiji Constitution

Some commentators, however, found in the Meiji Constitution the spirit of English constitutionalism. André Jean Louis Lebon (1858–1938), who met with Kaneko in Paris, drew attention to this:

> I believe it is true that the Japanese constitution was completely based on German doctrine. Yet if one really investigates its spirit, it contains within it a considerable measure of English constitutionalism.[8]

Lebon perceptively reveals aspects of parliamentarianism embedded within the Meiji Constitution by pointing out that the power to make laws does not reside with the emperor alone but always requires the consent of the Diet and that such consent is also necessary for increases in military expenditures and other budgetary matters.

Englishman William Reynell Anson (1843–1914) goes even further. He acknowledges the German aspects of the Meiji Constitution, saying, "The spirit [of the Japanese constitution] is to vest the rights of sovereignty completely with the emperor, giving the monarch control over all affairs of state. This is why people say that the Japanese constitution has learned from German doctrine." He adds, however, that "what I would like to argue is that the spirit of the Japanese constitution can be made completely compatible with the basic principles of the English constitution."[9]

Anson's assessment was based less on a purely legal argument than on his insight into the necessary tendencies of constitutional government. He states flatly, "It is probably the case with any government that, once a parliamentary system has been adopted, it cannot manage to govern by taking a stance aloof from and superior to the political parties.[10] That party governments had not been formed in Germany was solely due to Bismarck's political leadership. Once Bismarck passed on, Anson predicted, even Germany would not be able to avoid this development. According to Anson, once a constitutional government had been established, the road toward party politics was inevitable. His counsel was that what was important was to make this process as smooth as possible.

Historiography as a national enterprise

The commentators may have been divided in terms of emphasizing either the German or British aspects of the Meiji Constitution, but they were united in giving the document itself high marks. The question was what would happen next. In 1876, the Ottoman Empire in Turkey had established the first constitution outside the sphere of western European culture, but it did not function well and was suspended only a year later. Popular opinion in Europe and America was rife with the cynical assessment that no matter how modern its constitution, Japan was likely to follow in the wake of Turkey.

Stein, however, preached the value of historiography in eliminating this Western prejudice. "Surely, he wrote, "there must be a history behind the establishment of this constitution in Japan. If you do not accompany the constitution with an account of the history intimately related to it, then people are likely to simply view it in the same way as the Turkish constitution." Stein says that "history is undoubtably the most valuable and indispensable science for understanding the founding of the nation and the ancestry of its people," and asks rhetorically, "Without knowing the history of Japan, how can the independence and majesty of the imperial house be upheld?" Stein's advice was to make historiographical research a national enterprise.[11]

Herbert Spencer, the proponent of Social Darwinism, and Oliver Wendell Holmes, the star of American jurisprudence, also stressed the importance of history. Spencer's advice was along the same lines as Stein's: With the convening of the Diet only a year away, he argued that Japan's most urgent task was "to compile a history of Japan for translation and publication in the European languages."[12]

With regard to understanding national laws and institutions as the product of a country's history and culture, Spencer's concept of social evolution scarcely differed from the German historical school of jurisprudence. If it was demonstrated that the newly written constitution was not a complete departure from Japan's history, then the first hurdle in the introduction of a constitutional system would be cleared. This would leave the second hurdle, that of domesticating the constitutional system, of which Spencer wrote:

> With its history and customs as a foundation, Japan must at the same time adopt the constitutional thought of Europe and America, and adapt its traditional form of government to European constitutionalism.[13]

This "gradual conservatism" was the key point of Spencer's doctrine of social evolution—though in his vision it would culminate in "small government" founded on the principle of laissez-faire,[14] According to him, "the affairs of the government shall gradually diminish, leaving the people, as individuals, to manage their own affairs."[15] Spencer's ideal of a radical diminution of the functions of government was likely something that did not yet resonate with Kaneko's experience.

An exquisite blend of Japan and the West

Holmes offered opinions similar to Spencer's:

> The thing that makes me happiest about this constitution is that its roots are grounded in Japan's ancient history, institutions, and customs, though the logic of Western jurisprudence has been applied to embellishing it.[16]

Kaneko presented Holmes with the *Commentaries on the Constitution*, which in addition to citations from Western sources, made liberal reference to the *Kojiki*, *Man'yōshū*, and other Japanese classics. For Holmes, this was evidence that "the Japanese constitution could not but take its shape from Japan's history and its established institutional practices." At the same time, this constitution also guaranteed "a form of government that not even the emperor can willfully alter" and "in which the people also gain the right to participate in government."[17] The essence of constitutionalism—limitations on the rights of the sovereign and popular participation in government—was firmly upheld. While praising the Japanese constitution as the product of an exquisite blend of Japan's historical traditions with Western constitutionalism, Holmes offered this advice:

> After the Diet is convened this year, I hope that Japan's politicians, basing themselves on the spirit of this constitution, will in governing also study the ancient laws and customs, and using the nation's historical precedents as a standard, will gradually apply the logic of Western constitutionalism. In any case, as I have said before, European and American jurisprudence is in a state of flux, without fixed principles, completely dominated by the political realities and conditions pertaining in each country, and thus extremely volatile.[18]

Holmes fervently hoped that Western parliamentary politics would be established in Japan and believed that such an example would make a major contribution to Western jurisprudence. This was because the Japanese experience would assist in a broader examination of the legal principles making constitutional government possible. Holmes concluded by saying,

> I am firmly convinced that bringing an understanding of Japanese history and customs to the Western scholarly community would not only be in the interests of Japan, but would also serve to advance universal knowledge.[19]

"Truly gratifying"

That the Meiji Constitution won favorable reviews from all of the experts was not solely because of the quality of the document itself. *Commentaries on the Constitution*, carefully crafted to navigate the current of historicism sweeping Western scholarship at the time, contributed immensely to the constitution's widespread acceptance.[20] The presentation of the text of the constitution and the commentaries as a matching set was instrumental in winning an assessment from a number of Western experts that the constitution was a unique document authentically grounded in Japanese history and not merely an imitation of either the German or English models.

Upon hearing Kaneko's report following his return to Japan, Itō took satisfaction that things had gone according to his plan:

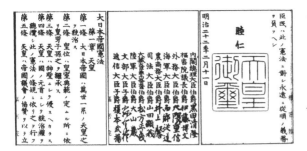

A portion of the official text of the Constitution of the Empire of Japan, showing the signature and seal of the emperor, the signatures of the cabinet ministers, and the first five articles.

From the time you left the country until your return I have been in my villa in Odawara, privately worrying both day and night about what the reaction of Western politicians and constitutional scholars would be, but having heard your detailed report I am much relieved. Not only to have escaped criticism, but to hear such praise is truly gratifying. Tomorrow I will hasten to Tokyo, request an audience with the emperor, and ask to be relieved of my responsibilities with regard to the drafting of the constitution.[21]

Constitutional gradualism

Even before dispatching Kaneko to Europe, Itō had written to Stein in Vienna asserting that the constitution was "in every respect, not merely an imitation of this or that other constitution" but "from beginning to end a completely Japanese affair."[22] He was keenly aware, without any Westerner pointing it out to him, that to be acknowledged in Europe and America, the constitution had to be "Japanese."

But what was it that Itō claimed to be "Japanese" about the document? Was this merely a matter of its surface historical trappings? Or did Itō think something more profoundly and authentically Japanese permeated its text? Thorough answers to these questions await further research, but it would be a mistake to conclude that Itō was merely trying to legitimize a superficially "constitutionalist" constitution that in fact reserved sweeping powers for the emperor and an almost mystical reverence for "the national essence" (*kokutai*). The evidence presented in this book confirms, rather, that Itō directed his "constitutional charisma" toward limiting the political prerogatives of the emperor and gradually implementing a parliamentary system.

As the Iwakura Embassy learned through experience, the logic of Western civilization was, above all, one of power. To join the ranks of the civilized nations required, through the constitution, a continual mobilization of the political energies of the people and their incorporation into the process of national government. It was therefore necessary to guarantee the parliamentary system as a forum for popular participation in politics and as a stimulus to the political energies of the nation-state.

This, however, was a double-edged sword. In Europe, Itō developed an appreciation for the difficulties of managing a parliamentary system. He sought, as a result, to develop a variety of institutional safeguards to ensure that the transplantation to Japan of these organs of civilization would not destroy the immune system of their host. The political energies of the people must be channeled in an orderly way. His basic lesson from Stein had been that the key to constitutional government lay in the balance of the three organs of government: the sovereign, the legislative, and the executive. This required the meticulous arrangement of a variety of institutions so that no one of the three could run riot politically.

This was why Itō gave such careful thought to the initially broad restraints on the powers of the Diet, the variety of measures to transform the emperor into a constitutional monarch, and the legal framework for the modernization of Japan's administrative system. It was the totality of these institutions constituting the national structure that Itō was probably referring to when he spoke of the Meiji Constitution as "a completely Japanese affair." Although it shared its ideals of civilization with the West, the constitution displayed a great deal of creative ingenuity in the methods and forms through which this Japanese-style constitutional state was to be expressed.

Initially, this did not go beyond defining the skeleton of the system. The practice of constitutional government that would flesh out the state, and the precedents it would establish were as yet unknown. The spirit of constitutional government would have to be gradually infused into the newly created framework of national institutions through ongoing political practice. As constitutional government matured, the institutions would change. For Itō, the constitutional order was not definitively established by the promulgation of the constitution; it would have to continually evolve in pace with historical developments. This, in the parlance of the times, was gradualism.

Kido and Ōkubo had discovered gradualism as a key concept for the importation of "civilization" and developed an argument for constitutional government around it after their return to Japan from the Iwakura Embassy. Itō, in turn, successfully guarded this gradualist approach through the crossfire of the memorials on the constitution submitted by Ōkuma Shigenobu and by Iwakura Tomomi and Inoue Kowashi and eventually launch the Meiji ship of state into international waters equipped with all the institutions of modern constitutional government.

A return to the spirit of the Meiji Restoration

It would not, however, be smooth sailing. As Itō pushed forward with his plans for constitutional government, Yamagata dragged his heels. The intense rivalry between these two men in their later years did much to define the Meiji constitutional order, but their skirmishing began earlier, during the process of drafting the constitution. Yamagata worked to create a network of constraints, using both personnel and institutions, to inhibit the development of the Meiji state as envisioned by Itō and succeeded in making them part of its very structure. It is worth pointing out some of the aspects of the Meiji state that were Yamagata's legacy.

In contrast to Itō's concept of the evolution of national institutions, Yamagata was adamant in seeking an unchanging national structure. This was a profound reflection of the differing mentalities of the two men, which the following anecdote emphasizes.

Every year Yamagata vacationed at his villa Murin'an in Kyoto. On each visit he would make a pilgrimage to Ryōzen, a shrine on a mountain in the Higashiyama district of the city dedicated to the activists who fell in the years of conflict leading up to the Meiji Restoration, to pray at the graves of his former comrades. He continued this custom to quite an advanced age, until his aides said that they would make the climb in his place while he offered his prayers from the foot of the mountain. Yamagata replied, "No, as long as I can still stand on my own two feet I won't be able to rest easy unless I go myself." And so, "he set off up that steep slope, climbing five paces and resting, climbing ten paces and stopping again to rest, until finally he was able to complete his pilgrimage."[23] Citing this episode, George Akita and Itō Takashi see in the elderly Yamagata "an extremely strong compulsion to protect the things that he had striven to create, not simply from external threats, but from internal disorder."[24]

It would seem that sentiments of this kind also drove him earlier in life, during the period covered by this book. When word of the constitution's promulgation reached him in Europe, Yamagata called the event "the third Restoration" (dai san no ishin)[25] Yet he did not use the term ishin in its original sense of "renovation" or "renewal."[26] Instead, he employed it to urge a return to the historical experience of the Meiji Restoration, which had attained mythic proportions. Yamagata's intent was to defend the great work of the Restoration from the internal disorder that he believed would result from the establishment of the constitution. His thought would constantly return to the myth of the Restoration. In this respect, he stands in marked contrast to Itō, whose thinking was evolutionary, and open to the future.

Unity and Harmony

The policies Yamagata envisioned for his "third Restoration" were the system of local government and the cabinet system touched on at the end of the last chapter.

Yamagata stated in a speech he made after returning to Japan from Europe and the United States that the significance of local government was to be found in combating the expanding power of the political parties. At the time, the local scene was becoming "an arena for political disputes." According to Yamagata,

> This stems from the fact that people are confusing local administration with central government, forgetting the public interests of the cities, towns, and villages and rushing about like madmen debating the great issues of the day.[27]

What Yamagata hoped to see from local self-government was not indulgence in a lot of abstract political argument but the fostering through participation in local affairs of "loyal subjects" who would serve as the cornerstones of the national interest: "Good citizens do not allow themselves to be distracted by public opinion, to the neglect of their true occupations."[28] Yamagata was seeking to rid the public sphere as much as possible of political debate and partisan conflict. "If," he said, "our legal system is not based upon a spirit of harmony and cooperation among the people, it will be impossible to administer it securely."[29]

Yamagata saw the essence of the cabinet system, meanwhile, as residing in a spirit of "unity and cooperation" among the men shouldering the burden of responsibility for governing the nation. What Yamagata devised to manifest that spirit was a revision of the Cabinet Law.

In December 1889, Yamagata formed his first cabinet as prime minister. He had accepted his appointment and the order to form a cabinet on one condition: a reform in the Cabinet Law that increased the autonomy of the individual ministers. This was a major alteration in the fundamental organizing principles of the cabinet. Previously, the issuance of an ordinance or directive from one of the government ministries had to be co-signed by the responsible minister and the prime minister. Yamagata's reform eliminated the need for the prime minister's signature. This change dispensed with the idea of a strong prime minister playing the role of chief executive in controlling the administrative machinery of the government and setting the course for national policy. Now, each cabinet minister would have a specific sphere of duties and be directly responsible to the emperor for the execution of those duties. This, presumably, would correct the dissension and wrangling that had plagued earlier cabinets over the issue of treaty revision and bring to the fore the idea, as a means of restoring "unity and cooperation," that the cabinet was empowered by and served the emperor.[30]

Creating loyal subjects

The character and the activities of individuals were crucial to the development of Yamagata's thinking on the cabinet.

> It is men who control it [government]. It is men who determine and implement it. And men alone have the power to elicit good results from it. Everything depends upon whether or not there is unity and harmony in the cabinet.[31]

What Yamagata demanded from the men who led the nation as members of the cabinet was that they set aside internal dissension and address the affairs of state "in unity and cooperation."

Yamagata's concept of order, extending from local government at the base to the cabinet at the top, consistently centered on the human factor. His "men" were good citizens or, perhaps more accurately, good subjects: apolitical and above all, loyal. To inculcate this spirit of the loyal imperial subject, Yamagata had the Imperial Rescript on Education drafted and issued in October 1890.[32] Earlier, in 1882, Yamagata was instrumental, as minister of the army, in the issuing of the Imperial Rescript to Soldiers and Sailors. It defined the basic stance to be adopted by loyal military men as "not to be misled by popular opinion, nor involve yourselves in politics."[33]

Yamagata liked to refer to himself as "a simple soldier," but the scope of his activities gradually expanded into virtually every area of national government. In the process, Yamagata sought to extend the spirit of the Imperial Rescript to Soldiers and Sailors to all facets of life in Japan. The system of local government and the Imperial Rescript on Education were both a part of this effort. Yamagata admitted as much in later years when he reminisced about working on the Imperial Rescript on Education: "Since I had the Imperial Rescript to Soldiers and Sailors on my mind, I thought something similar could be done with regard to education."[34]

Yamagata thus hoped to position his ideal men not only throughout the military but in every sector of national life. His vision was that this would create checks on the development of constitutional government, and in some cases, forestall it completely.

Centripetal and centrifugal forces

The Meiji constitutional order initially established in 1889 was far from monolithic. The fundamental law of any nation might be said to be the product of competition and compromise among a variety of political forces. The structure of the Meiji state as established by its constitutional system also embodied at least two contradictory forces at its inception.

It had a centripetal force pulling it toward the constitution and a centrifugal force pulling it away. The former resulted from the elements of the Meiji state identified with Itō, the latter from elements associated with Yamagata. By drafting a constitution and introducing the parliamentary system to Japan, Itō hoped to unify the people politically and, eventually, to achieve a full-fledged constitutional political order through the cooperation of the Diet and the government. In contrast, by seeding the central and local administrative bureaucracies and the military with the men of his clique, and by the permeation of primary education with the spirit of the Imperial Rescript on Education, Yamagata sought to isolate these institutions from constitutional government.

Itō's European trip had opened his eyes to the technique of using the executive to counterbalance a constitutional approach leaning too strongly in the direction of parliamentary politics. This, he had learned, achieved a more stable functioning of constitutional government. The executive, the sovereign, and the other state institutions outside the parliamentary framework were, to Itō, the organically connected parts from which the constitutional order was configured. For Yamagata, the thrust was to secure autonomy for the institutions outside the Diet, so that their unimpeded growth might neutralize the parliamentary system.

Meiji Japan contained within it the latent conflict between these two forces, and the shape of the nation developed and changed as a result of their clashes and competition. This book only sketches the beginning of this process. The later development of the Meiji constitution (in the sense of the structure of the nation-state) no doubt requires another book.

AFTERWORD

The late Kōsaka Masaaki, an eminent scholar of international politics, was fond of saying, "Constitutions are just conventions, you know."[1] It was a comment steeped in his profound understanding of British politics. To this day, Britain has no single legal document that can be called a constitution; instead, the corpus of its laws, including customary law, functions as a de facto constitution. Yet as Satō Kōji has also pointed out, there is an even deeper implication to Kōsaka's words.

It was Friedrich Carl von Savigny, founder of the German historical school of jurisprudence, who proclaimed that *all* law is customary law. He stressed that laws are but one part of the complex environment in which human beings are embedded—a part of a natural order that transcends human agency. The first task for the jurist was to gain a "living understanding" (*lebendige Anschauung*) of this aspect of the law.

German jurisprudence after Savigny did not fall victim to a simple determinism. In *The Struggle for Rights*, Jhering, though well-schooled in the historicist tradition, emphasized the birth of law out of the autonomous struggle of individual human actors. An evolutionist, he believed that human beings, while conditioned by their environment, also confronted it as autonomous agents. He understood law as a medium for the interaction between human beings and their environment. Savigny's immortal statement—"The essence of the law is the life of mankind regarded from a specific perspective"—should also be understood in these terms.

The Meiji Constitution was no exception to this. It was established in response to the far from peaceful international and domestic environments of the time, and behind its establishment were individuals willing to entrust the fate of their nation and its future to that constitution. Their efforts and experience in framing the constitution paved the way for the subsequent political life of the Japanese people. The various events and phenomena encountered on that path developed into practices and institutions that in turn either augmented or altered the constitution. Even with the discontinuity introduced by the postwar rewriting of Japan's constitution, we are not, in our times, cut off from the constitutional customs and practices that developed under the Meiji Constitution—some of which undoubtedly deserve to be ranked among "the achievements of the

Japanese people" (in the words of the *Final Report of the Committee on Administrative Reform*). Perhaps I have strayed a bit from the theme of this book in the foregoing remarks, but these are concerns I thought and spoke of frequently during the process of writing it.

I was abroad doing research in Vienna when, at the suggestion of Professor Yamanouchi Susumu of Hitotsubashi University, Mr. Shozawa Jun of the publishing company Kodansha, Ltd. first approached me about doing a history of the Meiji Constitution for the general reader. But there is already a rich historiographic tradition concerning the establishment of the Meiji Constitution, built upon the work of many eminent scholars, including Inada Masatsugu, Ōkubo Toshiaki, Osatake Takeki, Kojima Kazushi, Shimizu Shin, and Suzuki Yasuzō. I was initially reluctant, feeling that there was little reason for a young scholar such as myself to attempt to join their ranks. In conversations with Mr. Shozawa, however, I came to feel that I might be able contribute something to the historical writing on this subject by treating the Meiji Constitution in terms of the process of the reception and adaptation of Western civilization in Meiji Japan, and eventually agreed to the assignment.

As I began my research, however, I became painfully aware of what a blindly ambitious task I taken on. Moreover, in the nearly six years that have passed since the idea was first raised, a variety of other matters have diverted me from present volume: the publication of other work, joining the faculty at the university where I now teach, preparing for my classes there, sponsoring and participating in scholarly conferences, and so forth. However, this book (and anxiety over its completion) were never far from my mind, and I continued to work and struggle with it.

I write this afterword with the sense of liberation from that struggle. But I am also aware that this labor has propelled me a step forward in my scholarly work. The methods, arguments, and evidence of this book feel unfinished and rough-hewn, and it was not without hesitation that I let the manuscript leave my hands. Nevertheless, I hope that with the aid of rigorous criticism from my readers I will in future be able to bring theoretical and empirical refinement to the sketch presented here.

I am indebted to Professor Yamanouchi Susumu for the invaluable opportunity to publish in the Métier series. For years it appeared that this book might never see the light of day, and that I would betray the trust he had expressed with his recommendation to the publisher. Now that it is finally seeing print, I can only thank him for his patience and confess that it certainly does not approach in scope or quality his own masterpiece in this series, *Kita no jūjigun* (The Northern Crusade).

I must also mention three groups of professional colleagues who have provided me with a training ground: the Hikaku Hōshi Gakkai (Association for Comparative Legal History), the Kempōshi Kenkyūkai (Association for Research in Constitutional History), and the Nijū Seiki to Nihon Kenkyūkai (Research Association on Japan and the Twentieth Century). The stimulus and encouragement, both direct and indirect, that I received from all three groups always inspired me to return to the writing of this book with renewed spirits. I would like to take this opportunity to thank the gentlemen—each a faculty member of the Graduate School of Law at Kyoto University—who lead these associations: Professor Kawakami Rin'itsu (Western legal history), Professor Ōishi Makoto (constitutional law), and Professor Itō Yukio (Japanese political and diplomatic history). Professor Itō in particular gave me the chance to present an outline of this book to his association and to publish it in a collection of the association's research.[2] Time and again Professor Itō took me to task, saying, "Haven't you finished that book for Métier yet?" This, plus the example of his magisterial *Seitō seiji to tennō* (Party politics and the emperor), volume 22 in Kōdansha's Nihon no Rekishi (History of Japan) series, served as invaluable pressure and motivation for me to bring my own work to completion.

Finally, I would like to thank Misa, who became my wife while this book was in progress. Not only was she willing to put up with a new husband constantly busy with its preparation and writing, she even read the final manuscript, checking it for mistakes I had missed. No one more eagerly awaited this book's publication than Misa and Mr. Shozawa, and I thank the two of them, its first readers, from the bottom of my heart.

Takii Kazuhiro

January 3, 2003
The anniversary of the Constitution of Japan

The Constitution of the Empire of Japan
(Meiji Constitution)

PREAMBLE

Having, by virtue of the glories of Our Ancestors, ascended the Throne of a lineal succession unbroken for ages eternal; desiring to promote the welfare of, and to give development to the moral and intellectual faculties of Our beloved subjects, the very same that have been favoured with the benevolent care and affectionate vigilance of Our Ancestors; and hoping to maitain the prosperity of the State, in concert with Our people and with their support, We hereby promulgate, in pursuance of Our Imperial Rescript of the 12th day of the 10th month of the 14th year of Meiji, a fundamental law of State, to exhibit the principles by which We are to be guided in Our conduct, and to point out what Our descendants and Our subjects and their descendants are forever to conform.

The rights of sovereignty of the State, We have inherited from Our Ancestors, and We shall bequeath them to Our descendants. Neither We nor they shall in future fail to wield them, in accordance with the provisions of the Constitution hereby granted.

We now declare to respect and protect the security of the rights and of the property of Our people, and to secure to them the complete enjoyment of the same, within the extent of the provisions of the present Constitution and of the law.

The Imperial Diet shall first be convoked for the 23rd year of Meiji, and the time of its opening shall be the date when the present. Constitution comes into force.

When, in the future, it may become necessary to amend any of the provisions of the present Constitution, We or Our successors shall assume the initiative right, and submit a project for the same to the Imperial Diet. The Imperial Diet shall pass its vote upon it, according to the conditions imposed by the present Constitution, and in no otherwise shall Our descendants or Our subjects be permitted to attempt any alteration thereof.

Our Ministers of State, on Our behalf, shall be held responsible for the carrying out of the present Constitution, and Our present and future subjects shall forever assume the duty of allegiance to the present Constitution.

(His Imperial Majesty's Sign-Manual.)

(Privy Seal.)

The 11th day of the 2nd month of the 22nd year of Meiji.

(Countersigned)   Count Kuroda Kiyotaka,
                               Minister President of State.

Count Ito Hirobumi,
     President of the Privy Council.

Count Okuma Shigenobu,
     Minister of State for Foreign Affairs.

Count Saigo Tsukumichi,
     Minister of State for the Navy.

Count Inoue Kaoru,
     Minister of State for Agriculture and Commerce.

Count Yamada Akiyoshi,
     Minister of State for Justice.

Count Matsukata Masayoshi,
     *Minister of State for Finance and Minister of State
     for Home Affairs.*

Count Oyama lwao,
     Minister of State for War.

Viscount Mori Arinori,
     Minister of State for Education.

Viscount Enomoto Takeaki,
     Minister of State for Communications.

CHAPTER I

THE EMPEROR

ARTICLE I

The Empire of Japan shall be reigned over and governed by a line of Emperors unbroken for ages eternal.

ARTICLE II

The Imperial Throne shall be succeeded to by Imperial male descendants, according to the provisions of the Imperial House Law.

ARTICLE III

The Emperor is sacred and inviolable.

ARTICLE IV

The Emperor is the head of the Empire, combining in Himself the rights of sovereignty and exercises them, according to the provisions of the present Constitution.

ARTICLE V

The Emperor exercises the legislative power with the consent of the Imperial Diet.

ARTICLE VI

The Emperor gives sanction to laws, and orders them to be promulgated and executed.

ARTICLE VII

The Emperor convokes the Imperial Diet, opens, closes and prorogues it, and dissolves the House of Representatives.

ARTICLE VIII

The Emperor, in consequence of an urgent necessity to maintain public safety or to avert public calamities, issues, when the Imperial Diet is not sitting, Imperial Ordinances in the place of law.

Such Imperial Ordinances are to be laid before the Imperial Diet at its next session, and when the Diet does not approve the said Ordinances, the Government shall declare them to be invalid for the future.

ARTICLE IX

The Emperor issues or causes to be issued, the Ordinances necessary for the carrying out of the laws, or for the maintenance of the public peace and order, and for the promotion of the welfare of the subjects. But no Ordinance shall in any way alter any of the existing laws.

ARTICLE X

The Emperor determines the organization of the different branches of the administration and the salaries of all civil and military officers, and appoints and dismisses the same. Exceptions especially provided for in the present Constitution or in other laws, shall be in accordance with the respective provisions (bearing thereon).

ARTICLE XI

The Emperor has the supreme command of the Army and Navy.

ARTICLE XII

The Emperor determines the organization and peace standing of the Army and Navy.

ARTICLE XIII

The Emperor declares war, makes peace, and concludes treaties.

ARTICLE XIV

The Emperor declares a state of siege.

The conditions and effects of a state of siege shall be determined by law.

ARTICLE XV

The Emperor confers titles of nobility, rank, orders and other marks of honor.

ARTICLE XVI

The Emperor orders amnesty, pardon, commutation of punishments and rehabilitation.

ARTICLE XVII

A Regency shall be instituted in conformity with the provisions of the Imperial House Law.

The Regent shall exercise the powers appertaining to the Emperor in His name.

CHAPTER II

RIGHTS AND DUTIES OF SUBJECTS

ARTICLE XVIII

The conditions necessary for being a Japanese subject shall be determined by law.

ARTICLE XIX

Japanese subjects may, according to qualifications determined in laws or ordinances, be appointed to civil or military or any other public offices equally.

ARTICLE XX

Japanese subjects are amenable to service in the Army or Navy, according to the provisions of law.

ARTICLE XXI

Japanese subjects are amenable to the duty of paying taxes, according to the provisions of law.

ARTICLE XXII

Japanese subjects shall have the liberty of abode and of changing the same within the limits of law.

ARTICLE XXIII

No Japanese subject shall be arrested, detained, tried, or punished, unless according to law.

ARTICLE XXIV

No Japanese subject shall be deprived of his right of being tried by the judges determined by law.

ARTICLE XXV

Except in the cases provided for in the law, the house of no Japanese subject shall be entered or searched without his consent.

ARTICLE XXVI

Except in the cases mentioned in the law, the secrecy of the letters of every Japanese subject shall remain inviolate.

ARTICLE XXVII

The right of property of every Japanese subject shall remain inviolate. Measures necessary to be taken for the public benefit shall be provided for by law.

ARTICLE XXVIII

Japanese subjects shall, within limits not prejudicial to peace and order, and not antagonistic to their duties as subjects, enjoy freedom of religious belief.

ARTICLE XXIX

Japanese subjects shall, within limits of law, enjoy the liberty of speech, writing, publication, public meetings and associations.

ARTICLE XXX

Japanese subjects may present petitions, by observing the proper forms of respect, and by complying with the rules specially provided for the same.

ARTICLE XXXI

The provisions contained in the present Chapter shall not affect the exercise of the powers appertaining to the Emperor, in times of war or in cases of a national emergency.

ARTICLE XXXII

Each and every one of the provisions contained in the preceding Articles of the present Chapter, that are not in conflict with the laws or the rules and discipline of the Army and Navy, shall apply to the officers and men of the Army and of the Navy.

CHAPTER III

THE IMPERIAL DIET

ARTICLE XXXIII

The Imperial Diet shall consist of two Houses, a House of Peers and a House of Representatives.

ARTICLE XXXIV

The House of Peers shall, in accordance with the Ordinance concerning the House of Peers, be composed of the members of the Imperial Family, of the orders of the nobility, and of those persons, who have been nominated thereto by the Emperor.

ARTICLE XXXV

The House of Representatives shall be composed of Members elected by the people, according to the provisions of the Law of Election.

ARTICLE XXXVI

No one can at one and the same time be a Member of both Houses.

ARTICLE XXXVII

Every law requires the consent of the Imperial Diet.

ARTICLE XXXVIII

Both Houses shall vote upon projects of law submitted to it by the Government, and may respectively initiate projects of law.

ARTICLE XXXIX

A Bill, which has been rejected by either the one or the other of the two Houses, shall not be again brought in during the same session.

ARTICLE XL

Both Houses can make representations to the Government, as to laws or upon any other subject. When, however, such representations are not accepted, they cannot be made a second time during the same session.

ARTICLE XLI

The Imperial Diet shall be convoked every year.

ARTICLE XLII

A session of the Imperial Diet shall last during three months. In case of necessity, the duration of a session may be prolonged by Imperial Order.

ARTICLE XLIII

When urgent necessity arises, an extraordinary session may be convoked, in addition to the ordinary one.

The duration of an extraordinary session shall be determined by Imperial Order.

ARTICLE XLIV

The opening, closing, prolongation of session and the prorogation of the Imperial Diet, shall be effected simultaneously for both Houses.

In case the House of Representatives has been ordered to dissolve, the House of Peers shall at the same time be prorogued.

ARTICLE XLV

When the House of Representatives has been ordered to dissolve, Members shall be caused by Imperial Order to be newly elected, and the new House shall be convoked within five months from the day of dissolution.

ARTICLE XLVI

No debate can be opened and no vote can be taken in either House of the Imperial Diet, unless not less than one third of the whole number of Members thereof is present.

ARTICLE XLVII

Votes shall be taken in both Houses by absolute majority. In the case of a tie vote, the President shall have the casting vote.

ARTICLE XLVIII

The deliberations of both Houses shall be held in public. The deliberations may, however, upon demand of the Government or by resolution of the House, be held in secret sitting.

ARTICLE XLIX

Both Houses of the Imperial Diet may respectively present addresses to the Emperor.

ARTICLE L

Both Houses may receive petitions presented by subjects.

ARTICLE LI

Both Houses may enact, besides what is provided for in the present Constitution and in the Law of the Houses, rules necessary for the management of their internal affairs.

ARTICLE LII

No Member of either House shall be held responsible outside the respective House, for any opinion uttered or for any vote given in the House. When, however, a Member himself has given publicity to his opinions by public speech, by documents in print or in writing, or by any other similar means, he shall, in the matter, be amenable to the general law.

ARTICLE LIII

The Members of both Houses shall, during the session, be free from arrest, unless with the consent of the Houses, except in cases of flagrant delicts, or of offences connected with a state of internal commotion or with a foreign trouble.

ARTICLE LIV

The Ministers of State and the Delegates of the Government may, at any time, take seats and speak in either House.

CHAPTER IV

THE MINISTERS OF STATE AND THE PRIVY COUNCIL

ARTICLE LV

The respective Ministers of State shall give their advice to the Emperor, and be responsible for it.

All Laws, Imperial Ordinances and Imperial Rescripts of whatever kind, that relate to the affairs of the State, require the countersignature of a Minister of State.

ARTICLE LVI

The Privy Councillors shall, in accordance with the provisions for the organization of the Privy Council, deliberate upon important matters of State, when they have been consulted by the Emperor.

CHAPTER V

THE JUDICATURE

ARTICLE LVII

The Judicature shall be exercised by the Courts of Law according to law in the name of the Emperor.

The organization of the Courts of Law shall be determined by law.

ARTICLE LVIII

The judges shall be appointed from among those, who possess proper qualifications according to law.

No judge shall be deprived of his position, unless by way of criminal sentence or disciplinary punishment.

Rules for disciplinary punishment shall be determined by law.

ARTICLE LIX

Trials and judgements of a Court shall be conducted publicly. When, however, there exists any fear, that such publicity may be prejudicial to peace and order, or to the maintenance of public morality, the public trial may be suspended by provision of law or by the decision of the Court of law.

ARTICLE LX

All matters, that fall within the competency of a special Court, shall be specially provided for by law.

ARTICLE LXI

No suit at law, which relates to rights alleged to have been infringed by the illegal measures of the administrative authorities, and which shall come within the competency of the Court of Administrative Litigation specially established by law, shall be taken cognizance of by a Court of Law.

CHAPTER VI

FINANCE

ARTICLE LXII

The imposition of a new tax or the modification of the rates (of an existing one) shall be determined by law.

However, all such administrative fees or other revenue having the nature of compensation shall not fall within the category of the above clause.

The raising of national loans and the contracting of other liabilities to the charge of the National Treasury, except those that are provided for in the Budget, shall require the consent of the Imperial Diet.

ARTICLE LXIII

The taxes levied at present shall, in so far as they are not remodelled by a new law, be collected according to the old system.

ARTICLE LXIV

The expenditure and revenue of the State require the consent of the Imperial Diet by means of an annual Budget.

Any and all expenditures overpassing the appropriations set forth in the Titles and Paragraphs of the Budget, or that are not provided for in the Budget, shall subsequently require the approbation of the Imperial Diet.

ARTICLE LXV

The Budget shall be first laid before the House of Representatives.

ARTICLE LXVI

The expenditures of the Imperial House shall be defrayed every year out of the National Treasury, according to the present fixed amount for the same, and shall not require the consent thereto of the Imperial Diet, except in case an increase thereof is found necessary.

ARTICLE LXVII

Those already fixed expenditures based by the Constitution upon the powers appertaining to the Emperor, and such expenditures as may have arisen by the effect of law, or that appertain to the legal obligations of the Government, shall be neither rejected nor reduced by the Imperial Diet, without the concurrence of the Government.

ARTICLE LXVIII

In order to meet special requirements, the Government may ask the consent of the Imperial Diet to a certain amount as a Continuing Expenditure Fund, for a previously fixed number of years.

ARTICLE LXIX

In order to supply deficiencies, which are unavoidable, in the Budget, and to meet requirements unprovided for in the same, a Reserve Fund shall be provided for in the Budget.

ARTICLE LXX

When the Imperial Diet cannot be convoked, owing to the external or internal condition of the country, in case of urgent need for the maintenance of public safety, the Government may take all necessary financial measures, by means of an Imperial Ordinance.

In the case mentioned in the preceding clause, the matter shall be submitted to the Imperial Diet at its next session, and its approbation shall be obtained thereto.

ARTICLE LXXI

When the Imperial Diet has not voted on the Budget, or when the Budget has not been brought into actual existence, the Government shall carry out the Budget of the preceding year.

ARTICLE LXXII

The final account of the expenditures and revenue of the State shall be verified and confirmed by the Board of Audit, and it shall be submitted by the Government to the Imperial Diet, together with the report of verification of the said Board.

The organization and competency of the Board of Audit shall be determined by law separately.

CHAPTER VII

SUPPLEMENTARY RULES

ARTICLE LXXIII

When it has become necessary in future to amend the provisions of the present Constitution, a project to that effect shall be submitted to the Imperial Diet by Imperial Order.

In the above case, neither House can open the debate, unless not less than two thirds of the whole number of Members are present, and no amendment can be passed, unless a majority of not less than two-thirds of the Members present is obtained.

ARTICLE LXXIV

No modification of the Imperial House Law shall be required to be submitted to the deliberation of the Imperial Diet.

No provision of the present Constitution can be modified by the Imperial House Law.

ARTICLE LXXV

No modification can be introduced into the Constitution, or into the Imperial House Law, during the time of a Regency.

ARTICLE LXXVI

Existing legal enactments, such as laws, regulations, Ordinances, or by whatever names they may be called, shall, so far as they do not conflict with the present Constitution, continue in force.

All existing contracts or orders, that entail obligations upon the Government, and that are connected with expenditure, shall come within the scope of Article LXVII.

As translated by Baron Miyoshi Ito in
Commentaries on the Constitution of
the Empire of Japan, second edition
(Tokyo: Chuo Daigaku, 1906).

NOTES

Preface: The Meiji Constitution and Japan's Experience of the West

1. Nitobe Inazō (1862–1933) was a scholar, educator, and diplomat who later served as under-secretary general of the League of Nations and was the author of *Bushido: The Soul of Japan* (1899). At the time of the encounter described here, he was a doctoral student at a German university.

2. "Kigan no ashi" [Reeds for the wild geese], in *Nitobe Inazō zenshū* [Collected Works of Nitobe Inazō], 25 vols. (Tokyo: Kyōbunkan, 1969–2001), 6: 47ff.

3. Ienaga Saburō, *Nihon kindai kempō shisōshi kenkyū* [A historical study of modern Japanese constitutional thought (Tokyo: Iwanami Shoten, 1967), 78–79.

4. "Jinshin kyōdō iken an" [A proposal for educating the minds of the people], in *Inoue Kowashi den* [Biography of Inoue Kowashi], 7 vols. (Tokyo: Kokugakuin Daigaku Toshokan, 1986–94), 1: 251.

5. Helmut Coing, *Yōrropa hōshi ron* [European legal history] trans. Sasaki Yūshi, (Sōbunsha, 1980); and Coing, *Yōroppa hō bunka no nagare* [Currents of European legal culture] trans. Ueyama Yasutoshi (Kyoto: Mineruba Shobō, 1983).

6. Satō Kōji, *Kempō to sono "monogatari" sei* [The constitution and its "narrativity"] (Tokyo: Yūhikaku, 2003), 128–29. See also Satō, *Nihon kempō shi to "hō no shi-hai"* [Japanese constitutional history and "the rule of law"] (Tokyo: Yūhikaku, 2002), 191ff.

7. Lorenz von Stein, "Nihon teikoku shi oyobi hō shi no kenkyū" [A historical study of the Japanese Empire and its laws] trans. Takii Kazuhiro, in *Jurisprudentia: kokusai hikaku hōsei kenkyū* [Jurisprudentia: comparative studies in international legal systems] (Kyoto: Mineruba Shobō, 1995), no. 4, 59.

8. Titus Livius, "Rōma-shi kensetsu irai no rekishi (IX)" [A history of Rome from the founding of the city (IX)], trans. Suzuki Kazukuni, in *Ronshū* (*Kobe Daigaku Kyōyōbu kiyō*), no. 33 (1984): 130. See also Funada Kyōji, *Rōma hō* [Roman law] (Tokyo: Iwanami Shoten, 1986), vol. 1: 116.

9. Shiono Nanao, *Rōmajin no monogatari* [The story of the Roman people] (Shinchōsha, 1992), 88ff.

10. See the previously cited works by Satō Kōji, who has been a central figure in this series of reforms.

Chapter One: The Iwakura Embassy

1. A number of valuable books and monographs have been published on the Iwakura Embassy by such scholars as Ōkubo Toshiaki, Tanaka Akira, Haga Tōru, Nishikawa Nagao, and Izumi Saburō. Among them, Tanaka Akira's *Iwakura shisetsudan no rekishiteki kenkyū* [A historical study of the Iwakura

163

Embassy] (Tokyo: Iwanami Shoten, 2002) is especially valuable, as it represents the current position of a scholar who has been a leader in research in this field for many years. Fundamental source materials related to the mission are collected in Ōkubo Toshiaki, ed. *Iwakura shisetsu no kenkyū* [Research on the Iwakura Mission] (Kyoto: Munetaka Shobō, 1976). In addition, the vast collection of materials in the National Archives of Japan related to the mission has been converted to microfilm under the supervision of Tanaka Akira (Tokyo: Yumani Shobō, 1994) and made available for general use. In addition to the work by Tanaka mentioned above, other notable recent publications include the reports of international conferences on the Iwakura Embassy organized by Ian Nish, Izumi Saburō, and Haga Tōru, repectively: Ian Nish, ed., *The Iwakura Mission in America and Europe: A New Assessment* (Richmond, Surrey: Curzon Press, 1998); Ō-Bei Kairan no Kai, ed., *Iwakura shisetsudan no saihakken* [Rediscovering the Iwakura Embassy] (Kyoto: Shibunkaku Shuppan, 2003); and Haga Tōru, ed. *Iwakura shisetsudan no hikaku bunkashiteki kenkyū* [The Iwakura Embassy as comparative cultural history] (Kyoto: Shibunkaku Shuppan, 2003).

2. Takahashi Hidenao, "Haihan seifu ron—kūdetā kara shisetsudan e" [The government that dissolved the domains—from coup d'état to overseas mission], *Nihonshi kenkyū*, no. 356 (1992).

3. Ōkubo Toshiaki, ed. *Iwakura shisetsu no kenkyū* [Research on the Iwakura Embassy] (Tokyo: Munetaka Shobō, 1976), 161.

4. Ibid., 161–62.

5. Quoted in Kengi Hamada, *Prince Itō* (Tokyo: Sanseido, 1936; Washington, D.C.: University Publications of America, 1979), 66.

6. Takahashi, "Haihan seifu," 76.

7. Ōkubo, *Iwakura shisetsu,* 176.

8. For an example of leading research in this area, see Hamashita Takeshi, *Chōkō shisutemu to kindai Ajia* [The tribute system and modern Asia] (Tokyo: Iwanami Shoten, 1997). The national seclusion policies of the Tokugawa shogunate were an attempt to construct a world order with Japan at the civilized center as an antithesis to the Chinese world order. In this regard, see Ronald Toby, *State and Diplomacy in Early-Modern Japan: Asia in the Development of the Tokugawa Bakufu* (Princeton University Press, 1984; Stanford University Press, 1991).

9. Ōkubo, *Iwakura shisetsu,* 164.

10. Yamanouchi Susumu, "Meiji kokka ni okeru 'bummei' to kokusai hō" ["Civilization" and international law in the Meiji state], *Hitotsubashi ronsō*, vol. 115, no. 1 (1996).

11. James Lorimer, *The Institutes of the Law of Nations*, 2 vols. (Edinburgh and London: W. Blackwood and sons, 1883), 1: 101–02. See also Yamanouchi, "Meiji kokka," 24.

12. William Edward Hall, *A Treatise on International Law* (Second edition, Oxford: Clarendon Press, 1884), 40. Quoted in Yamanouchi, "Meiji kokka," 23.

13. Izumi Saburō, *Dōdōtaru Nihonjin—shirarezaru Iwakura shisetsudan: kono kuni no katachi to shinro o kimeta otokotachi* [Magnificent Japanese—the unknown

Iwakura Embassy: the men who determined the shape and course of our nation] (Tokyo: Shōdensha, 1996).

14. Ōkubo, *Iwakura shisetsu*, 187.

15. Ōkubo, *Iwakura shisetsu*, 174.

16. *Hogo hiroi: Sasaki Takayuki nikki* [The scrap collector: The diary of Sasaki Takayuki], 5 vols. (Tokyo: University of Tokyo Press, 1974), 5: 240.

17. Ōyama Shikitarō, ed., *Wakayama Norikazu zenshū* [Collected works of Wakayama Norikazu], 2 vols. (Tokyo: Tōyō Keizai Shimpōsha, 1940), 2: 498. Wakayama Norikazu (1840–91) was an economist of the early Meiji period. He accompanied the Iwakura Embassy to America and Europe, and remained in the West to study economics.

18. *Kume hakushi kūjūnen kaikoroku* [A record of Professor Kume's recollections of his ninety years] (Tokyo: Munetaka Shobō: 1985; Tokyo: Waseda Daigaku Shuppanbu, 1934), vol. 2: 186.

19. Ibid., 181.

20. Ibid., 185.

21. See Kanai Madoka, *Tomii to iu na no Nihonjin* [A Japanese named Tommy] (Tokyo: Bun'ichi Sōgō Shuppan, 1979); Imai Ichirō, "Kanazawa han chūgaku higashikō kyōshi Nagano Keijirō den—Man'en kembei shisetsu Tomii shōnen no shōgai" [A biography of Nagano Keijirō, instructor at the east campus of the Kanazawa Domain Middle School—the life of Tommy, the boy who went with the 1860 mission to America], in *Ishikawa kyōdoshi gakkai kaishi*, no. 14 (1981); Akatsuka Yukio, *Kimi wa Tomii poruka wo kiita ka* [Have you heard the Tommy Polka?] (Nagoya: Fūbaisha, 1999).

22. *Hogo hiroi*, vol. 5: 244.

23. Ibid., 244.

24. *Kido Takayoshi kankei monjo* [Kido Takayoshi papers], vol. 4: 33 (Tokyo: University of Tokyo Press, 2007). Letter of Meiji 4.12.20 to Sugi Magoshichirō, Kashiwamura Shin, and Kubo Danzō.

25. *Hogo hiroi*, vol. 5: 243.

26. Ibid., 251.

27. Ibid., 251.

28. For an earlier discussion of the changes in Iwakura's style of dress during the course of the embassy, see Tanaka Akira, *"Datsu A" no Meiji ishin—Iwakura shisetsudan o ou tabi kara* [The Meiji Restoration as an "escape from Asia"—in the footsteps of the Iwakura Embassy] (Tokyo: Nihon Hōsō Shuppan Kyōkai, 1984).

29. *Hogo hiroi*, vol. 5: 289.

30. On Meiji 5.1.13, just as the embassy was departing San Francisco for Washington, the Japanese government revised its rules for official dress, switching to Western-style formal attire. So Iwakura's abandonment of Japanese dress was mandated by law. According to Hayashi Tadasu, when the leaders of the mission met with the president in Washington they wore Japanese court dress, but for their next

stop, Great Britain, it was decided to wear Western formal attire in keeping with the recent government decree. Hayashi was sent ahead to Britain to have the clothing made to order, and Hayashi says that the style and design selected at that time became, almost without alteration, the new court dress of Japan. Hayashi Tadasu, *Nochi wa mukashi no ki nari—Hayashi Shigeru kaikoroku* [The rest is history—the memoirs of Hayashi Shigeru] (Tokyo: Heibonsha, 1970), 171.

31. *Kume kaikoroku*, 184–85.

32. *Hogo hiroi*, vol. 5: 245.

33. *Itō Hirobumi den* [Biography of Itō Hirobumi], 3 vols. (Tokyo: Shumpo-kō Tsuishōkai, 1940), 1: 591ff.

34. The English text of the speech is reproduced in *Itō den*, vol. 1: 1013–17, from which the following quotations are taken.

35. *Hogo hiroi*, vol. 5: 253, 290–91. Opinions vary as to Itō's English ability, but a British diplomat who received him at the British consulate in Tokyo before the embassy's departure reported to his government that Itō was quite fluent. William G. Beasley, *Japan Encounters the Barbarians* (New Haven, CT.: Yale University Press, 1995), 161.

36. Itō Shin'ichi, "Chichi, Hirobumi o kataru" [Speaking of my father, Hirobumi] in Muramatsu Takeshi, *Nihon bunka o kangaeru (taidan shū)* [Considerations on Japanese Culture (A Collection of Dialogues)] (Tokyo: Nihon Kyōbunsha, 1979), 41.

37. *Itō den*, vol. 1, 708–09.

38. Itō Shin'ichi, "Chichi, Hirobumi."

39. *Hogo hiroi*, vol. 5: 291.

40. Shimomura Fujio, *Meiji shōki jōyaku kaisei shi no kenkyū* [A historical study of treaty revision in the early Meiji period] (Tokyo: Yoshikawa Kōbunkan, 1962); and Ishii Takashi, *Meiji shōki no kokusai kankei* [International relations in the early Meiji period] (Tokyo: Yoshikawa Kōbunkan, 1977).

41. Ishii, *Meiji shōki no kokusai kankei*, 38.

42. Ibid., 50.

43. Ibid., 51.

44. Nihon Shiseki Kyōkai, ed., *Kido Takayoshi nikki* [Kido Takayoshi diary], 3 vols. (Tokyo: Nihon Shiseki Kyōkai, 1932; Tokyo: University of Tokyo Press, 1985), 2: 148–49 (entry for Meiji 5.2.18). Translated by Sidney Devere Brown and Akiko Hirota as *The Diary of Kido Takayoshi*, 2 vols. (Tokyo: University of Tokyo Press, 1983), 2: 142 (entry for March 26, 1872).

45. Ibid., vol. 2: 179–80 (entry for Meiji 5.4.20). Brown and Hirota, vol. 2: 168–69 (May 26, 1872)]

46. Ibid., vol. 2: 154–55 (entries for Meiji 5.2.30 and 5.3.1). Brown and Hirota, vol. 2: 147–48 (April 7 and 8, 1872).

47. *Itō den*, vol. 1: 709–10.

48. According to Itō's conversation cited in the previous note, when the mission reached Germany Aoki Shūzō and Shinagawa Yajirō were so concerned about

the relationship between Kido and Itō that they offered to mediate between the two, but Itō declined the offer.

49. *Kido monjo*, vol. 4: 431. Letter of Meiji 5.2.11 to Sugiyama Takatoshi.

50. *Kido monjo*, vol. 4: 346. Letter of Meiji 5.3.11 to Inoue Kaoru.

51. *Kido monjo*, vol. 4: 366. Letter of Meiji 5.7.1 to Kashimura Shin.

52. *Kido monjo*, vol. 4: 374. Letter of Meiji 5.7.2 to Sugi Magoshichirō.

53. Makino Nobuaki, *Kaikoroku* [Memoirs], 2 vols. (Chūkō Bunko, 1977), 1: 25.

54. Interview with Kume Kunitake in Matsubara Chion, ed., *Ōkubo Toshimichi*, second edition (Matsuno Shoten, 2003; 1st ed., Tokyo: Shinchōsha, 1912), 119ff.

55. Ibid.

56. Ibid., 120.

57. Ibid.

58. Ibid., 121.

59. Ibid., 125–26.

60. Takahashi, "Haihan seifu," 91.

61. Nihon Shiseki Kyokai, ed. *Ōkubo Toshimichi monjo* [Ōkubo Toshimichi papers], 10 vols. (Tokyo: University of Tokyo Press, 1973; 1st edition 1928), 4: 484. Letter to Nishi Tokujirō of Meiji 6.1.17.

62. Matsubara, ed., *Ōkubo Toshimichi*, 123–24.

63. Kume Kunitake, *Tokumei zenken taishi Bei-Ō kairan jikki* [A True Account of a Journey of Observation through the United States and Europe], ed. and annotated by Tanaka Akira, 5 vols. (Tokyo: Iwanami Shoten, 1977–82), 5: 149. A complete English translation of this work is now available: *The Iwakura Embassy, 1871–73: A True Account of the Ambassador Extraordinary & Plenipotentiary's Journey of Observation Through the United States of America and Europe*, 5 vols., compiled by Kume Kunitake; Graham Healey and Chūshichi Tsuzuki, editors-in-chief (Matsudo, Chiba: The Japan Documents, 2002).

64. Kume, *Jikki*, vol. 5 149; trans. in *Iwakura Embassy*, vol. 5: 149.

65. Fukuzawa Yukichi, *Bummeiron no gairyaku* [Outline of a theory of civilization] (Iwanami Bunko, 1962), 229ff. The passages quoted are from pages 254 and 259, respectively.

66. Kume, *Jikki*, vol. 5: 160; trans. in *Iwakura Embassy*, vol.5: 161.

67. Ibid., vol 5: 149, trans. in *Iwakura Embassy*, vol. 5: 149.

68. Nishikawa Nagao, "Tōgō sareta Europa" in Nishikawa Nagao and Matsumiya Hideharu, eds., *Bei-Ō kairan jikki o yomu—1870 nendai no sekai to Nihon* [Reading the *Bei-Ō kairan jikki*—The world of the 1870s and Japan] (Kyoto: Hōritsu Bunkasha, 1995), 244.

69. Kume, *Jikki*, vol. 5: 160; trans. in *Iwakura Embassy*, vol. 5: 161.

70. Ibid., vol 5: 146; trans. in *Iwakura Embassy*, vol. 5: 146.

71. Ibid., vol. 3: 116; trans. in *Iwakura Embassy*, vol. 3: 105.

72. Ibid., vol. 5: 221; trans. in *Iwakura Embassy*, vol. 5: 234.

73. Ibid., vol. 2: 195; trans. in *Iwakura Embassy*, vol. 2: 206.

74. Ibid., vol. 1: 297; trans. in *Iwakura Embassy*, vol. 1: 311

75. Ibid., vol. 3: 167; trans. in *Iwakura Embassy*, vol. 3: 159.

76. Ibid., vol. 2: 114; trans. in *Iwakura Embassy*, vol. 2: 109.

77. Ibid., vol. 5: 21ff; trans. in *Iwakura Embassy*, vol. 5: 9ff.

78. Ibid., vol. 2: 114; trans. in *Iwakura Embassy*, vol. 2: 110.

79. Ibid., vol. 3: 221; trans. in *Iwakura Embassy*, vol. 3: 213–14.

80. Ibid., vol. 2: 114; trans. in *Iwakura Embassy*, vol. 2: 109–10.

81. Ibid., vol. 3: 71; trans. in *Iwakura Embassy*, vol. 3: 59.

82. Ibid., vol. 2: 331.

83. Fukuzawa Yukichi, *Bummeiron no gairyaku*, 30.

84. Kume, *Jikki*, vol. 5: 158; trans. in *Iwakura Embassy*, vol. 5: 159.

85. Recent research focusing on Kido's investigation into Western constitutions includes Sidney Brown, "Iwakura shisetsudan ni okeru Kido Takayoshi no yakuwari" [The role of Kido Takayoshi in the Iwakura Embassy], trans. Ōta Akiko, in Haga, ed., *Iwakura shisetsudan no hikaku bunkashiteki kenkyū*, 195ff.

86. *Kido nikki*, vol. 2: 142 (entry for Meiji 5.1.22). Brown and Hirota, vol. 2: p. 134 (entry for March 1, 1872).

87. Ibid., (entry for Meiji 6.4.23). Brown and Hirota, vol. 2: p. 133–34 (entry for April 23, 1873).

88. *Kido monjo*, vol. 4: 424. Letter of Meiji 5.11.27 to Watanabe Kōki.

89. Ibid., vol. 5: 15. Letter of Meiji 6.3.20 to Miura Gorō.

90. Ibid., vol. 4: 371. Letter of Meiji 5.7.2 to Yamada Akiyoshi.

91. The memorials on the constitution submitted by Kido and Ōkubo have been given a comparative analysis by Toriumi Yasushi in *Nihon kindaishi kōgi* [Lectures in modern Japanese history] (Tokyo: University of Tokyo Press, 1988), 50ff. Toriumi points to the more progressive nature of Ōkubo's memorial compared with Kido's.

92. *Kido monjo*, vol. 8, 123. "Kempō seitei no kengen sho" [Memorial on the establishment of a constitution].

93. Ibid., 118.

94. Ibid., 119.

95. Ibid., 118.

96. *Kido nikki*, vol. 2: 420 (entry for November 20, 1873). in Brown and Hirota, vol. 2: 398. Kido uses the English word *despotic* in *katakana*.

97. *Kido monjo*, vol. 8: 123. "Kempō seitei no kengensho."

98. Ibid., 121–22.

99. Ibid., 123–34.

100. Ibid., 128.

101. *Kido nikki*, vol. 2: 420 (entry for September 3, 1873). Brown and Hirota, vol. 2: 371.

102. *Ōkubo monjo*, vol. 4: 484. Letter of January 27, 1873 to Nishi Tokujirō.

103. Ibid.

104. *Ōkubo monjo*, vol. 4: 492. Letter of March 21, 1873 to Saigō Takamori and Yoshii Tomozane.

105. *Ōkubo monjo*, vol. 4: 501. Letter of March 27, 1873 to Nishi Tokujirō.

106. Kume, *Jikki*, vol. 3: 329; trans. in *Iwakura Embassy*, vol. 3: 323.

107. Ibid.

108. Ibid.

109. Ibid., 330; trans. in *Iwakura Embassy*, vol. 3: 324

110. *Itō den*, vol. 1: 798.

111. *Ōkubo monjo*, vol. 5: 184. "Rikken seitai ni kansuru ikensho" (Memorandum on constitutional government).

112. Ibid., 188.

113. Ibid., 186.

114. See Toriumi, *Nihon kindaishi kōgi*, 51. Fujita Masaharu's *"Seijika" Ōkubo Toshimichi* [The politician Ōkubo Toshimichi] (Tokyo: Kōdansha, 2003) contains a discussion of Ōkubo's memorandum beginning on p. 154. Sasaki Suguru's *Ōkubo Toshimichi to Meiji ishin* [Ōkubo Toshimichi and the Meiji Restoration] (Tokyo: Yoshikawa Kōbunkan, 1998) raises some important points on p. 163.

115. *Ōkubo monjo*, vol. 5: 188. "Rikken seitai ni kansuru ikensho" (Memorandum on constitutional government).

116. Ibid., vol. 5: 206.

117. The lecture was published in book form as Rudolf von Jhering, *Der Kampf ums Recht*, 1872. Translated by Murakami Jun'ichi as *Kenri no tame no tōsō* (Iwanami Bunko, 1982). For the background of this speech and its place in Western legal history, see Murakami Jun'ichi, *"Kenri no tame no tōsō" o yomu* [Reading *The Struggle for Rights*] (Tokyo: Iwanami Shoten, 1983).

118. Yamanouchi, "Meiji kokka," 19.

Chapter Two: Itō Hirobumi's European Research

1. For concise and balanced overviews of these developments, see Toriumi, *Nihon kindaishi kōgi*, 57ff; and Ōishi Makoto, *Nihon kempōshi* [Japanese constitutional history] (Tokyo: Yuhikaku, 1995), 25ff.

2. On the Political Crisis of 1881, see Sakamoto Kazuto, *Itō Hirobumi to Meiji kokka keisei* [Itō Hirobumi and the formation of the Meiji state] (Tokyo: Yoshikawa Kōbunkan, 1991), 41ff. I have also written previously on this subject; see Takii Kazuhiro, *Doitsu kokkagaku to Meiji kokusei* [German political economy and the constitution of the Meiji state] (Kyoto: Mineruba Shobō, 1999), 186ff. The present volume expands upon the theme of chapter 5 in this previous book, reworking it and adding material on Germany and Austria from the perspective of comparative constitutional history.

3. *Itō den*, vol. 2: 207. Letter of Meiji 14.7.2 to Iwakura Tomomi.

4. Inada Masatsugu, *Meiji kempō seiritsushi no kenkyū* [History of the establishment of the Meiji Constitution], 2 vols. (Tokyo: Yuhikaku, 1960–62), 1: 525.

5. *Kido nikki*, vol. 2: 452ff (entry for Meiji 6.11.20).

6. Ōkuma-kō Hachijūgonenshi Hensankai eds., *Ōkuma kō hachijūgonen shi* [An 85-year history of Count Ōkuma], 3 vols. (Tokyo: Hara Shobo, 1970), 1: 261.

7. Ōkubo Toshiaki, "Meiji 14-nen no Seihen—Sat-Chō hambatsu seiken no kaku-ritsu"[The Political Crisis of 1881—the establishment of the Satsuma-Chōshū clique government] (first published in 1952), in *Meiji kokka no keisei: Ōkubo Toshiaki rekishi chōsaku shū* [The formation of the Meiji state: The historical works of Ōkubo Toshiaki] (Tokyo: Yoshikawa Kōbunkan, 1986), vol. 2. This is a classic analysis of the Political Crisis of 1881 and Inoue Kowashi's emergence on the political scene. Sakamoto, *Itō Hirobumi to Meiji kokka keisei* also discusses Inoue's pivotal role.

8. Tada Kōmon, ed., *Iwakura kō jikki* [The true record of Prince Iwakura] (Tokyo: Hara Shobō, 1968), 715ff.

9. Hogo Hiroi, vol. 11: 22–23

10. Inada, *Seiritsushi*, vol. 1: 545.

11. The nine official members were: Yamasaki Naotane (Dajōkan secretary), Itō Miyoji (assistant to a member of the Sanjikan), Kawashima Atsushi (secretary to the Minister of Finance), Yoshida Masaharu (secretary in the Foreign Office), Hirata Tōsuke (junior secretary in the Ministry of Finance), Miyoshi Taizō (judge in the Daishin'in), and Saionji Kimmochi, Iwakura Tomosada, and Hirohashi Kenkō (all assistants to councillors of the Sanjiin).

    At the time, prior to the establishment of a cabinet system, the Meiji government was headed by the Dajōkan, which functioned as a kind of cabinet office for the *dajō daijin* (grand minister of state), assisted by the ministers of the left and right, who presided over a council called the Sanjiin, a legislative bureau comprised of the *sangi*, or councillors, who concurrently served as heads of the various government ministries. The term Dajōkan was also often used loosely to refer to the government as a whole.

12. *Itō den*, vol. 2: 256ff.

13. Ikeda Hiroshi, ed., *Ōmori Shōichi* (privately published, 1930), 102.

14. Inoue Kaoru Monjo [Papers of Inoue Kaoru] (Collection of the Modern Japanese Political History Materials Room of the National Diet Library), 255-(2). Letter of February 22, 1882 from Fukuchi Gen'ichirō to Inoue.

15. Inoue Kaoru Monjo, 255-(3). Letter of February 26, 1882 from Fukuchi Gen'ichirō to Inoue.

16. Takii, *Doitsu kokkagaku to Meiji no kokusei*.

17. "Ryūkakusai nikki" [Ryūkakusai diary], in *Ono Azusa zenshū* [The complete works of Ono Azusa], 6 vols. (Tokyo: Waseda University Press, 1982), 3: 388.

18. As recollected by Yoshida Masaharu in Osatake Takeki, *Nihon kensei shi* [History of the Japanese constitutional system] (Tokyo: Nihon Hyōron Sha, 1930), 338.

19. Kawakami Rin'itsu, *Hō no bunka shakai shi* [A sociocultural history of law] (Kyoto: Mineruba Shobō, 1989).

20. Osatake, *Nihon kensei shi*, 338–39.

21. *Itō den*, vol. 2: 271. Letter of Meiji 15.5.24 to Matsukata.

22. Ibid., vol. 2, 314. Letter of Meiji 15.9.6 to Matsukata.

23. Ibid.

24. The following discussion owes much to Ernst Rudolph Huber, *Deutsche Verfassunggeschichte*, Bd. IV (Stuttgart, u.a., 1969), 142ff; and Lothar Gall, *Bismarck: der weisse Revolutionar*. Translated by Ōuchi Hirokazu as *Bismarck: Hakushoku no kakumeika* [Bismarck, the White Revolutionary] (Tokyo: Sōbunsha, 1988), 68off.

25. *Itō den*, vol. 2: 271–22. Letter of Meiji 15.5.24 to Matsukata.

26. "Mosse-shi kogi hikki" [Notes on Mr. Mosse' lectures], manuscript in Itō Miyoji Kankei Monjo [Ito Miyoji Papers] (Collection of the Modern Japanese Political History Materials Room of the National Diet Library); later published in Shimizu Shin, *Meiji kempō seiteishi* (jō): *Doku-Ō ni okeru Itō Hirobumi no kempō chōsa* [History of the establishment of the Meiji Constitution (vol. 1): Itō Hirobumi's constitutional research in Germany and Austria] (Tokyo: Hara Shobō, 1971).

27. Inoue Kaoru Monjo, 628-29. Letter of Meiji 15.7.5 from Itō to Inoue Kaoru.

28. Hiratsuka Atsushi ed., *Itō Hirobumi hiroku* [Private Records of Itō Hirobumi] (Tokyo: Shunjūsha, 1929), 292.

29. Inoue Kaoru Monjo, 628-29. Letter of Meiji 15.7.5 from Itō to Inoue Kaoru.

30. Shimizu, *Seiteishi*, 36.

31. Ito Hirobumi Kankei Monjo Kenkyukai, ed., *Ito Hirobumi kankei monjo* [Itō Hirobumi papers], 9 vols. (Tokyo: Hanawa Shobō, 1973–81), 7: 218ff.

32. *Itō den*, vol. 2: 271. Letter of Meiji 15.5.24 to Matsukata.

33. *Aoki Shūzō jiden* [The autobiography of Aoki Shūzō], ed. and annotated by Sakane Yoshihisa (Tokyo: Heibonsha, 1970), 234ff.

34. Ibid.

35. *Itō den*, vol. 2: 282ff. Letter of Meiji 15.8.4 to Yamagata Aritomo, Inoue Kaoru, and Yamada Akiyoshi.

36. "Tai Ō chū kokujō tō ni kansuru tsūshin bun no an" (Draft of a communiqué on national affairs written in Europe), Ito Hirobumi Kankei Monjo [Ito Hirobumi Papers] (Collection of the Modern Japanese Political History Materials Room of the National Diet Library), 112.

37. *Itō den*, vol. 2: 283. Letter of Meiji 15.8.4 to Yamagata Aritomo, Inoue Kaoru, and Yamada Akiyoshi.

38. Yoshino Sakuzō, "Sutain Gunaisuto to Itō Hirobumi" [Stein, Gneist, and Itō Hirobumi], in *Yoshino Sakuzō senshū* [Selected works of Yoshino Sakuzō], 16 vols. (Tokyo: Iwanami Shoten, 1995–97; first published 1933), vol. 11: 342–63.

39. "Hyakusei no chi wa gakusei o kaisei shite ikkoku no shisō o itsu ni suru ni shikazaru gi" ["Why government that will endure for a hundred generations must reform the educational system and unify the thought of the nation,"] in *Kawakami Atsushi ko "Gakusei kaisei ni tsuki Kawashima Atsushi no kengi oyobi hon kengi ni tsuki Fukuoka Monbukyō Kuki Ryūichi Katō Hiroyuki tō no shuhi*

["Kawakami Atsushi's memorial on reform of the educational system, with annotations by Minister of Education Fukuoka, Kuki Ryūichi, Katō Hiroyuki, and others,"] manuscript in the collection of Tōsho Bunko, catalogue no. 110/11.

40. Yoshida in Osatake Takeki, *Nihon kensei shi*, 338.

41. Shimizu, *Seiteishi*, 37.

42. Satō Takashi, "Meiji shoki ichi gaikōkan no kiseki: Homma Kiyoo" [Homma Kiyoo: the legacy of an early Meiji diplomat], in *Yokohama Kaikō Shiryōkan hō*, no. 12 (1985), 67. Letter of Meiji 15.8.10 from Ida to Homma Kiyoo.

43. *Itō monjo*, vol. 1: 114. Letter of Meiji 15.8.19 from Ida to Itō.

44. Keio University ed., *Fukuzawa Yukichi zenshū* [Collected works of Fukuzawa Yukichi], 24 vols. (Tokyo: Iwanami Shoten, 1958–64), 21: 368.

45. *Itō den*, vol. 2: 296–97. Letter of Meiji 15.8.11 to Iwakura Tomomi.

46. *Itō den*, vol. 2: 300. Letter of Meiji 15.8.27 to Yamada Akiyoshi.

47. Two sets of manuscript notes on the lectures Stein gave to Itō have been preserved among the Itō Miyoji Papers in the collection of the Kensei Shiryōshitsu (Modern Japanese Political History Materials Room of the National Diet Library). The first is "Junri shakuwa" [Lectures on (legal) principles], and the second, "Dai hakase Sutein shi kōgi hikki" [Manuscript notes on lectures by the great Doctor Stein]. The latter has been reprinted in Shimizu, *Seiteishi*, vol. 1, 233ff, and that is the version cited here.

In addition, though not of the same period, there is a set of notes in the Itō Hirobumi Papers, again in the collection of the Kensei Shiryōshitsu, entitled "Sutain shi no kōgi hikki" [Manuscript notes on Mr. Stein's lectures]; and the Kanagawa Prefectural Kanazawa Bunko has in its collection an archive entitled "Itō Hirobumi Kizō Kempō Shiryō" [Documents on the constitution donated by Itō Hirobumi] which includes a collection of Stein's lectures entitled "Kempō oyobi gyōsei hō kōgi" [Lectures on the constitution and administrative law], edited and translated by Kawashima Jun, and the English originals upon which those translations was based, "Inquiries into Constitutions" and "Some Remarks on the Principles of Administrative Organization." Moreover, we also have notes taken on Stein's lectures by the numerous Japanese who made the famous "Stein pilgrimage."

48. "Junri Shakuwa."

49. "Supplementary Notes on State-Science," in Kazuhiro Takii, ed., *Lorenz von Steins Arbeiten für Japan* (Frankfurt a. M., u.a. 1998), S. 115f. The original manuscript of these lecture notes is preserved in the Kanagawa Prefectural Kanazawa Bunko. My Japanese translation of them has been published as *Sutain kokkagaku nōto* [Notes on Stein's *Staatswissenschaft*], Nihon Kempōshi Sōsho [Library of Japanese Constitutional History] (Tokyo: Shinzansha, 2005).

50. Ibid., S. 143 f.

51. Shimizu, *Seiteishi*, 353.

52. Ibid., 364.

53. Ibid., *Seiteishi*, 365.

54. "Junri Shakuwa."

55. Shimizu, *Seiteishi*, 416.

56. *Itō den*, vol. 2: 320. Letter of Meiji 15.10.22 to Inoue Kaoru.

57. Hiratsuka Atsushi ed., *Zoku Itō Hirobumi hiroku* [Additional private records of Itō Hirobumi] (Tokyo: Shunjūsha, 1930), 46–47.

58. Ibid., 45–46.

59. Hiratsuka Atsushi, ed., *Itō Hirobumi hiroku* [Private records of Ito Hirobumi] (Tokyo: Shunjūsha, 1929), 307.

60. *Itō den*, vol. 2: 314. Letter of Meiji 15.9.6 to Matsukata.

61. *Itō den*, vol. 2: 305. Letter of Meiji 15.8.27 to Yamada Akiyoshi,

62. For Austria under the Ausgleich, see Wilhelm Brauneder, *Österreichische Verfassunggeschichte*, 8.Aufl., 2001, S. 154ff.

63. For constitutional government in Austria during this period, in addition to the aforementioned sources, see Brauneder, *Österreichische Verfassunggeschichte*; and Brauneder "Die Verfassungsentwicklung in Österreich 1848 bis 1918," in *Die Habsburgermonarchie 1848–1918*, Bd. VII (Wien, 2000). In addition, Kaneko Kentarō, who traveled in Europe in 1889 to publicize the Meiji Constitution (see the concluding chapter of this book), offers the following observations on contemporary Austria:

> Of the contemporary European empires, the one most likely to experience political difficulties in the future is Austria. This is easily imaginable when one sees that at present, because the country includes within its territory eighteen different languages and a tangle of ethnic groups, all with differing manners and customs, when a law is promulgated, the official government version is in the German language, while the people are informed of this in the language of their particular region. Whether or not Austria will in future be able to further develop its constitutional government and achieve national unity is a question I hope to investigate at some other time. (Kaneko Kentarō, *Ōbei giin seido torishirabe junkaikii* [Record of an inspection tour of European and American legislative systems] ed. and annotated by Ōbuchi Kazunori (Tokyo; Shinzansha Shuppan, 2001), 53.

64. Mark Twain produced a hilarious piece of reportage on the depressing state of parliamentary affairs in Austria at the end of the nineteenth century: "Stirring Times in Austria," *Harper's New Monthly Magazine*, March 1898, vol. 96: 530-40. It was translated by Nagao Ryūichi as "Austria gikai kembunroku," *Seikei kenkyū*, vol. 37: no. 3 (2000), 239–85.

65. On Franz Joseph as a ruler, see the classic work by Joseph Redlich, *Kaiser Franz Joseph von Österreich* (Berlin, 1929); and Steven Beller, *Francis Joseph* (New York and London: Addison Wesley Longman, 1996.)

66. Eric W. Streissler and Monika Streissler, eds., *Carl Menger's Lectures to Crown Prince Rudolf of Austria*, trans. by Monica Streissler and Davic F. Good (Aldershot, Hants, England: E. Elgar, 1994), 5. It appears that Stein's sympathies lay more with Crown Prince Rudolf of Austria, who held more liberal views and clashed with his father, Franz Joseph. When a tutor was being selected to teach the crown prince statecraft, Stein recommended one of his own students, Inama-Sternegg. But the person actually appointed to the post was Carl Menger

(1840–1921), famous as one of the founders of modern economics. Rudolf, under the psychological stress of his strained relationship with his father, among other factors, ended his life in a scandalous manner, committing suicide along with his lover, a young actress, at Mayerling on the outskirts of Vienna.

67. Hiratsuka, *Itō Hirobumi hiroku*, 307ff.

68. Shimizu, *Seiteishi*, 36–37.

69. Ritsumeikan Daigaku Saionji Kimmochi Den Hensan Iinkai, eds., *Saionji Kimmochi den* [Biography of Saionji Kimmochi], 6 vols. (Tokyo: Iwanami Shoten, 1990), 1: 411ff; and Iwai Tadakuma, *Saionji Kimmochi* (Iwanami Shinsho, 2003), 51ff.

70. The "Stein pilgrimage" is discussed in chapter 3.

71. Alexander Freiherrn von Siebold, "Personliche Erinnrungen an den Fürsten Itō Hirobumi," *Deutsche Revue*, Jg. 35, Bd. 2, 1910, 226ff. This was a remembrance of Itō published at the time of his death. I understand that there is a pamphlet containing an English translation of this text, entitled "Personal Reminiscences of Itō Hirobumi," in the collection of the Siebold Memorial Museum in Nagasaki.

72. Siebold's diary from this period has been preserved, and from it we have a clear picture of Itō's movements during his second stay in Berlin. Vera Schmidt, *Alexander von Siebold: Der Tagebucher, A 1866–1892 (Acta Sieboldiana VII)*, 1992, Wiesbaden, S 338ff.

73. Ibid. See also a letter from Itō to Siebold dated Meiji 16.3.22, in Arcadio Schwade (Hrsg.), *Briefe aus dem Familienarchiv von Brandenstein: der Kreis um Alexander und Heinrich von Siebold (Acta Sieboldiana IV)*, Wiesbaden, 1991, S. 48–49. In that letter Itō acknowledges receipt of Siebold's English translation of a lecture by Gneist.

74. For Japan-related documents in the Gneist Papers, see my "Gunaisuto monjo saihō" [Revisiting the Gneist Papers] in *Shosai no mado*, no. 480, 1998.

75. Schmidt, *Alexander von Siebold*, 342.

76. *Itō den*, vol. 1: 73.

77. This may have been William E. Grigsby, a British national who was the first professor of law at Tokyo Kaisei Gakkō from 1874–78, before it became the University of Tokyo.

78. *Itō den*, vol. 2, 362. Letter from Itō Miyoji to Itō Hirobumi of Meiji 16.9.

79. Itō Hirobumi Paper, "Ōshū taizaichū no shukan no ichibu" [A portion of the correspondance during the European tour], 121.

Chapter Three: Yamagata Aritomo's European Tour

1. For Itō's role in the reform of national institutions prior to the promulgation of the Meiji Constitution, see Sakamoto, *Itō Hirobumi to Meiji kokka keisei*, chapter 4 and following, and my *Doitsu kokkagaku to Meiji kokusei*, chapter 6 and following.

2. See Nakano Minoru, *Kindai Nihon daigaku seido no seiritsu* [The formation of the modern Japanese university system] (Tokyo: Yoshikawa Kōbunkan, 2003).

3. Inoue Kowashi Denki Hensan Iinkai, *Inoue Kowashi den* [Biography of Inoue Kowashi], 6 vols. (Tokyo: Kokugakuin University Library, 1969–77), 5: 37. Letter of Meiji 21.4.20 from Itō to Inoue Kowashi. See also Sakamoto, *Itō Hirobumi to Meiji kokka keisei*, 248ff.

4. "Sutain-shi kōgi bunsho" [Transcripts of Stein's lectures], entry for February 15, 1887. The original manuscript is in the collection of the Archives and Mausolea Department of the Imperial Household Ministry. A manuscript copy is available in the Modern Japanese Political History Materials Room of the National Diet Library. See also Horiguchi Osamu, "Komatsu no miya Akihito shinnō to Shutain oyobi Gunaistu kōgi" [Prince Komatsu and the Stein and Gneist Lectures] in *Shoryōbu kiyō* [Proceedings of the Archives and Mausolea Department], no. 54.

5. Essential sources on this process include three works by Itō Yukio, *Rikken kokka no kakuritsu to Itō Hirobumi* [Itō Hirobumi and the establishment of a constitutional state] (Tokyo: Yoshikawa Kōbunkan, 1999); *Rikken kokka to Nichi-Ro sensō* [The Russo-Japanese War and the constitutional state] (Tokyo: Bokutakusha, 2000); and "Kindai Nihon no gikaisei no hatten to rikken kunshusei no keisei" [The development of the modern Japanese parliamentary system and the formation of a constitutional monarchy], in Hikaku Hōshi Gakkai, eds., *Hō seikatsu to bummei shi* [Legal life and the history of civilization] (Kyoto: Hikaku Hōsei Kenkyūjo, 2003)

6. Ōishi, *Nihon kempō shi*, chapter 4ff. This is an outstanding account of the process by which this body of law—"the constitution in practical terms"—was conceived and established.

7. This is the language used in the Imperial Rescript on the Promulgation of the Constitution.

8. Kojima Kazushi, *Kempōgaku kōwa* [Lectures on constitutional studies] (Tokyo: Yūhikaku, 1984) is a splendid introduction to constitutional studies from this perspective.

9. See Shiyake Masanori, "Seijiteki tōgō toshite no kempō" [The constitution as political unifier], in Satō Kōji and Ōishi Makoto, *Kempō gojūnen no tembō* [A perspective on the constitution after fifty years], 2 vols. (Tokyo: Yūhikaku, 1998), 1. Shiyake's discussion is concerned with constitutionalism under the present system rather than constitutional monarchy, but a certain amount of what he has to say applies to the Meiji Constitution as well.

10. For the various ceremonies conducted on the day the constitution was promulgated, see the official bulletins and special editions of the newspapers for February 11, 1889; Imperial Household Agency, *Meiji tennō ki* [Record of the Meiji Emperor], 12 vols. (Tokyo: Yūhikaku, 1968–75), 7, 205ff; Sashihara Yasuzō, *Meiji seishi* [A political history of the Meiji period], 3 vols. (Tokyo: Fuzambō Shoten, 1892–93; in Meiji Bunka Kenkyūkai, eds., *Meiji bunka zenshū* [Library of Meiji culture], 30 vols. (Tokyo: Nihon Hyōronsha, 1955–1970), 10: 6ff.

11. Ottmar von Mohl, *Am japanischen Hofe* (Berlin: D. Reimer, 1904), translated by Kanamori Seiya as *Doitsu kizoku no Meiji kyūtei ki* [A German nobleman's account of the Meiji imperial court] (Tokyo: Shin Jimbutsu Ōrai Sha, 1988), 191.

12. Meiji Nyūsu Jiten Hensan Iinkai, eds., *Meiji nyūsu jiten* (Encyclopedia of Meiji news] (Tokyo: Mainichi Communications, 1983–86), 476.

13. He is probably referring to the members of the nobility and to the chairmen of the prefectural assemblies, as the members of the Diet had yet to be appointed or elected.

14. Mohl, *Doitsu kizoku*, 191–92.

15. Elisabeth Kraus, *Albert u. Lina Mosse Fast wie mein eigen Vaterland: Briefe aus Japan 1886–1889* (München, 1995), 416. The source is a letter of February 14 to her parents from the wife of Albert Mosse, the German legal expert retained by the Japanese government.

16. See Hayashida Kametarō, *Meiji Taishō seikai sokumen shi* [Sidelights on the political world of the Meiji and Taishō periods] (Tokyo: Ōzorasha, 1991; first published 1926 by Dai Nihon Yūbenkai), 201ff; and Ōishi Makoto, *Nihon kempō shi no shūhen* [The margins of Japan's constitutional history] (Tokyo: Seibundō, 1995), 244. Quotations in the rest of this section came from these sources.

17. It is tempting to surmise that Itō's haggardness that morning owed itself to a bit of early celebration in the company of geisha the night before, for which Itō was notorious.

18. Erwin Baelz, *Das Leben eines deutschen Arztes im erwachenden Japan* (Yokohama: Japan Times, 1883) Trans. in Toku Baelz, ed. and Suganuma Ryūtarō trans., *Baelz no nikki* [Baelz's diary], 2 vols. (Tokyo: Iwanami Shoten, 1979), I: 134.

19. Letter of February 15, 1889, in the possession of Mr. Barthold Witte.

20. Ibid.

21. Inada, *Seiritsu shi*, vol.2: 912 ff.

22. Osatake Takeki, *Nihon kempō shi taikō* [An outline history of the Japanese constitution], 2 vols. (Tokyo: Munakata Shobō, 1939), 2: 797.

23. Ibid., 796.

24. Inada, *Seiritsu shi*, vol.2: 921.

25. See Jürgen Habermas, *Strukturwandel der Offentlichkeit* (Neuwied, Berlin: Luchterhand, 1965), [The structural transformation of the public sphere] trans. by Hosoya Sadao and Yamada Masayuki as *Kōkyōsei no kōzō tenkan* (Tokyo: Miraisha, 1994).

26. Sashihara, *Meiji seishi*, 41.

27. This passage appeared in the official list of Home Ministry promotions and retirements for 1888 and is reproduced in Mikuriya Takashi, *Meiji kokka keisei to chihō keiei* [The formation of the Meiji state and regional management] (Tokyo: University of Tokyo Press, 1980), 178. With regard to the issues involved in the concept of the public sphere from the perspective of media studies, I will cite two works by Satō Takumi as especially helpful: Kingu no jidai: Kokumin taishū zasshi no kōkyōsei [The *King* era: Nationalism, mass magazines, and the public sphere] (Tokyo: Iwanami Shoten, 2002), and his co-translation with Satō Yasuko of George Mosse's *The Nationalization of the Masses* as *Taishū no kokuminka* (Tokyo: Kashiwa Shobō, 1994).

It is worth mentioning that George Mosse's great-grandfather was Gneist's student Albert Mosse, later a legal consultant to the Japanese government, whose name comes up several times in this book. See Satō's translator's note in *Taishū no kokuminka* and the following sources: Elisabeth Kraus, *Albert u. Lina Mosse Fast wie mein eigen Vaterland* (München, 1995), 534; and Elisabeth Kraus, *Die Familie Mosse* (München, 1999).

28. "Daitōryō oyobi sho daijin menwa oboegaki" [Memoranda on interviews with the president and various ministers] in Nakayama Kanrokurō Kankei Monjo [Nakayama Kankurō papers], in the Collention of the Center for Historical Materials on Modern Japanese Law in the Faculty of Law at the University of Tokyo, 6-128, "Nijūni-nen ichigatsu muika: Futsukoku gaimu daijin Goblet to ōsetsu no taii" [January 8, 1889: Outline of meeting with Foreign Minister Goblet of France].

29. For the classic interpretation of Yamagata's place in the political history of modern Japan, see Oka Yoshitake, *Yamagata Aritomo*, in *Oka Yoshitake chōsakushū* [The writings of Oka Yoshitake], 8 vols. (Tokyo: Iwanami Shoten, 1993; first published 1958), vol. 5. For a more recent perspective, see Kawada Minoru, *Hara Takashi to Yamagata Aritomo* [Hara Takashi and Yamagata Aritomo](Chūō Kōronsha, 1998).

30. Tokutomi Sohō, *Kōshaku Yamagata Aritomo den* [The biography of Yamagata Aritomo], 3 vols. (Tokyo: Hara Shobō, 1968; 1st edition 1933), 2: 1027–28. Accompanying Yamagata on the voyage were Furuichi Kimitake, Arakawa Kunizō, Terasaki Son, and Nakayama Kanrokurō from the Home Ministry and Hirasa Korezumi, Nakamura Yūjirō, Kosaka Chihiro, and Kako Tsurudo of the Army Ministry.

31. Mikuriya, *Meiji kokka keisei to chihō keiei*, 184; and Nagai Jun'ichi, "Yamagata Aritomo to chihō jichi seido kakuritsu jigyō—Meiji 21-nen no yōkō o chūshin ni" [Yamagata Aritomo and the efforts to establish a system of local government—focusing on his European tour of 1888], *Shigaku zasshi*, vol. 100, no. 4 (1991), 4–5. Yamagata was in conflict with Inoue Kaoru, Inoue Kowashi, and Itō Hirobumi over a variety of issues, from plans to privatize government-owned forests and agricultural land to Inoue Kaoru's plan to found a political party called the Jichitō (Self-Government Party) as well as the various proposals being considered with regard to the restructuring of local government at the prefectural level and below. It has been suggested that in the midst of this tumult, Yamagata decided to temporarily relinquish the reins of leadership and travel to Europe in order to spend some time observing domestic developments from a distance.

32. Takii, *Doitsu kokkagaku to Meiji kokusei*, 134ff.

33. Hayashi Tadasu, *Nochi wa mukashi no ki nari*, 214.

34. An archive of documents (the Nakayama Papers) left by Nakayama Kanrokurō, who was Yamagata's private secretary and accompanied him on this voyage, has been preserved at the Center for Historical Materials on Modern Japanese Law in the Faculty of Law at the University of Tokyo. This chapter makes extensive use of these materials, which provide thorough documentation of the tour.

35. Sashihara, *Meiji seishi*, 41.

36. "Jinshin kyōdō iken an," in *Inoue Kowashi den*, vol. 1: 251. Quoted in the introduction.

37. Yamamuro Shin'ichi, *Hōsei kanryō no jidai* [The era of the legal bureaucrats] (Tokyo: Bokutakusha, 1984), 250ff; Katada Tsuyoshi, *Doitsugaku kyōkai to Meiji hōsei* [The Association for German Studies and the Meiji legal system] (Tokyo: Bokutakusha, 1999); and Morikawa Jun, *Inoue Kowashi no Doitsuka kōsō* [Inoue Kowashi's ideology of "Germanification"] (Tokyo: Yūshōdō Shuppan, 2003). These sources discuss the process of the introduction of German studies and its significance. I consider this subject in chapter 6 of *Doitsu kokkagaku to Meiji kokusei.*

38. "Doitsu kaze fukikitareri" [The German wind is blowing], *Kokumin no tomo*, no. 2 (1887). See also Yamamuro, *Hōsei kanryō no jidai*, 313.

39. Takii, *Doitsu kokkagaku to Meiji kokusei.*

40. Nakamura Takeshi, *Shinsetsu Meiji rikugun shi* [A new interpretation of the history of the Meiji army] (Tokyo: Azusa Shobo, 1973), 162ff.

41. Entry for January 17, 1889, in *Hara Takashi nikki* [Diaries of Hara Takashi], Hara Keiichirō, ed., 9 vols. (Tokyo: Fukumura Shuppan, 2000; first published 1965), 1: 137.

42. *Yamagata den*, vol. 2: 1031–33. After his meeting with Goblet, Yamagata wrote the following in a letter to Matsukata dated January 16, 1889:

> Of course prior to my departure I had learned from the both the foreign minister and the minister of the army of the trouble that had arisen, and being aware of this, was determined to approach everything cautiously. I consulted with chargé d'affaires Tanaka and took all precautions to ensure there were no missteps in approaching the meeting. The fact that in spite of all this the French brought up the change in policy was unpleasant, but I don't think it would do for us to get our back up in response.

43. Yamagata's visit to France is explained in precisely this manner in Akiyama Yoshifuru Taishō Denki Kankōkai, eds., *Akiyama Yoshifuru* (Akiyama Yoshifuru Taishō Denki Kankōkai, 1936), 62 ff.

44. *Yamagata den*, vol. 2: 1032. Letter dated January 16, 1889 from Yamagata to Matsukata.

45. In the previously cited "Daitoryō oyobi sho daijin menwa oboegaki," see the entry "Nijūni-nen ichigatsu nijūichi-nichi: Futsukoku rikugun daijin Freycinet to ōsetsu no taii" (January 21, 1889: Outline of meeting with Minister of War Freycinet of France).

46. Ibid.

46. Inoue Kaoru Papers, 639-4. Letter dated February 16, 1889 from Yamagata to Yoshikawa Akimasa.

48. "Nijūni-nen nigatsu nijūichi-nichi: Futsukoku naikaku gichō ken naimu daijin Floquet to ōsetsu no taii" [February 21, 1889: Outline of meeting with prime minister and interior minister Floquet] in the previously cited "Daitōryō oyobi sho daijin menwa oboegaki."

49. For Boulangism, I have relied upon Jean-Jacques Chevalier, *Histoire des institutions des régimes politiques de France de 1789 à 1958*, 9th edition (Paris, 2000), 386ff; and Shibata Michio, Kabayama Kōichi, and Fukui Norihiko, eds., *Furansu shi* [History of France], 3 vols. (Tokyo: Yamakawa Shuppansha, 1996), 3: 135ff.

50. Inoue Kaoru Papers, 639-4. Letter dated February 16, 1889 from Yamagata to Yoshikawa Akimasa.

51. "Jun'Ō nisshi" [Daybook of the European Tour], Nakayama Papers, 6-127.

52. A manuscript of Prince Fushimi's lecture notes is preserved as part of the Itō Miyoji Papers as "Gneist-shi danwa" [Conversations with Gneist]; Prince Komatsu's lecture notes are preserved in the Archives and Mausolea Department of the Imperial Household Agency as "Gneist-shi kōgi bunsho" (Transcripts of Professor Gneist's Lectures).

53. "Lectures by Prof. Gneist" (4-40-7); "Lectures by Prof. Gneist" (4-40-8); "Gunaihito [sic]-shi tōgi (Hōritsu meirei no kubetsu / Teishitsu narabi ni kōshitsu zaisan)" [Responses from Prof. Gneist (On the distinction between laws and ordinances / On imperial household finances)] (6-377); and "Gunaihito-shi kōgi" [Lectures by Prof. Gneist]. These records of the Gneist lectures in the Nakayama Papers are supplemented by related materials in the "Doitsu chōsa shorui" [Papers of the German Study Tour; 6-150], including "Ro-shi to Gu-shi to no romben" [A debate between Roessler and Gneist] and "Gneist kōgi" [Gneist lectures].

54. "Lectures by Prof. Gneist." This notebook is dated May 3.

55. Ibid. The English phrasing is that of the original notes.

56. "Gunaihito-shi tōgi."

57. Ibid.

58. "Gunaihito-shi kōgi."

59. "Sutei-shi ikensho" [Opinions of Professor Stein], Nakayama Papers, 6-137. The "Jun'Ō nisshi" contains no mention of a meeting with Stein, so it is possible that this information was conveyed in writing rather than an interview. On June 1, Yamagata and company left Vienna for Russia.

60. Katō Yōko, Sensō no Nihon kin-gendai shi [War in Modern and Contemporary Japanese History] (Kōdansha Gendai Shinsho, 2002), 85ff.

61. "Sutei-shi ikensho."

62. "Shissei hōshin enzetsu" [Policy address], in Yamagata Aritomo ikensho [Position papers of Yamagata Aritomo], Ōyama Azusa, ed. (Hara Shobō, 1966), 203.

63. "Sutei-shi ikensho."

64. Ōishi, Nihon kempō shi no shūhen, 172ff; and Giin hō seitei shi no kenkyū [A historical study of the establishment of the Law of the Houses] (Tokyo: Seibundō, 1990), 107ff.

65. The original document is contained in the Itō Miyoji Papers. Documents with essentially the same content may be found in the Inoue Kaoru Papers and in Itō Hirobumi, ed., Hisho ruisan: kempō shiryō [Materials on the Constitution] under the titles "Nihon kempō o sōsetsu suru ni kansuru ikensho ippan no rikai" (in vol. 2) and "Kurumetsuki-shi Nihon kempō shikō ni kansuru ikensho" (in vol. 3). See Ōishi, Nihon kempō shi no shūhen, 174.

66. Ōishi, Nihon kempō shi no shūhen and Giin hō seitei shi no kenkyū.

67. Takii, "Cheko ni nokoru Itō Hirobumi no tegami—Buruno ni Kurumetsuki-ke Monjo o tazunete" [A letter by Itō Hirobumi preserved in the Czech Republic—

Visiting the Chlumecky Family Archive in Brno], parts 1 and 2, in *Shosai no mado*, nos. 475-6 (1998).

68. "Ōchirii kokkai daiichi fukugichō fuon Kurumetsuki-shi danwa (kokkai un'ei kankei)" [Conversation with first vice-president von Chlumecky of the Austrian national assembly (relating to management of the national assembly)], in Nakayama Papers, 6-136.

69. *Yamagata den*, 1040.

70. *Hara Takashi nikki*, vol. 1: 139.

71. Inoue Kaoru Papers, 639-4. Letter of February 16, 1889 from Yamagata to Yoshikawa Akimasa.

72. Ibid.

73. Nagai, "Yamagata Aritomo to chihō jichi seido kakuritsu jigyō." Letter of April 22, 1885 from Nomura Yasushi to Yamagata.

74. *Yamagata den*, vol. 2: 1033. Letter of January 14, 1889 to Matsukata Masatoshi.

75. *Yamagata den*, vol. 2: 1051. Letter of April 5, 1889 from Yamagata to Yoshikawa Akimasa and Tanaka Mitsuaki.

76. Ibid.

77. *Yamagata den*, vol. 2, 1033. Letter of June 5, 1889 to Yamada Akiyoshi, *Yamagata den*, vol. 2: 1060.

78. Mutsu Munemitsu Kankei Monjo [Mutsu Munemitsu Papers] (Collection of Modern Japanese Political History Materials Room of the National Diet Library, 41-3. Letter of May 12, 1889 from Yamagata to Mutsu Munemitsu.

79. "Jun'Ō chū shokan an" [Draft of a letter from the European tour], Nakayama Papers, 6-149.

80. Ibid.

81. Inoue Kaoru Papers, 639-3. Letter of June 22, 1899 from Yamagata to Yoshikawa Akimasa.

82. "Jun'Ō chū shokan an."

83. Inoue Kaoru Papers, 576-1. Letter of March 21, 1889 from Yamagata to Inoue Kaoru.

84. Inoue Kaoru Papers, 639-3. Letter of June 22, 1899 from Yamagata to Yoshikawa Akimasa.

85. Inoue Kaoru Papers, 576-1. Letter of March 21, 1889 from Yamagata to Inoue Kaoru.

86. Inoue Kaoru Papers, 639-1. Letter of May 22, 1889 from Yamagata to Yoshikawa Akimasa,

87. *Yamagata den*, vol. 2, 1040.

88. Oka, *Yamagata Aritomo*, 35.

89. Inoue Kaoru Papers, 576-1. Letter of March 21, 1889 from Yamagata to Inoue Kaoru.

90. Inoue Kaoru Papers, 628-28. Letter of March 18, 1889 from Sufu Kōhei to Inoue Kaoru. Prior to Yamagata's letter, Sufu himself had written an appeal to Inoue.

Conclusion: The Meiji Constitution Seen from Abroad

1. Kaneko Kentarō, *Kempō seitei to Ō-Bei jin no hyōron* [The establishment of the constitution and the opinion of Europeans and Americans] (Tokyo: Nihon Seinenkan, 1937), 197; and Kaneko Kentarō, *Ōbei giin seido torishirabe junkaiki*, 195.

2. To understand the constitution from this perspective, it is also interesting to consider the gala held on April 17, 1889, at Johns Hopkins University to celebrate the promulgation of the Meiji Constitution, two months after that event. Daniel C. Gilman, president of Johns Hopkins, and Japanese ambassador to the United States Mutsu Munemitsu attended, and Woodrow Wilson (1856–1924), then a professor at Wesleyan University, and later president of the United States, sent a congratulatory letter. At the gathering, Ienaga Tomikichi, then studying political science at Johns Hopkins, gave an address entitled "Japan's Preparations for the Present Constitution." This speech, the doctoral dissertation that Ienaga submitted to Johns Hopkins entitled "The Constitutional Development of Japan 1853–1881," and Wilson's letter have all been translated into Japanese as part of an important work edited and supervised by Ōta Masao, *Ienaga Tomikichi to Meiji kensei shiron* [Ienaga Tomikichi and the historiography of the Meiji constitutional order] (Tokyo: Shinsensha, 1996]. In his letter, Wilson notes that the Meiji Constitution was clearly based on the Prussian model, concluding:

   > And I think that, considering the state of development in which Japan now finds herself, the Prussian constitution was an excellent instrument to copy. Her choice of it as a model is but another proof of the singular sagacity, the singular power to see and learn, which is Japan's best constitution and promise of success. (Letter from Wilson to Daniel C. Gilman, in Arthur S. Link, ed., *The Papers of Woodrow Wilson*, vol. 6 [Princeton University Press, 1969], 172.)

3. Kaneko, *Ōbei giin seido torishirabe junkaiki*.

4. Ibid., 98.

5. Ibid., 99.

6. Ibid., 137.

7. Ibid., 137.

8. Ibid., 76.

9. Ibid., 115.

10. Ibid., 115.

11. Ibid., 48.

12. Ibid., 107.

13. Ibid., 104.

14. Ibid., 106.

15. For this aspect of Spencer's thought, see Herbert Spencer, *The Man versus the State* (London, 1884). Like Stein, Spencer was a sociologist who had gained wide acceptance in Japan. Highly recommended for understanding his reception in Japan is Yamashita Jūichi, *Spencer to Nihon kindai* [Spencer and Japanese modernity] (Tokyo: Ochanomizu Shobō, 1983).

16. Kaneko, *Ōbei giin seido torishirabe junkaiki*, 177.

17. Ibid., 176.

18. Ibid., 177.

19. Ibid., 178.

20. For the process of compiling *Commentaries on the Constitution*, see Inada, *Seiritsushi*, vol. 2: 859ff.

21. Kaneko, *Kempō seitei to Ō-Bei jin no hyōron*, 390.

22. Letter of March 1, 1889 from Itō to Stein, in Der Nachlass Lorenz von Steins in the collection of the Central State Library of Schleswig-Holstein.

23. Irie Kan'ichi, *Yamagata kō no omokage* [The face of Prince Yamagata] (Kaigyōsha Hensanbu, 1930), 55.

24. George Akita and Itō Takashi, "Yamagata Aritomo to 'jinshu kyōsō' ron" [Yamagata Aritomo and the theory of "racial competition"] in Kindai Nihon Kenkyūkai, eds., *Nempō: Kindai Nihon Kenkyū 7*—Nihon gaikō no kiki ishiki [Annual report: research on modern Japan 7—Crisis consciousness in Japanese diplomacy] (Tokyo: Yamakawa Shuppansha, 1985), 111.

25. Yamagata saw the second Restoration as being the dissolution of the feudal domains and the establishment of prefectures under the control of the central government (*haihan chiken*) in 1871. See the previously cited letter dated June 5, 1889 from Yamagata to Yamada Akiyoshi in *Yamagata den*, vol. 2: 1061.

26. The term *ishin* is drawn from a classical phrase that means "make it new," so its standard translation as "restoration" has always been problematic).

27. *Yamagata den*, vol. 2, 1099.

28. Ibid., vol. 2: 1102.

29. Ibid., vol. 2: 1103.

30. A cabinet order promulgated in 1907 restored the earlier position on ministerial responsibility by requiring that all ordinances issued by ministries other than military be co-signed by the prime minister.

31. *Yamagata den*, vol. 2: 1061.

32. For Yamagata's role in the framing of the Imperial Rescript on Education, see Umetani Noboru, *Kyōiku chokugo seiritsu shi* [A history of the establshment of the Imperial Rescript on Education] (Tokyo: Seishi Shuppan, 2000).

33. For Yamagata and the Imperial Rescript to Soldiers and Sailors, see Umetani Noboru, *Gunjin chokugo seiritsu shi* [A history of the establishment of the Imperial Rescript to Soldiers and Sailors] (Tokyo: Seishi Shuppan, 2000].

34. Kokumin Seishin Bunka Kenkyūjo, eds., *Kyōiku chokugo kampatsu kankei shiryō shū* [Collection of materials related to the promulgation of the Imperial Rescript on Education], 3 vols. (Kompanion Shuppan, 1985), 2: 453.

Afterword

1. Satō Kōji, *Kempō to sono "monogatari" sei* (The constitution and its "narrativity"), 56.

2. Itō Yukio and Kawada Minoru, eds., *Nijū seiki Nihon no tennō to kunshusei* [Emperor and monarchy in twentieth-century Japan] (Tokyo: Yoshikawa Kōbunkan, 2004).

PRIMARY SOURCES

Hiratsuka Atsushi, ed. *Itō Hirobumi hiroku* [Private Records of Itō Hirobumi]. Tokyo: Hara Shobō, 1982 (1st edition, 1929).

———. *Zoku Itō Hirobumi hiroku* [Additional private records of Itō Hirobumi]. Tokyo: Hara shobō, 1982 (1st edition 1929).

Inada Masatsugu. *Meiji Kempō seiritsushi* [History of the establishment of the Meiji Constitution]. 2 vols. Tokyo: Yūhikaku, 1960–62.

Inoue Kowashi Denki Hensan Iinkai. *Inoue Kowashi den: shiryōhen* [Biography of Inoue Kowashi: Supplementary Documents]. 6 vols. Tokyo: Kokugakuin University Library, 1969–77.

Ito Hirobumi Kankei Monjo Kenkyūkai, ed. *Itō Hirobumi kankei monjo* [Itō Hirobumi papers]. 9 vols. Tokyo: Hanawa Shobō, 1973–81.

Kaneko Kentarō, ed. and annotated by Ōbuchi Masanori. *Ō-bei giin seido torishirabe junkaiki* [Record of an inspection tour of European and American legislative systems]. Tokyo: Shinzansha, 2001.

Kokuritsu Kokkai Toshokan Kensei Shiryōshitsu zō [Collection of the Modern Japanese Political History Materials Room of the National Diet Library]. *Inoue Kaoru kankei monjo* [Inoue Kaoru papers].

Kokuritsu Kokkai Toshokan Kensei Shiryōshitsu zō [Collection of the Modern Japanese Political History Materials Room of the National Diet Library]. *Itō Hirobumi kankei monjo* [Itō Hirobumi papers].

Kume Kunitake, ed. and annotated by Tanaka Akira. *Bei-Ō kairan jikki* [A true account of a journey of observation through the United States and Europe]. 5 vols. Tokyo: Iwanami Shoten, 1977–82.

Kume Keiichirō, et al. eds. *Kume Hakushi kyūjū-nen kaikoroku* [A record of Professor Kume's recollections of his ninety years]. 2 vols. Tokyo: Hanawa Shobō, 1985 (1st edition, 1934).

Nihon Shiseki Kyokai, ed. *Kido Takayoshi monjo* [Kido Takayoshi papers]. 8 vols. Tokyo: Tokyo Daigaku Shuppannkai, 1971 (1st edition, 1929).

Nihon Shiseki Kyokai, ed. *Ōkubo Toshimichi monjo* [Okubo Toshimichi papers]. 10 vols. Tokyo: University of Tokyo Press, 1973 (1st edition, 1928).

Shimizu Shin. *Meiji Kempō seiteishi, jō: Doitsu ni okeru Ito Hirobumi no kempō chōsa* [History of the establishment of the Meiji constitutional system, vol. 1: Itō Hirobumi's constitutional research in Germany and Austria]. Tokyo: Hara Shobō, 1972.

Shunpo-kō Tsuishōkai, ed. *Itō Hirobumi den* [Biography of Itō Hirobumi], 3 vols. (Tokyo: Hara Shobō, 1972).

Tokutomi Sohō. *Kōshaku Yamagata Aritomo den* [Biography of Prince Yamagata Aritomo]. 3 vols. Tokyo: Hara Shobō, 1969. (1st edition, 1933).

Tokyo Daigaku Hōgakubu Fuzoku Kindai Nihon Hōsei Shiryō Sentā shozō [Collection of the Center for Historical Materials on Modern Japanese Law in the Faculty of Law at the University of Tokyo]. *Nakayama Kanrokurō kankei monjo* [Nakayama Kanrokurō papers].

Tokyo Daigaku Shiryō Hensanjo [Center for Historical Materials on Modern Japanese Law in the Faculty of Law at the University of Tokyo], ed. *Hogo hiroi: Sasaki Takayuki nikki* [The scrap collector: The diary of Sasaki Takayuki]. 5 vols. Tokyo: University of Tokyo Press, 1974.

INDEX

A

Academy of the German Studies
Association, 109
Adams, Francis, 20
administrative law: as foundation of constitution, 69; mission members see as
beneath dignity to research, 69
administrative reform: Its Vienna memo
on, 78–79
American Revolution, xii, xvii
Americans, hidden ulterior motives of, 20
ancient Rome and Meiji Japan, xv–xvii
Anson, William Reynell, 133, 134
Aoki Shūzō, 36, 60, 85, 86; advises Itō to
investigate administrative law, 69
army: shift from French to German
model, 110
Atami Conference, 53, 89
Austro-Hungarian Empire: complex
dual-state structure and vastness
of, 81; parliament fraught with
difficulties, 81
"autocratic constitution," 39, 40

B

Baelz, Erwin: on public reception of
constitution, 101, 103
Bismarck, 41, 42, 46, 83, 115, 134; decries
"disease of factionalism," 65; German
Empire and imperial constitution and,
64; hails Germany as model for Japan,
43; ideals for parliament abandoned, 81;
legitimation of Realpolitik, 42–43; on law
of nations, 42; Prussian constitutional
crisis instigated by, 64
Bloch, Maurice, 36
Boulanger, Charles, 114
Boulangism, 126; drama of exposes
Yamagata to parliamentary
weakness, 114–115
Brandt, Max von, 20
British Museum, 33, 34
British-style politics: countered by Prussian
model, 54

budget: Gneist decries legislative authority
over, 62–63
Bureau for the Investigation of
Constitutional Systems, Itō appointed
director of, 92
bureaucracy: system for building, 92–93

C

Cabinet Law: Yamagata seeks revision
of, 141
cabinet system: introduced in Japan, 92
capitalism, 45
caretaker government: broken promises
and overhasty reforms, 37; radical initiatives in domestic and foreign policy, 50;
shaky foundations of, 50
Charter Oath of 1868, 36, 38, 98
China: hegemony of ended, 4
Chinese world order, 4
Chlumecky Family Archive, 122
Chlumecky, Johann Freiherr von, 121, 132
civil war, 50
civilization: as virtue of law of nations, 5;
brilliant comparative analysis of, 27; conflict as principle of, 46; energy expended
on trappings of, 13; Japan's search for,
xvii; Japanese realize cunning underlay
politesse of, 30; Kume sees ethos of, 35;
law of nations misconceived as other
name for, 46; naive imitation of, 12;
nineteenth-century clash of, xv; reaction
against by incorrigibles (gankōron), 10;
sequence of stages of, 33; tense dynamic
generated by, 13; unique perspective
on, 1–2
civilization and antiquity, 7
"civilization and enlightenment," program
of, xv, 10
civilized nation, 100
Code Civil of France, xiii
Coing, Helmut, xiii
Commentaries on the Constitution, 131, 135;
instrumental in garnering acclaim for
constitution, 136

competition, 43; and conflict 29; bolstering
national capacity for, 49–50; individual
to social to national, 31
Compromise of 1867, 81
conservatism, Confucian and German
blend of, xi
constititution: as clothing, 16–17; as
composition or structure, xiv; as goal
of reform of national institutions,
xvii; as heart of political system, xviii;
as integral to institutionalizing nationalism, 32; as legal document, xiv; as
national structure, 3; as political
proclamation, xiii; as "shape of the
nation" (kuni no katachi), xiv, xv, xviii;
as symbol of civilized nation, xviii; at
apex of consistent legal system, 97;
establishment of gains speed, 52;
insufficient in and of itself, 91; Itō
sees as just one element, 79; its
unifying and symbolic roles, 97;
Kido and Ōkubo share grand plan
for, 44; Kume and Kido see as
backbone of national unity, 38;
national survival hinges on state
of, 38; nineteenth century age of,
xvii; proclamations of ideals in
need of supplementary materials,
69; significant as nation's most
fundamental law, 96; signified Japan's
intent to joined "civilized" nations,
97; subtle nuance of word, xiii–xv; symbolic domestically and internationally,
97; symbolizes Japan's civilization
and enlightenment, 100
"constitutional charisma," 137
constitutional government, xi; administrative support for, 93; as form of civilization, xvii; Austrian style not affirmed by
Itō, 83; balance of three organs Stein's
key lesson for Itō, 138; democracy and
gradualism as organizing principles of,
44; Europe deepened Itō's insight into
pitfalls of, 95; gradualist argument for,
44; Kido's two central pillars of, 40–41;
Ōkuma's radical memorial on, 51; parliamentary system inevitable but with
requirements, 95; premised on overhaul
of national institutions, 91; realities of in
Germany, 64–65; strengthen nation to
support, 49

constitutional gradualism, 137–138
constitutional history, significant aspect
of, xii
constitutional law: German, xi
constitutional monarchy: as advocated by
Kido, 40; emperor encouraged to develop into, 94; executive branch and, 76; Itō
follows own blueprint to establish,
94–95; pivotal role in for Privy Council,
93
constitutional system: creation of, 47; government by popular will fundamental to,
39; gradual implementation of, 50;
Stein's overview exceeds drafting constitution, 78
constitutionalism, inaugural era of, xii;
orthodox interpretation of, xii
"cooperative impulse": Kume preaches
necessity of, 31–32

D

democracy and gradualism, 44
despotism, rejection of, xii, xiii
development, laws of, 34
developmental dictatorship, 118–119
Dicey, Albert Venn, 132
Diet: fraught with difficulties at outset, 95;
Itō's consistent leadership of, 95; Itō
devotes thought to restraining, 138
diplomacy, traditional definition of, 3
diversity: of national institutions and political systems, 37
domestic stability: political priority for
Iwakura Embassy, 50–51

E

emperor: granted sweeping powers under
constitution, 96; institutional constraints
on political activity of, 93–94; Itō aimed
for limited monarchy of, 96–97; Itō
indicates decision-making authority
of, 94
Emperor Franz Joseph I: as contrast to
Stein's vision, 82; as linchpin of Austro-
Hungarian Empire, 82–83; Itō strongly
impressed with, 82–83
Emperor Meiji, 38; Itō takes step to turn
into constitutional monarch, 92; letter of
credence from, 3

English constitutionalism: Meiji
Constitution and, 133
Equality: study policies for restoring, 5
ethnic conflict: paralyzes Austro-
Hungarian parliament, 81
Etō Shimpei, 49; driven out of
government, 50
Eurocentric model, 6
European civilization: "shape of
the nation" and, 6; standards
of, 5–6
European law, xiii
executive branch: center stage in Stein's
theory, 76; Itō learns value of from Stein,
83, 92; selected by but autonomous from
sovereign, 76

F

Fish, Hamilton, 20
Floquet, Charles, 114, 115
Franco-Prussian War of 1870–71, 41
Freedom and Popular Rights Movement
(Jiyū Minken Undō), xi, xvii, xviii, 50, 51,
127; activists freed as sign of reconcilia-
tion, 104; boosted by Pink Pamphlet
Incident, 116; denigrated by Yamagata,
128; enthusiasm unmatched by govern-
ment leaders, 106; government's deep-
rooted antipathy for, 105; publications
of welcome constitution, 103; see consti-
tution as legitimizing, 104; suppression
of, 116
French civil code, xiii
French Declaration of the Rights of
Man, xii
French military advisers: dismissal of at
heart of discord with France, 110–111
French Revolution, xii, xvii
Freycinet, Charles Louis de Saulces de, 113
Fuisting, Bernhard, 85
Fukuchi Gen'ichirō: request to accompany
Itō becomes public, 56–57
Fukuzawa Yukichi, 28, 35, 51; letter to hints
of Stein's ambitions, 72–73

G

"Germanification," 109
German civil code, xiii
German constitution, ix, x, xi

German Imperial Constitution of 1871
(Bismark Constitution): universal suffrage and, 64
German Studies Association, 109
German thought, institutionalization
of, 110
Germany: as model for Japan, xi, 41; breakdown of politics of compromise in, 65;
Japan deepening friendship with, 109
Gneist Papers: reveal regular correspondence with Japan, 86–87
Gneist, Rudolf von, 36, 60, 65, 70, 80, 132;
advocates Japan follow French model in
local administration, 119; "democratic"
aspect of Yamagata lectures, 117; dim
appraisal of Japan, 61–62; emphasizes
policy implementation through strong
executive power, 118; fundamental relationship with constitution, 116; Itō and
Meiji Japan and, 85–86; Savigny's
thought and, 61
Goblet, Rene-Marie: Yamagata's surprisingly cold meeting with, 108
Gotō Shōjirō, 85
government: aims and intentions of,
2; British-style system of, 51; establishment of autonomous executive
branch of, 92; manners and customs
of people and, 35; republican or monarchical form of, xii
gradualism, 33, 34, 40–41, 52, 138–139; as
approach to establishing constitution,
49; in ethos of civilization, 35

H

Habermas, Jürgen: "public sphere" concept of, 105
Haga Tōru, 27
Hatakeyama Yoshinari [Sugiura Kōzō],
24–25, 36
Hiraga Yoshitada, 10; Iwakura's favor and
Western table manners, 9
Hirata Tōsuke, 86, 87
historiography: as national enterprise, 134
Hokkaido Colonization Office: sale of
assets of inflames popular rights movement, 51; sale of assets suspended, 52
Holmes, Oliver Wendell, 132; appraisal of
and advice on constitution, 134–135;
stresses importance of history, 134

I

Ida Yuzuru: former envoy suggests legation have Itō meet Stein, 71–72; writes Itō about inviting Stein to Japan, 72
Ienaga Saburō, xi, xvii
Imperial Household Department, Itō appointed minister of, 92
Imperial Household Law, 52, 93
imperial palace: as venue where entrenched politics ameliorated, 104
imperial proclamation of April 1875, 50
imperial rescript of 1881, 52, 53, 101, 109
Imperial Rescript on Education: Yamagata and, 142
Imperial Rescript to Soldiers and Sailors: Yamagata and, 142
Imperial University Order, 92–93
Imperial University system: comprising Imperial University Order and other regulations, 93
Imperial University, 102
imperial will: Austrian government ministers subservient to, 82
individual, autonomy and self-reliance of, 28. See Fukuzawa Yukichi
industrialization, 45
Inoue Kaoru, 23, 53, 78, 109, 128, 129; intense irritation of, 56–57; on Itō's mental state, 54
Inoue Kowashi, xi, 56, 59, 80, 100, 139; considered author of Meiji Constitution, 54; date mistake of, 101; drafts Iwakura's counter to Ōkuma's memorial, 54; explanation to by Itō of Privy Council, 93–94; provides draft constitution with Iwakura memorandum, 54; resourcefulness of, 54; submits position paper encouraging German studies, 109; under Itō's command, 95
Institutes of the Law of Nations, The (Lorimer): "three concentric zones or spheres" of humanity, 5–6
interest-based politics, Western principle of, 28
international law, 46
international politics, essential nature of, 31
Ishii Takahashi, 20
Itagaki Taisuke: driven out of government, 50

Itō Hirobumi, xv, xvii, xviii, 1, 22, 37, 39, 86, 109, 131; 1882 mission of, xvii; advocate of "enlightenment," 36; alarmed response to Ōkuma's memorial, 51; and intellectuals inside and outside government, 80; angered by Gneist's remarks, 62; argues for delay of parliamentary government and party cabinets, 106; as antagonist, 17; as equal of former shogunal retainers, 17; as lively leader, 17; as odd man out, 25; as originator of Iwakura Embassy, 18; attends coronation of tsar, 88; August Vienna trip improves mood of, 68; aware that constitution had to be "Japanese," 137; blamed for embassy's difficulties, 21; central to reform of national political system, 53; close early relationship with Ōkuma, 53; committed to partnership with parliament, 83; competitive atmosphere and friction surrounding mission of, 56; confidence to confront popular rights activists, 79; confidentiality of mission, 56; connects constitution to administrative law, 69–70; correspondence with Chlumecky, 122; departure of compared with Iwakura Embassy, 56; designated central to drafting constitution, 52; difficulty understanding Mosse, 66; difficulty with mission members, 66–67; dismisses intellectual opponents, 79; distinguishes between conflicting positions, 89; distress in Berlin combines dissatisfaction and discontent, 68; ebullient with Stein's teachings, 73; entrance to party politics of, 95; expert in constitutional systems, 79; failure in Berlin, 62; faithful to Stein's teachings, 95; gains insight into national structure, 79; guards gradualism, 139; humiliating failure of, 21; initiates institutional and palace reforms, 92; invokes limited version of Franz Joseph, 95; laid tracks for first party cabinet under Hara Takahashi, 95–96; lesson acquired in Europe, 91–92; letters to Gneist reveal familiarity, 87; limits emperor's political prerogatives and gradually implements parliamentary system, 137; misplaces constitution, 100–101; mission secrecy arouses public suspicion, 58–59; mock trial of Nagano,

12; no shared understanding of mission's purpose, 68; notes reconstruct Stein's teachings, 74; on Ōkubo's memorandum, 44; ordered to investigate form of government, 43; priority on national structure not constitution, 95; proposal to regain tariff autonomy and promote Japan's industry, 21; rationale for European trip and, 55; regains control of mission through Stein, 84; registers satisfaction with Kaneko's mission, 136–137; rejects Aoki's advice on use of mission members, 70; "Rising Sun" speech, 18–19, 21; seeks to regain leadership of and unique position in constitutional process, 55, 70; selected for constitutional research in Europe, 52; shares Kido's concerns about Korean expedition, 52; Shitty Speech of, 10–11; shock on of Ōkuma's memorial, 53; sidelined by Iwakura and Ōkuma, 53; small but elite research team for clandestine journey of, 55–56; sole authority in formulating constitution, 91; sought cooperation of government and parliament, 97; supple policy helps overcome Diet crises, 95; treated harshly by Gneist, 60; treaty revision boast of, 20; two points for constitutional government, 83–84; unfinished letter to Ōkuma exudes confidence, 88–89; variation on Stein's teachings, 84; Western extravagances of, 19

Itō Miyoji, 85, 88, 100

Itō Papers, 88

Iwakura Embassy, xvii, 1, 4, 50, 53, 55, 107, 126, 139; as fact-finding mission, 3; as national pageant, 18; at standstill for four months, 21; completion of, 49; confidence and optimism before dispatch of, 26; decision on attire, 13–14; departure of, 98; diplomatic ineptitude of, 21; embarrassing display by, 8–9; focused on national structure, 32–33; historical context of, 6; initial emphasis on law of nations, 46; instructions on civilized manners and, 7; itinerary of, 12–13; sees logic of Western civilization is power, 138; national survival as new mission of, 31; overestimation of American goodwill, 19–20; overlooks nonreciprocal most favored nation clause, 21; scrutiny of

Western civilization and, 8; suspends treaty negotiations, 21; treaty discussions in Washington and, 19–20; understanding of contemporary civilization, 46; Western contact compels reassessment of views, 26

Iwakura Tomomi, 1, 51, 59, 80, 88, 139; abandons Japanese dress, 14–15; anxiety of, 8; death of, 91; harsh lesson for in diplomatic reality, 20–21; official government instructions and, 8; return to Japan, 49; traditional court dress of, 6–7

Izumi Saburō, 27

J

Japanese civilization, major task facing, 28

Japanese legation in Vienna: high regard for Stein, 71

Japanese spirit, Western learning, 15, 97–100

Jhering, Rudolf von, 45, 132

"Jiyūsho" (Statement of Purpose), 2, 4, 5, 46

Jiyūtō (Liberal Party), 95, 115

jurisprudence, historical school of, 61

K

Kaeda Nobuyoshi, 121

Kaiser Wilhelm I, 65, 80; decries national assembly and financial control of, 63

Kaiser Wilhelm II, 115

Kaishintō (Progressive Party), 103, 104

Kaneko Kentarō, 100, 101; debuts constitution in West, 131; eminent Westerners' impressions recorded in diary of, 132; European and U.S. study tour of, 131

Katō Yōko, 119

Kawashima Atsushi, 85; influences Itō to meet Stein, 71; memorial on government reform learned from Stein, 70–71; selected to Itō's mission, 71

kempō, definition of, xiv. *See also* constitution: as legal document

Kiba Sadanaga, 66, 67; on Kawashima's familiarity with Stein, 71

Kido Takayoshi, xviii, 1, 13; as budding constitutionalist, 36; built argument for constitutional government on gradualism, 139; changed relationship with Itō, 23, 35;

distanced self from radical modernizers, 23; distress of, 36; endorsement of absolutist rule, 38, 39, 44; first to return to Japan, 37; gradualism and, 49; importance for of constitution, 38–39; impressed by Gneist, 60; leads recrimination against Itō, 21–22; linguistic difficulties as source of frustration for, 23; memorandum as political manifesto, 47; memorial on constitutional government, 37, 38; national institutions and, 35; paradigm shift for, 46; priority on internal administration, 40; regrets joining embassy, 23; revaluates advocacy of "enlightenment," 24; search for new guiding principle for Japan, 24; study of Western civilization and malaise and, 26; Western-style attire of, 6–7

Korea, punitive expedition against, 50. *See also* Saigo Takamori

Kōsaka Maasaki, xiv

Kume Kunitake, 10, 36, 38, 43; as eyes and ears of Kido and Ōkubo, 27; "autonomous people" and national strength and, 28; discourse on comparative political culture, 27–28; discovery of role of interest politics, 29; enabling of individual autonomy and, 29; notes Ōkubo's self-criticism in England, 26; *Ō-Bei kairan jikki* (A true account of a journey of observation through the United States and Europe), 27, 28, 29, 30, 31, 32, 33, 34, 35; on U.S. rail travel, 24; on Western dress, 16–17; reveals serious issues in button incident, 11; view of "justice" and "society," 29–30

Kuroda Kiyotaka, 51, 111, 113; of Satsuma faction, 53; speech rejecting party government, 106

L

laissez-faire, 135; Yamagata views as evil, 127

law of nations, 4, 49; assimilating "virtue" demanded by, 5; definition of, 2; naive faith in, 3–5, 42; requirements for application of as international law, 6; shift from, 46, 47

Law of the Houses, 121, 122

Lebon, André Jean Louis, 133

legal systems: formulation of individual, xiii

legislature: kaiser and Gneist oppose budgetary control of, 64

local assemblies: Yamagata impressed by moderation of, 128

Lorimer, James, 6

loyal subjects: Yamagata and, 141–142

M

Makino Nobutero, 24

Matsukata Matsuyoshi, 107, 109

Meckel, Klemens Wilhelm Jacob, 110–111

Meiji government, intent of, 3

Meiji Restoration, return to spirit of, 139–140

Meiji state, xv, 46; Chlumecky influenced development of, 121–122; collective body of laws fundamental to, 96; constitution as fundamental legal principle for, 47; in world historical perspective, xvii–xviii; overhauled to turn into constitutional order, 94; positive connection with Gneist, 87; public sphere formed in, 105; three study missions of, xvii; two contradictory forces shaping, 142–143; Western civilization and, 6

Miyoshi Taizō, 85; Berlin memo remonstrating with Itō, 67–68; questions Itō's fixation on Germany, 68

Mohl, Ottmar von: account of Western-style promulgation ceremony, 98

Moltke, 41

Mori Arinori, assassination of, 100; advocate of "enlightenment," 36; antagonized by advocating radical modernization, 22–23; introduced to Gneist by Itō, 86; Yamagata's condolences on assassination of, 130

Mosse, Albert, 65, 70, 117; Itō takes lectures seriously, 85; Itō refers to derisively as "the little monk," 66

Mutsu Munemitsu, 127; notes on limitations of sovereign, 75

N

Nagano Keijirō, mock trial of, 11–12

Nakamura Takeshi, 111

Nakano Minoru, 93

Nakayama Kanrokurō, 117
Napoleonic Wars: repercussions of, xii
nation: defined by legislation, 17; diverse character of, 33–34; independence tested by struggle for profit, 45; reassessment of foundations of, 37
nation building: administrative autonomy as theme for, 76–77; Japan engages in program of, xvii; shift in paradigm of policies for, 49
national assembly: demand for popularly elected, 50; Gneist strongly conservative about, 118; hopes for the convening of, 104–105; promise of, 52
national independence, naked force to preserve, 43; sphere of interests as essential to, 119–120
national institutions: avoid hasty imitation of Western, 35; different nature as reason for treaty inequality, 5; framework of, 32; Itō takes lead role in reforming, 91; Itō's broad vision for reform of, 78–79; Itō's concept of evolution of, 139; Iwakura Embassy's perspectives on, 27–48; program for reform of, 3; reform of culminates in promulgation of constitution, 96; vision for civilized, 35
national institutions and political customs: need to alter and reform, 5
national legal codes, compilation of, xiii
national politics: constitution as symbol of, 50; establishing true form of, 49
national power, buildup of, 46
national structure, evolution of, 84
national unification: Bismarck and, 64–65
nationalism, age of, xii, xiii, xvii; in ethos of civilization, 35; institutionalization of, 31–32
nation-state, as ultimate form of cooperative impulse, 32; constitution a symbol of, 97; evolution of, xiii; Itō gains clear definition of from Stein, 78; priority on building political structure of, 47; product of Europe, xvii; toward creation of, 46–47
Nishikawa Nagao, 27, 29
Nitobe Inazō, ix, x, xi, xii, xiii, xiv,
nonreciprocal most favored nation clause: Iwakura and Kido and, 20
normative values: constitution significant in codifying, 97

O

Ōbuchi Kazunori, 132
Ōishi Makato, 101, 121
Ōkubo Toshimichi, xviii, 1, 12, 22, 24; advocates constitution on return to Japan, 43; as "taciturn" and melancholic, 25; as progressive, 44; as silent contrast to talkative Kido, 25; built argument for constitutional government on gradualism, 139; emphasizes domestic administration, 44; endorses shared sovereignty, 44; eyes opened by Bismarck, 43; gradualism and, 49 ; memo to Itō on constitutional government, 43; memorandum as political manifesto, 47; memorial on constitutional government, 53; national institutions and, 35; on Prussia and Russia, 41; paradigm shift for, 46; shared Kido's irritation at linguistic incompetence, 26; shocked by gap between West and Japan, 26; study of Western civilization and malaise and, 26; Western-style attire of, 6–7
Ōkuma faction, 59
"Ōkuma plot," 52
Ōkuma Shigenobu, xi, 23, 59, 88–89, 109, 139; and Fukuzawa wing of popular rights movement, 51–52; disparaged by Itō, 80; forced from government, 52; Kaishintō leader and elected to cabinet, 104; national assembly and, 51; shock of memorial by, 51–52
Ono Asuza: forced from office with Ōkuma, 59
"Opinions of Dr. Stein," 119
"Opinions on the Diet": Chlumecky position paper causes "about-face" in Japan, 121
Ordinance on Public Assembly: Yamagata opposes revision of, 127
Osaka Conference, 53
Ozaki Saburō, 20

P

parliamentarianism, 133–134
parliamentary system: Bismarck and, 64–65; gap between Japanese and German perceptions of, 65; government open to idea of, 50; Itō lays groundwork

for, 91; Itō sees difficulties of in Europe, 81, 138; Itō undeterred from despite warnings, 83; Itō unshaken by German and Austrian examples, 95; Japan's first in Asai, 95; necessary for popular participation and political energy, 138; Stein, Gneist, kaiser see as threat to national order, 80; Yamagata apprehensive of, 126–127

patriotism and nationalism: arousing and developing feelings of, 32, 40; as backbone of national unity, 83

Peace Preservation Ordinance of 1887, 116

people, guarantees for rights of, xii; Kido defines rights and duties of, 40; Ōkubo and Kido share view on position of, 44; political and social autonomy of, 40; unifying political and social energies of, 49

Pink Pamphlet Incident, 115–116; Gneist and, 116

Political Crisis of 1881, xi, 49, 51, 59, 89, 108; ends with purge of Ōkuma faction, 52

political enlightenment, promotion and protection of, 40

political parties: growing power of in Germany, 64

political system: constitution as framework for, 44

political thought: as antithesis of East Asian thinking, 29

politics and economics: Itō connects to national life, 79; public sphere of, xiii

politics and morality: Western political culture's separation of, 29

politics: expansion of personal gain as role of, 31; popular participation in, 105; sacred dimension to Japan's, 7

power politics, 29

power, balance of, 43

prefectural assemblies: political battlegrounds of popular rights activists, 128

prefectural assemblymen: admonished by Itō, 105–106

Prince Arisugawa Taruhito, 51, 53; attends Stein lecture with Itō, 85

Prince Fushimi: Gneist lecture notes clandestinely published, 115–116; visits Gneist with Yamagata, 87

Prince Komatsu, 86, 87, 115; attends Stein's lectures, 94; visits Gneist with Yamagata, 87

private interest: as guiding principle of Western politics, 28–29

Privy Council: as advisory body in event of deadlock, 94; as check on emperor's intrusion in politics, 94; established with Itō as first president, 93; initial role of, 93; institutionalized sovereign's political activity, 94; Itō claims as his "completely new invention," 94

profit: struggle for, 45

progressive constitutionalism, advocacy of, 43–44

progress, marrow of, 36–37

promulgation ceremony: and popular imagination, 104; as glimpse of constitution's symbolism, 97–100; clear impression of Western learning on display, 99; prefectural assemblymen and, 104; presence of Westerners significant, 100; symbolically moves from ancient to Western, 98; symbolism of holding in new palace, 97; unforeseen events before, 100–101

Prussian [constitutional] theory, xi

Prussian absolutism: Meiji constitutional order and, 76

Prussian Diet, 64

Prussian model: as object of Itō's mission, 60

Prussian-style constitution: Itō's passive stance toward, 80

Prussian-style constitutional monarchy: desired by Japan, 109

public sphere: inclusiveness of feared, 106; tension over creation of, 105–106; Yamagata seeks to rid of public debate and partisanship, 140

R

Rathgen, Karl: on public reception of constitution, 101–103

Realpolitik, 42–43, 46

rights of people, promotion and protection of, 40; struggle for as ethical duty to nation, 45–46

Rikken Seiyūkai (Friends of Constitutional Government), 107; party organized by Itō, 95

Roesler, Hermann: doubt cast on by Itō, 80
Roman law, xiii

S

Saga Rebellion, 50
Saigō Takamori, 41; driven out of government, 50; proposal for punitive expedition against Korea, 37, 40
Saigō Tsugumichi, 109
Saionji Kimmochi, 84
Sakamoto Kazuto: Itō's "constitutional charisma," 80, 91
Sasaki Takayuki, 8–9; decries imitation of "civilization and enlightenment," 15; denunciation of Itō Hirobumi and associates, 16; detestation of Itō, 12; disdain for Western dress, 14; irritation with Itō, 17; on Itō's increased power through English, 19; on Iwakura's Western attire, 15
Satō Kōji, xiv
Satsuma faction, 53
Satsuma Rebellion of 1877, 50
Savigny, Friedrich Carl von, 61
separation: of imperial household and government, 92, 94
"shape of the nation": Kido and Ōkubo share vision of, 40–41
Shiba Ryōtarō, xiv
Shimbun zasshi (News digest): "Kido sangi kichōgo no enzetsu" (Speech by Councillor Kido upon his return to Japan), 38, 39–40
Shimomura Fujio, 20
Sidgwick, Henry, 132, 133
Siebold, Alexander Freiherrn von: as aide and friend to Itō, 85; relates Itō's confession in diary, 87–88
Social Darwinism, 88, 134
social evolution: "gradual conservatism" key point of Spencer's doctrine of, 135
sovereign, Stein describes as mediating force in politics, 94
Spencer, Herbert, 88, 132; stresses importance of history, 134, 135
"stages of civilization," 34
Stein, Lorenz von, xv, xvi, 70, 94, 132, 137; advises vigilance over legislative dominance, 74–75; answer to Itō's prayers, 80; characterized as world-famous scholar in Japan, 72; critical of British parliamentary system, 76; critical of German bureaucracy's subservience, 76; evolutionary theory of state, 77, 83; international relations driven by power politics, 120; Itō mission members stay in contact with, 84–85; lectures Yamagata on independence in international affairs, 120; limits sovereign to organ and symbol of state, 76; preached value of historiography to eliminate Western prejudice, 134; rejects despotism by sovereign, 75; relationship with Japan and, 73; responsible for emperor-system ideology, 76; saw Japan as fertile ground for his theories, 72; teachings and attitude contrast with Gneist, 84; unenthused with parliamentary system, 75; unique, three-element organic theory of state, 74; visited by numerous high-ranking Japanese, 107
"Stein pilgrimage," xv, 84, 85, 107, 115, 121
"Struggle for Rights, The" (Jhering), 45
suffrage, 105
Sugiura Kōzō. See Hatakeyama Yoshinari
superficiality, 36, 37

T

Takahashi Hidenao, 2, 3, 26
Tanaka Akira, 27
temperament: differences in Japanese government leaders, 101; ethnic difference in Eastern and Western peoples', 30
Terashima Munenori: ordered to investigate form of government, 43
Tokugawa shogunate, xvii, 85, 110; antiforeign agitation in last years of, 9; Iwakura Embassy members veterans of fall of, 9; national seclusion policy of, 4
Tosa Memorial, 50
tradition: continuity of, 34–35; Kume decries modernization at expense of, 35
traditional virtues: Yamagata extols over Western civilization, 130
transcendental cabinet system, 106
treaty revision, xviii, 2; postponement of negotiations on, 3; Japanese and American interpretations of, 20
tribute system: fundamental to East Asian order, 4
Tsarist Russia: as model for Japan, 41

U

U.S. constitution, x, xiii, xiv
unitary legal code: famous German debate
over, 61. *See also* Savigny, Friedrich Carl
von
virtue: as ultimate manifestation of politics
and civilization, 29, 30
voluntarism: espoused by Gneist in lectures to Yamagata, 118

W

"war in peacetime," 31
Western civilization, in upheaval, 45;
Kume grasped essence of, 31; salient
characteristic of, 28
Western etiquette: Iwakura Embassy mem-
bers and, 9
Western governmental structures: Kido
and embassy immersed in study of, 36
Western impact: nineteenth century era of,
xv, xvii
Western nations: childlike dependence
on, 3
Western political thought: consistent spirit
of, 35; two major aspects of, 28; unique-
ness of, 27–29
Western politics, savage reality of, 46
Western travel: de rigueur for government
officials since Itō's mission, 107
Western-dominated international system:
submit to, 4
Western-style suit: and shape of the
nation, 16
world system: centered on Europe and
North America, xvii

Y

Yamada Akiyoshi, 73
Yamagata Aritomo, xvii, xviii, 56, 86, 109;
acquires lines of sovereignty and influence policy from Stein, 119–120; devel-
ops countermeasures for growing
mayhem, 128; drags heels on constitutional government, 139; emphasizes
quality of "men," 129–130; European
tour unquestionably for constitutional
research, 124–125; expresses foreboding
for future, 125; focuses on local government and cabinet system, 140; gains
valuable advice on Diet from Chlumecky,
123–124; learns bottom-up structure of
national politics from Gneist, 117; learns
sphere of interests concept from Stein,
120; leaves legacy of constraints on Meiji
state, 139–140; letters reference position
papers from Chlumecky, 122–123; not
unaware of military adviser situation,
112; overawed by Western civilization,
125; political factors underlie journey,
107; private Gneist lectures highlight
stay in Berlin, 115; proposes powerful
cabinet, 128; reasons for fact-finding tour
to Europe, 106–107; relieved after meeting with French war minister, 113; shares
Gneist's concern about national assembly, 127; taken aback by brusque treatment, 112; to become It's principal rival,
107; tour of France proceeds smoothly,
113–114; views West as negative example,
127; visit to France possibly diplomatic,
112; Western model not to be followed
without question, 126
Yamaguchi Hōshun, 6, 14
Yamaguchi Masuka, 1
Yamaguchi Naoyoshi, 24
Yamanouchi Susumu, 46
Yamazaki Naotane, 84
Yoshida Masaharu: on Kawashima's anger
at Gneist, 71
Yoshii Tomozane, 41
Yoshino Sakuzō, 70